$$P.O. = \frac{V_{max} - V_{final}}{V_{final}} \times 100\%$$

Damped frequency $(F_D) = \frac{1}{2} T_p$

$T = 2 T_p$

$$F(s) = X_L = sL$$
$$F(s) = X_c = \frac{1}{sC}$$
$$F(s) = R = R$$

If: ZATA $= .707 \Rightarrow$ Butterworth

(damping factor) 
$Z < .707 \Rightarrow$ Chebyshev

$Z > .707 \Rightarrow$ slower Transition

$Z = \frac{b_1/2}{\sqrt{b_0}}$ where, $b_0 = \frac{1}{R_1 R_2 C_1 C_2}$

$+ b_1 = \frac{1}{R_1 C_1} + \frac{1}{R_2 C_2} - \frac{R_4}{R_2 R_3 C_1}$

damping ratio $= 2 z \, w_n$

damping freq. $= w_d = w_n \sqrt{1 - z^2} = w$

$w_p = w_n \sqrt{1 - 2 z^2}$

$$M_p = \frac{A_0}{2 z \cdot \sqrt{1 - z^2}}$$

$$M_n = \frac{A_0}{2 z}$$

$$M_1 O_1 = C^{\left(\frac{-z\pi}{\alpha}\right)}$$

$$I_1 = \frac{V_1 - V_2}{R_T} = V_1(A) + V_2(C)$$

$$S = jw = w \angle 90°$$
$$S^2 = -w^2 = w^2 \angle 180°$$
$$S^3 = -jw^3 = w^3 \angle 270°$$
$$S^4 = w^4 = w^4 \angle 0°$$

# Transform Analysis and Electronic Networks with Applications

## Joseph Kulathinal

**DeVry Institute of Technology**
**Toronto, Ontario**

**Merrill Publishing Company**
**A Bell & Howell Information Company**
**Columbus   Toronto   London   Melbourne**

Published by Merrill Publishing Company
A Bell & Howell Information Company
Columbus, Ohio 43216


This book was set in Times Roman
Administrative Editor: Stephen Helba
Production Editor: JoEllen Gohr
Production Coordination: Carnes Publication Services
Art Coordinator: Mark Garrett
Cover Designer: Jolie Muren

Library of Congress Catalog Card Number: 87-62376
International Standard Book Number: 0-675-20765-7
Printed in the United States of America
2 3 4 5 6 7 8 9 — 92 91 90

To Claramma, Rina, Ron and Rob

# Preface

This book is written with the following three objectives in mind:

1. to help the student develop the necessary math skills for transform analysis
2. to enable the student to analyze and design analog and digital networks
3. to prepare the student for a course in control systems

Because this text includes a comprehensive coverage of the Laplace transformation, an introductory course in calculus is a prerequisite. The student must also have a thorough background in network theorems and their applications in network analysis, preferably from a technology-based course in circuit analysis. It is hoped that the student will continue with one or more courses in analog and digital control systems. Consequently, control systems topics beyond an introductory level are not covered.

These three objectives are integrated throughout the text rather than handled sequentially. The mathematics used in this text will enhance the student's understanding of the networks or physical systems that a technologist is likely to encounter.

Several excellent laboratory exercises are included in Appendix A. They are cross-referenced at the ends of Chapters 7 through 11. These labs can be postponed to a later semester (preferably in a control systems course) if a balanced lab schedule is desired. Exercises in computer-aided design are encouraged, since they are helpful in actual job situations; thus, some computer programs are included.

Some good books on the market cover one or two objectives of this book. Most of these texts are oriented toward communications systems, however, and use the Fourier series as the primary mathematical tool and frequency domain analysis as the dominant mode of analysis. This text is oriented toward control systems and uses the Laplace transformation as its primary mathematical tool and mode of analysis.

### Supplements

A diskette containing the programs in Appendix B of the text (written in Applesoft for Apple II computers) is available upon adoption of the text. An IBM version is also available. These interactive, fully menu-driven programs, which follow the design/analysis procedure described in the text, enable the user to design six different kinds of active filter networks as well as to obtain an inverse transform function. The design parameters in these programs can be changed easily or similar programs can be written for other circuits, depending on the user's needs.

These programs enable the user to perform analysis and design of certain networks described in the text, greatly reducing the mathematical procedures that are required.

Solutions to problems have been worked out in the accompanying Solutions Manual. Your Merrill representative can provide you with a copy.

## Acknowledgments

The author wishes to acknowledge the following reviewers for their suggestions and comments:

| | |
|---|---|
| Donald Abernathy | DeVry Institute of Technology — Dallas, Texas |
| Russell E. Puckett | Texas A & M University |
| Jim Stewart | DeVry Institute of Technology — Woodbridge, N.J. |
| Les Thede | Ohio Northern University |

# Contents

## CHAPTER 9   State Variable Networks

## CHAPTER 10   Gyrators

## CHAPTER 11   Network Synthesis

# CHAPTER 1

# Analog Signals and Systems

## 1.1  Introduction

*Signals* are the functions of time that are usually the input and output variables of physical systems. Voltage, current, and charge are examples of electric signals. *Systems* are used to manipulate the input signals, so as to extract the useful information in them. Amplifiers, filters, modulators, and multivibrators are examples of electric systems. Nonelectric signals, such as torque, force, velocity, and pressure are not covered in this text; however, it is important to recognize that the behavior of systems and signals outside electric technology is similar to that of electric systems and signals.

## 1.2  Linear Time-Invariant (LTI) System

In defining a physical system, we say it is linear if it obeys the superposition theorem. That is, the output of such a system, when excited by several inputs, can be considered to be made up of parts, where each output part is caused by one of the inputs of the system. Further, a system is time-invariant because its parameters are independent of time. For example, resistance is an electric parameter that remains the same with respect to time. In contrast, the mass of a rocket is an example of a time-*variant* parameter. The mass of a rocket depends on the amount of fuel expended, which in turn depends on the duration of the flight. In this book we will deal with linear time-invariant (LTI) systems only. Therefore, coverage will include LTI analog and LTI discrete systems.

## 1.3  Analog Signals

Any continuous signal $f(t)$ that has no abrupt changes in amplitude is an *analog signal*. When the signal exists for all time $t$, including $t < 0$, it is said to be an *eternal signal*. An eternal signal exists for all values of time $t$ from negative infinity to positive infinity. Unless boundary conditions are specified for an analog signal, it is assumed to be an eternal signal.

A signal $f(t)$ can be expressed by a mathematical function of the form

$$f(t) = 2t \tag{1.1}$$

This signal has no specified boundary condition; therefore, it is assumed to be an eternal signal. This same signal can be described by the graphical plot in the time domain of Figure 1.1(a). The graph of $f(t)$ versus $t$ is said to be the time-domain response of the signal $f(t)$.

Another type of analog signal, a *causal signal*, starts at $t = 0$ and continues to positive infinity. A typical example of a causal signal is the *unit step* $u(t)$, shown in Figure 1.1(b). Boundary conditions for the unit step are

$$\text{for } t < 0 \qquad f_2(t) = 0$$
$$\text{for } t > 0 \qquad f_2(t) = 1$$

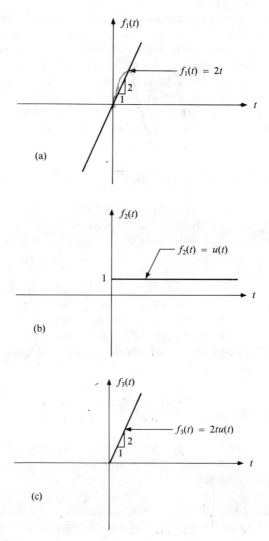

(a)

(b)

(c)

FIGURE 1.1. Time-domain response curves for: (a) $f_1(t) = 2t$. (b) $f_2(t) = u(t)$. (c) $f_3(t) = 2t\, u(t)$.

In Figure 1.1(b), an amplitude of 1 unit exists from $t = 0$ to positive infinity, but does not exist for values of $t < 0$. One way to indicate a causal signal is to multiply its eternal function by a unit step. If $f(t)$ is an eternal signal, $f(t)u(t)$ becomes a causal signal. Figure 1.1(a), (b), and (c) illustrate how multiplying by a unit step makes an eternal signal $f(t)$ a causal signal.

There is yet another type of analog signal — the *delayed causal signal*. These signals start with a time delay. A delayed signal can be indicated by multiplying an eternal signal by a delayed unit step $u(t - T_d)$. In Figure 1.2(a), the response of $f(t) = \cos 2\pi t$ is shown. Figure 1.2(b) is the delayed

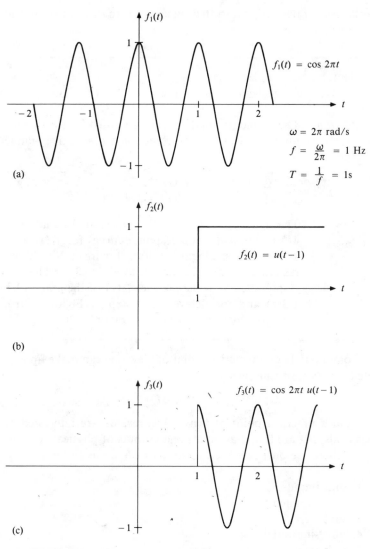

FIGURE 1.2. Time-domain response curves for: (a) $f_1(t) = \cos 2\pi t$. (b) $f_2(t) = u(t - 1)$. (c) $f_3(t) = \cos 2\pi t \, u(t - 1)$.

unit step $u(t-1)$, that is, a unit step delayed by 1 second (s). The response of $\cos 2\pi t$ delayed by 1 s is given in Figure 1.2(c). All three types — eternal, causal, and delayed causal signals — continue on to infinity.

A signal $f(t-T_S)$ is a time-shifted signal, where $T_S$ is the time shift. A time-shifted signal can be eternal, causal, or delayed causal.

| | |
|---|---|
| $f(t-T_S)$ | shifted and eternal |
| $f(t-T_S)u(t)$ | shifted and causal |
| $f(t-T_S)u(t-T_d)$ | shifted and delayed causal |
| $f(t-T_S)u(t-T_S)$ | shifted and delayed causal |

A special case of delayed and shifted signal is where the time delay and time shift are equal.

---

### Example 1.1

Draw the response curve for $f(t) = 4(t-2)u(t-2)$.

*Solution.* The boundary conditions are specified for the signal by the multiplicant $u(t-2)$. Stated in a descriptive manner, we have

when $t < 2$ $\quad f_1(t) = 0$

when $t > 2$ $\quad f_1(t) = 4(t-2)$

The signal $f_2(t) = 4(t-2)$ is the shifted signal of $f_1(t) = 4t$. The time-domain response curves for $f_1(t)$ and $f_2(t)$ are shown in Figure 1.3(a). Figure 1.3(b) shows the response of a unit step delayed by 2 s. The required response curve is the product $f_2(t)$ of the graph of Figure 1.3(a) and the delayed unit step of Figure 1.3(b). The response curve is presented in Figure 1.3(c).

---

From a purely mathematical point of view one can make up any complicated function of time, such as

$$f(t) = \tan^2(t^3 + 3t + 8) \tag{1.2}$$

From a practical point of view, however, we are interested only in those signals that are found as inputs and outputs of physical systems. Fortunately, there are only few such signals, which are as follows:

1. unit impulse
2. unit exponential
3. unit step
4. unit sinusoidal
5. unit ramp

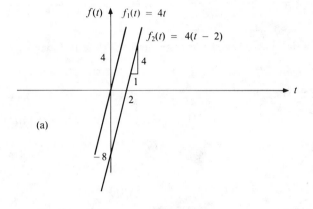

(a)

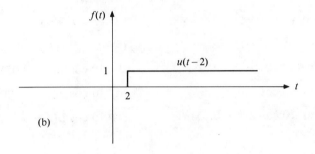

(b)

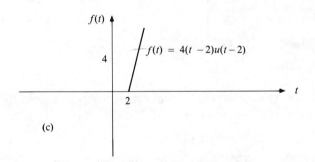

(c)

FIGURE 1.3. Time-domain response curves for: (a) $f_1(t) = 4(t-2)$. (b) $f_2(t) = u(t-2)$. (c) $f_3(t) = 4(t-2)u(t-2)$.

These signals are very important and need to be studied in detail. We have already discussed the unit step function. Later in this chapter we will look at sinusoidal and exponential signals. Unit impulse function is presented in Chapter 2 and again in Chapter 3.

## Problems

**1.1**  Draw the time-domain response curves for the following sets of signals.

A. (a) $\sin 2t$                                        (b) $\sin 2(t - 0.1)$

    (c) $\sin 2tu(t)$                           (d) $\sin 2tu(t - 0.1)$

    (e) $\sin 2(t - 0.1)u(t)$            (f) $\sin 2(t - 0.1)u(t - 0.1)$

B. (a) $3t + 1$                                     (b) $(3t + 1)u(t)$

    (c) $3t$                                           (d) $3tu(t)$

    (e) $(3t + 1)u(t - 1)$              (f) $3tu(t - 1)$

C. (a) $e^{2t}$                                         (b) $e^{2(t-1)}$

    (c) $e^{2t}u(t)$                              (d) $e^{2t}u(t - 1)$

    (e) $e^{2(t-1)}u(t)$                (f) $e^{2(t-1)}u(t - 1)$

D. (a) $10 \cos 2t$                           (b) $10 \cos 2(t - 0.05)$

    (c) $10 \cos 2tu(t)$              (d) $10 \cos 2tu(t - 0.05)$

    (e) $10 \cos 2(t - 0.05)u(t)$      (f) $10 \cos 2(t - 0.05)$
                                                      $\times u(t - 0.05)$

E. (a) $2t^2$                                       (b) $2(t - 0.5)^2$

    (c) $2t^2u(t)$                            (d) $2t^2u(t - 0.5)$

    (e) $2(t - 0.5)^2u(t)$            (f) $2(t - 0.5)^2u(t - 0.5)$

F. (a) $20$                                          (b) $20u(t)$

    (c) $20u(t - 5)$

**1.2**  Select the appropriate choice for each of the signals given for Problem 1.1:

The signal is shifted/not shifted

The signal is eternal/causal/delayed causal

## 1.4  Exponential Signals

The *exponential signal* is very unique among analog signals for the following reason: Its derivative and its integral yield the function, itself, as indicated in equation (1.3).

$$\frac{de^t}{dt} = \int e^t \, dt = e^t \tag{1.3}$$

This important characteristic of the exponential signal can be used to advantage in system analysis. If one can only express all signals (at least the ones we are interested in as the input and output of physical systems) in terms of exponential functions, the mathematical simplification implied in equation (1.3) can be then universally applied. As a matter of fact, our wishful thinking happens to be true. Most of the input/output signals encountered in physical systems can be converted to exponential signals. The time-domain response of exponential signals is shown in Figure 1.4.

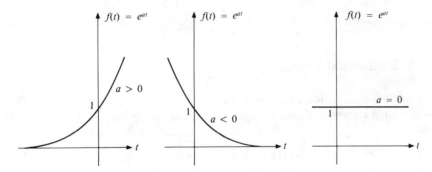

FIGURE 1.4. Time-domain response curve for $f(t) = e^{at}$

The unit step function $u(t)$ is a special case of causal exponential function where the exponent coefficient is zero. The unit step function will be discussed in greater detail in Chapter 2.

$$e^{at} = u(t) \quad \text{when } a = 0 \quad \text{for } t > 0 \tag{1.4}$$

Sinusoidal signals, $\sin \omega t$ and $\cos \omega t$, can be expressed as sums of exponentials as given by equations (1.5) and (1.6), respectively.

$$\sin \omega t = \left(\frac{1}{2j}\right) (e^{j\omega t} - e^{-j\omega t}) \tag{1.5}$$

$$\cos \omega t = \left(\frac{1}{2}\right) (e^{j\omega t} + e^{-j\omega t}) \tag{1.6}$$

Most signals, analog or discrete, encountered in practice can be expressed as a sum of various exponential functions. Since all linear systems obey the superposition theorem, it is possible to consider an output as the sum of several component outputs, each of which is the result of an exponential component of the input signal.

**Problems**

**1.3**   Find the initial value $f(0)$ and the time constant of the following exponential functions. [**Hint:** Exponential function $e^{-at}$ can be stated as $f(t) = e^{-(t/\tau)}$ where $\tau = 1/a$ is the time constant.]

(a) $e^{-3t}$   (b) $-4e^{-t/8}$   (c) $20e^{-50t}$   (d) $(t-1)e^{-20t}$

**1.4**   Draw the time-domain response curves for the following:

(a) $2e^{4t}$   (b) $2e^{4t}u(t)$

(c) $2e^{4t}u(t-0.5)$   (d) $2e^{4(t-0.5)}$

(e) $2e^{4(t-0.5)}u(t)$   (f) $2e^{4(t-0.5)}u(t-0.5)$

## 1.5 Sinusoidal Signals

A sine wave, a cosine wave, or a sum of sine wave and cosine wave of the same frequency is a *sinusoidal* signal. A typical sinusoidal signal is expressed as

$$f(t) = A \sin (\omega t - \phi) \tag{1.7}$$

where   $A$   is the amplitude or the peak value of the sinusoidal
      $\omega$   is the frequency in radians per second (rad/s)
      $\phi$   is the phase shift (lag) in radians (r) or degrees (°)
      $f$   is the frequency in hertz (Hz)
      $T$   is the period of the sinusoidal

An angle is expressed in units of radians or degrees. These units are dimensionless, as can be seen from the defining equation of an angle.

$$\phi = \frac{\text{arc length (length)}}{\text{radius (length)}} \tag{1.8}$$

The relationship between radians and degrees is expressed as

$$180° = \pi \text{ radians} \tag{1.9}$$

Radians per second (rad/s) and hertz (Hz) are units of frequency or angular velocity. The relationship between these units is expressed as

$$\omega = 2\pi f \tag{1.10}$$

Expressing an angle in degrees or radians and expressing a frequency in radians per second or hertz is similar to expressing distance in kilometers or miles. The units of quantity can be used interchangeably, with proper correction of magnitudes.

The phase shift can be stated as either a *phase-lead* or a *phase-lag* angle depending on the start of the sine wave cycle within the range of $-T/2$ and $T/2$. A sine wave crosses the time axis twice during every period. Of the two crossings, the one with the positive slope is said to be the start of the sine wave cycle (see Figure 1.5). Recall that a sine wave cycle starts within any one-period interval. If the cycle starts between $-T/2$ and zero seconds the sinusoidal is said to have a phase lead. If the start of the cycle is between zero and $T/2$ seconds, the sinusoidal is phase lagging. Equation (1.7) is an example of a sinusoidal with a phase lag. With causal signals, it is better to *Note:* assume a phase-lag signal; i.e., a lag angle indicating the start of a sine wave cycle between zero and $T$ seconds. Note that a sinusoidal with a phase lag between 180° and 360° is a phase-lead signal. The time corresponding to the phase-lag angle is called *time shift*.

$$T_s = \frac{\phi}{\omega} \tag{1.11}$$

where $T_s$ is the time shift in seconds and $\phi$ is the phase shift in radians.

A sinusoidal function can be reduced to a sine function and a cosine function. Conversely, sine and cosine functions with the same frequency can *Note:* be combined to form a sine function with a phase shift (sinusoidal function).

$$A_1 \sin \omega t + A_2 \cos \omega t = A \sin(\omega t - \phi) \tag{1.12}$$

where

$$A = \sqrt{A_1^2 + A_2^2} \tag{1.13}$$

$$\phi = \arctan\left(\frac{-A_2}{A_1}\right) \tag{1.14}$$

Note that equation (1.14) will give two phase angles of which only one is the correct answer. The correct phase angle can be identified by the quadrant in which it lies.

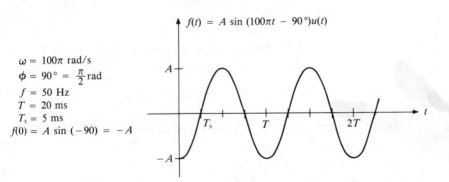

$\omega = 100\pi$ rad/s
$\phi = 90° = \frac{\pi}{2}$ rad
$f = 50$ Hz
$T = 20$ ms
$T_s = 5$ ms
$f(0) = A \sin(-90) = -A$

$f(t) = A \sin(100\pi t - 90°)u(t)$

FIGURE 1.5. Time-domain response curve for $f(t) = A \sin(100\pi t - 90°)u(t)$

## Example 1.2

Find the amplitudes and the phase lags of the following functions.

(a) $f_1(t) = 3 \sin 100t + 4 \cos 100t$
(b) $f_2(t) = -3 \sin 100t + 4 \cos 100t$
(c) $f_3(t) = 3 \sin 100t - 4 \cos 100t$
(d) $f_4(t) = -3 \sin 100t - 4 \cos 100t$

*Solution.*    (a) $A_1 = 3$, $A_2 = 4$    $A = (9 + 16)^{0.5} = 5$

$$\phi = \arctan -4/3 = 360° - 53.13° = 306.87°$$

Since $A_1$ is positive and $-A_2$ is negative, the angle belongs to the fourth quadrant of a full cycle. The tangent (tan) of an angle is the ratio of rise ($y$) and run ($x$). In this case $y$ is negative ($-4$) and $x$ is positive (3), hence the angle is in the fourth quadrant.

(b) $A_1 = -3$, $A_2 = 4$    $A = 5$

$$\phi = \arctan(-4/-3) = 180° + 53.13° = 233.13°$$

Both $A_1$ and $-A_2$ are negative, hence the angle lies in the third quadrant. Most calculators will give the answers in two quadrants, first or fourth. And as is evident from this example, this can lead to the wrong results.

(c) $A_1 = 3$ and $A_2 = -4$    $A = 5$

$$\phi = \arctan 4/3 = 53.13°$$

The angle lies in the first quadrant of the full cycle.

(d) $A_1 = -3$ and $A_2 = -4$    $A = 5$

$$\phi = \arctan(4/-3) = 180° - 53.13° = 126.13°$$

Arctan(4/3) and arctan($-4/-3$) are two different angles. A calculator cannot recognize the difference since the ratio is numerically identical.

The time-domain response curves are shown in Figure 1.6.

## Example 1.3

Draw the approximate time-domain response curves for the following:

(a) $f_1(t) = 3 \sin 2\pi t u(t)$
(b) $f_2(t) = 3e^{-2t} \sin 2\pi t u(t)$
(c) $f_3(t) = 3 \sin 2\pi t \sin 6\pi t u(t)$
(d) $f_4(t) = 3e^{-2t}(-4 \cos 2\pi t + 3 \sin 2\pi t)u(t)$

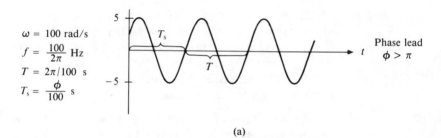

$\omega = 100$ rad/s

$f = \dfrac{100}{2\pi}$ Hz

$T = 2\pi/100$ s

$T_s = \dfrac{\phi}{100}$ s

Phase lead
$\phi > \pi$

(a)

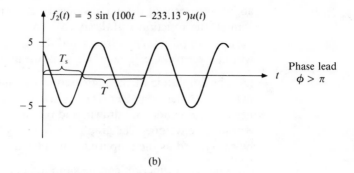

$f_2(t) = 5 \sin (100t - 233.13°)u(t)$

Phase lead
$\phi > \pi$

(b)

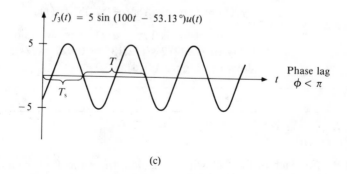

$f_3(t) = 5 \sin (100t - 53.13°)u(t)$

Phase lag
$\phi < \pi$

(c)

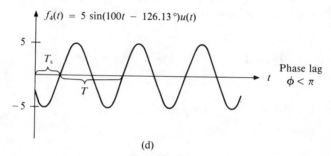

$f_4(t) = 5 \sin(100t - 126.13°)u(t)$

Phase lag
$\phi < \pi$

(d)

FIGURE 1.6. Time-domain response curves of sinusoidals for Example 1.3 (a), (b), (c), and (d)

*Solution.* (a) The amplitude of the sinusoidal is $3u(t)$. The positive and negative amplitudes are drawn ($3u(t)$ and $-3u(t)$). The sine wave is now drawn within the positive and negative amplitudes. The frequency of the sinusoidal is $2\pi$ rad/s or 1 Hz. The period of the sinusoidal is $1/f = 1$ s. The graph is shown in Figure 1.7(a).

(b) The amplitude of the sinusoidal is $3e^{-2t}u(t)$. It is a decaying exponential signal of an initial value 3 and a time constant of $\frac{1}{2} = 0.5$ s. In 0.5 s, the function will decay by about 63 percent of the initial value. In 2.5 s (five time constants), the function will decay to zero. The positive and negative amplitudes are drawn and the sine wave is drawn within the envelope. The graph is shown in Figure 1.7(b).

(c) The amplitude of the high-frequency sinusoidal is another sinusoidal, $3 \sin 2\pi tu(t)$. As always, the positive and negative amplitudes are drawn, and the sinusoidal is drawn within the envelope. The graph shown in Figure 1.7(c) can be recognized as the amplitude modulated (A.M.) signal.

(d) The given function can be simplified as

$$f_4(t) = 15e^{-2t} \sin(2t - 52.13°)u(t)$$

The amplitude is $15e^{-2t}u(t)$. The sinusoidal has a phase delay of $0.927/2$ s ($52.13° = 0.927$ rad/s). The graph is shown in Figure 1.7(d).

## Problems

**1.5** For each of the following sinusoidal functions find the amplitude, frequency in rad/s, period, phase shift, and time shift. Also draw the approximate time-domain response curves. All functions are causal.

(a) $20 \cos 200t$

(b) $10 \sin 40t - 20 \cos 40t$

(c) $8t \sin 500t$

(d) $40 \cos(10t - \pi/6)$

(e) $(2 - t)\sin 400t$

(f) $-20 \sin 7t + 10 \cos 7t$

(g) $e^{-20t}(20 \sin 2000t - 40 \cos 2000t)$

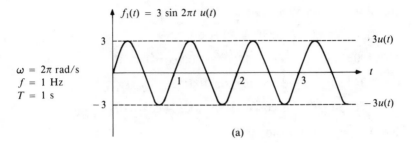

$$f_1(t) = 3 \sin 2\pi t \; u(t)$$

$\omega = 2\pi$ rad/s
$f = 1$ Hz
$T = 1$ s

(a)

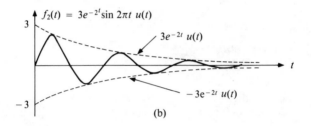

$$f_2(t) = 3e^{-2t} \sin 2\pi t \; u(t)$$

$3e^{-2t} u(t)$

$-3e^{-2t} u(t)$

(b)

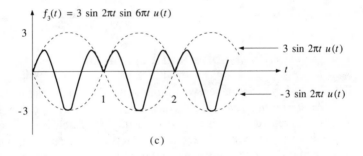

$$f_3(t) = 3 \sin 2\pi t \sin 6\pi t \; u(t)$$

$3 \sin 2\pi t \; u(t)$

$-3 \sin 2\pi t \; u(t)$

(c)

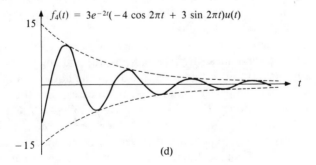

$$f_4(t) = 3e^{-2t}(-4 \cos 2\pi t + 3 \sin 2\pi t)u(t)$$

(d)

FIGURE 1.7. Time-domain response curves for Example 1.4
(a), (b), (c), and (d)

(h)  $20t\,(-4\sin 500t - 20\cos 500t)$

(i)  $50e^{20t}(-40\sin 2000t + 30\cos 2000t)$

(j)  $100\sin 20t\,(-400\sin 1000t - 300\cos 1000t)$

(k)  $10(4\sin 10t + 3\cos 10t)\sin 100t$

(l)  $10(4\sin 10t + 3\cos 10t)(\sin 100t - \cos 100t)$

(m)  $(10 + 3\sin 10t)\sin 100t$

(n)  $t\sin 2t$

(o)  $e^{-12t}\cos 100t$

(p)  $e^{12t}\cos 100t$

(q)  $-10\sin 100t$

(r)  $1 - 2\sin 100t$

(s)  $20 + t\sin t$

(t)  $4 - e^{-2t}\sin 4t$

(u)  $20 + 10e^{2t}\sin 4t$

## 1.6  System Variables and Parameters

All physical systems have two fundamental variables, the *driving function* and the *driven function*. The driving function is a net or difference function and the driven function is a quantity function. In electric systems, *voltage* is the driving function. Voltage is more accurately termed voltage difference or potential difference, although the term is often shortened to voltage. The driven function in electric systems is the *electric charge* $(q)$. It depends on the number of charged particles such as electrons, each of which carries a specified quantity of electric charge.

In comparison, here are a few driving/driven variable pairs in nonelectric systems: force and linear displacement, torque and angular displacement, pressure and mass of air, liquid level (height of the liquid column) and volume of liquid, and temperature and heat. In all cases, note the missing term of the driving functions – the "net" or "difference" – such as net force or temperature difference.

The terms, driving function and driven function, are often used to indicate input signal and output signal, respectively. However, we are using these terms simply as names of a system model. Any signal, voltage, current, or charge can be the input or the output of a system.

There are two dependent variables for all systems: The *rate* of the driven function and the *second rate* or *rate of rate* of the driven function.

The term *rate* means derivative with respect to time. In electric systems, the current $i(t) = dq/dt$ is the rate function and the rate of current $di/dt$ the rate of rate function. The four system variables for electric systems are as follows:

1. Driving function—voltage difference in volts
2. Driven function—charge in coulombs
3. Rate function—current in amperes
4. Rate of rate function—rate of current in amperes/second (A/s)

A *parameter* is the slope of the graph between two variables. Since we have four variables, it is possible to define twelve parameters; three will suffice, however. If the graph is a straight line passing through the origin, the slope, hence the parameter, is simply the ratio of the variables. This is usually true in the case of electrical parameters. As a matter of fact, the defining laws of electrical parameters are based on the *proportionality* of the system variables. It should be kept in mind, however, that the parameters are slopes; hence, they need not be constants.

The parameter *resistance* $(R)$ is defined as the slope of the graph between the driving function and the rate function. Electrical resistance is defined by Ohm's law. It is the slope of the graph between voltage and current (see Figure 1.8(a)).

$$R = \frac{dv}{di} = \frac{V}{I} \tag{1.15}$$

Note that Ohm's law as stated by equation (1.15) assumes that the graph of voltage $(V)$ versus current $(I)$ is a straight line passing through the origin. This is not always true. For a diode, the *V-I* graph is a curve and its slope is not a constant (see Figure 1.8(b)).

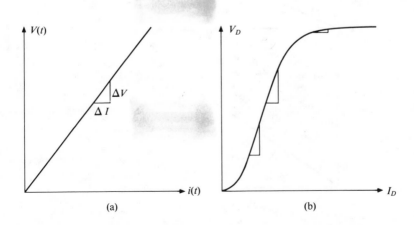

FIGURE 1.8. (a) *V-I* curve. (b) *V-I* curve for diode.

**Example 1.4**

The current through a diode is given as

$$i = I_{sat} e^{v/0.026}$$

where $i$ is the diode current, $I_{sat}$ is the saturation current or scale current, and $v$ is the diode voltage.

Find an expression for the dynamic resistance of the diode.

*Solution.* The dynamic resistance $(r)$ of the diode is $r = dv/di$.

$$\log_e i = \log_e I_{sat} + \frac{v}{0.026} \qquad \text{or} \quad v = 0.026(\log_e i - \log_e I_{sat})$$

$$r = \frac{dv}{di} = \frac{0.026 \, d(\log_e i - \log_e I_{sat})}{dt}$$

---

$$\text{If } y = \log_e x, \quad \text{then } \frac{dy}{dx} = \frac{1}{x}$$

---

$$r = 0.026 \left( \frac{1}{i} - 0 \right) = \frac{0.026}{i}$$

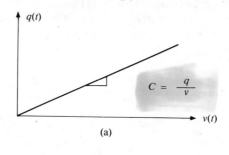

(a)

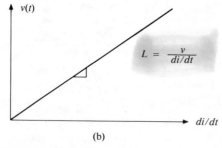

(b)

FIGURE 1.9. (a) $q$-$V$ curve. (b) $V$-$di/dt$ curve.

*Inductance* ($L$) is the slope of the graph between the driving function and the rate of rate function. In electric systems, the inductance is defined by Lenz's law, which is stated as

$$V = L \frac{di}{dt} \tag{1.16}$$

*Capacitance* ($C$) is the slope of the graph between the driven function and the driving function. In electric systems, the capacitance is defined by Faraday's law, which is stated as

$$q = CV \tag{1.17}$$

As in the case of Ohm's law, both Lenz's law and Faraday's law assume a proportional relationship between the variables. The graphical representations of Lenz's law and Faraday's law are given in Figure 1.9(a) and (b), respectively.

The devices that exhibit the properties of resistance, inductance, and capacitance are called *resistor*, *inductor*, and *capacitor*. Of the three devices, the capacitors and inductors are capable of storing energy. The resistor is an energy-dissipating device. A capacitor, for example, can be compared to a tank of certain dimensions that is capable of storing liquid. Likewise, a capacitor can store charge. The de-energized capacitor is like an initially empty tank in a liquid-level system. The *initial condition* is the state of the system output just before $t = 0$. Often, the initial condition would have been zero if the energy-storing elements had been de-energized. The cause of non-zero initial conditions is very often the energized capacitors and inductors.

The three electrical parameters are listed below:

1. Electrical Resistance
   - volt/ampere (V/A)
   - volt/coulomb/second (V/C/s)
   - volt·second/coulomb (V·s/C)
   - ohm ($\Omega$)
2. Electrical Inductance
   - volt/ampere/second (V/A/s)
   - volt/coulomb/second$^2$ (V/C/s$^2$)
   - volt·second$^2$/coulomb (V·s$^2$/C)
   - henry (H)
3. Electrical Capacitance
   - coulomb/volt (C/V)
   - farad (F)

**Example 1.5**

Prove that $(L/C)^{0.5}$ is an impedance.

*Solution.*

$$\frac{L}{C} = \frac{\text{Volt} \times \text{Second}^2 \times \text{Volt}}{\text{Coulomb} \times \text{Coulomb}} = \left(\frac{\text{Volt}}{\text{Coulomb/second}}\right)^2$$

$$= (\text{ohm})^2$$

$$\left(\frac{L}{C}\right)^{0.5} = \text{ohm}$$

**Problems**

**1.6**  From the defining equations, prove that:

(a) $R \cdot C$ is time

(b) $L/R$ is time

(c) $(L \cdot C)^{-0.5}$ is frequency

(d) $R^2 C$ is inductance

**1.7**  For the following systems, find the units of system resistance, inductance, and capacitance.

(a) Linear mechanical system, where the driving function is force in newton (N) and the driven function is linear displacement in meter (m).

(b) Rotary mechanical system, where the driving function is torque in newton-meter (N-m) and the driven function is the angular displacement in radian (r).

(c) Pneumatic system, where the driving function is pressure in Pascal (P) and the driven function is the mass in kilograms (kg).

(d) Thermal system, where the driving function is the temperature in degrees Celsius (°C) and the driven function is heat in calorie (cal).

(e) Liquid level system, where the driving function is height in meters (m), and the driven function is volume in cubic meters (m³).

## 1.7  Analog Systems

The block diagram in Figure 1.10 represents a physical system. In this diagram the input signal $r(t)$ and the output signal $c(t)$ are related. The relationship between the output variable and the input variable can be mathematically expressed. The mathematical expression for an LTI analog system 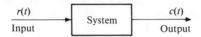 is, in general, an integro-differential equation, which may contain integration, differentiation, and algebraic terms.

r(t)
Input → System → c(t)
Output

FIGURE 1.10. Block diagram representation of a physical system

Consider the *LRC* network of Figure 1.11(a). The input signal is $V_a(t)$. The loop current $i(t)$ is the output signal in this case. It is important to state the input and output of a given system. The input of the network $V_a(t)$ is somewhat obvious. The output, however, is not so obvious. The output could have been the voltage across the capacitor or anything else for that matter. The input and output of a system must be specified, preferably as indicated in Figure 1.11(b).

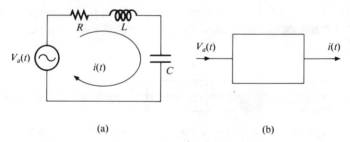

(a)                                  (b)

FIGURE 1.11. (a) *LRC* network. (b) Block diagram of (a).

The inductance $L$, the capacitance $C$, and the resistance $R$ are time-invariant electrical parameters. The relationship between the input $V_a(t)$ and the output $i(t)$ is given by the loop equation of the network.

$$V_a(t) = L\left(\frac{di}{dt}\right) + Ri(t) + \left(\frac{1}{C}\right)\int i\, dt \qquad (1.18)$$

Equation (1.18) is a typical integro-differential equation. An integro-differential equation can be changed to a differential equation by differentiating both sides of the equation. For (1.18), the above process yields

$$\frac{dV_a}{dt} = L\frac{d^2i}{dt^2} + R\frac{di}{dt} + \left(\frac{1}{C}\right)i(t) \qquad (1.19)$$

Thus, finding the output of a system requires solving for the output variable of an integro-differential equation or a modified differential equation. Both equations represent the mathematical description of the system.

In system analysis and design, knowing what the output will be under the influence of various inputs is essential. This task points to the understanding of the relationship of the input and output signals of the system. This in turn requires the solution of differential equations. Before trying to solve for the current $i(t)$ of Figure 1.11(a), we will first look at solutions of various differential equations.

*Leod*

## 1.8  Differential Equations

In this section, the procedure of solving a second-order linear differential equation is illustrated using a typical example. It is assumed that this topic was previously covered in a calculus course. Consider the typical second-order linear differential equation in (1.20).

$y(t) = t, \frac{dy}{dt} = 1$

$y(t) = \otimes, \frac{dy}{dt} = \otimes$

$$A \frac{d^2y}{dt^2} + B \frac{dy}{dt} + Cy = f(t) \tag{1.20}$$

$$Y(0) = 0, \ Y'(0) = 0$$

where $Y(0)$ is $y(t)$ when $t = 0$ and $Y'(0)$ is $dy/dt$ when $t = 0$. Solving this equation means finding an expression for $y(t)$. The equation implies that $y(t)$ is the output signal and $f(t)$ the input signal, as indicated in Figure 1.12.

$$f(t) \longrightarrow \boxed{\text{System}} \longrightarrow y(t)$$

FIGURE 1.12. Block diagram representation of the system

In equation (1.20) the constants $A$, $B$, and $C$ are the system parameters. Two conditions are given for $t = 0$. They are called *initial conditions* and are needed to find $y(t)$. Out of the three system parameters, two of them, the *capacitor* and *inductor*, are energy-storing elements. The third parameter, *resistor*, is an energy-dissipating element. At $t = 0$ it is possible that the energy-storing elements are not fully de-energized. In electrical systems, the capacitor may have a voltage across it or the inductor may have a current through it at $t = 0$. This condition will create the initial conditions for the system equations. At the start, i.e., when $t = 0$, if the energy-storing elements are de-energized, the initial conditions will simply be zeros. As a specific problem, consider the differential equation in (1.21).

$$\frac{d^2y}{dt^2} + 4 \frac{dy}{dt} + 3y = 1 \tag{1.21}$$

$$Y(0) = 0, \ Y'(0) = 0$$

The output signal is $y(t)$ and the input signal is 1. The input can be recognized as a unit step input $u(t)$. It would have been preferable to indicate it as such in equation (1.21). However, it is often stated as a given and should be interpreted as a unit step. The two initial conditions are given as zeros, meaning that the energy-storing parameters are de-energized at $t = 0$. The output signal $y(t)$ is made up of two parts, $y_1(t)$ and $y_2(t)$, as indicated by equation (1.22).

$$y(t) = y_1(t) + y_2(t) \qquad (1.22)$$

In order to find $y_1(t)$, we arbitrarily assume the input to be zero, as given in equation (1.23). Equation (1.23) is then solved for $y_1(t)$.

$$\frac{d^2y}{dt^2} + 4\frac{dy}{dt} + 3y = 0 \qquad (1.23)$$

To find $y_1(t)$ the so-called $m$-equation (characteristic equation) is set up. The characteristic equation is obtained by letting the input signal equal zero and by replacing $y(t)$ by 1, $dy/dt$ by $m$, $d^2y/dt^2$ by $m^2$, and in general, $d^ny/dt^n$ by $m^n$. The roots of the characteristic equation determines the form of the solution of $y_1(t)$. All possible forms of the transient component of the output signal for a second-order system are given in Table 1.1.

If the characteristic equation is quadratic, there are two roots. For the quadratic equation $m^2 + bm + c = 0$, the two roots are

$$m_1 = \frac{-b}{2} + \left[\frac{b^2}{4} - c\right]^{0.5} = Root_1 = \frac{-b}{2} + \sqrt{\frac{b^2}{4} - c} \quad (1.24)$$

$$m_2 = \frac{-b}{2} - \left[\frac{b^2}{4} - c\right]^{0.5} = Root_2 = \frac{-b}{2} - \sqrt{\frac{b^2}{4} - c} \quad (1.25)$$

Depending on the coefficients $b$ and $c$, the roots can take different forms.

1. $m_1$ and $m_2$ (two real numbers)
   For example, the roots of $m^2 + 6m + 8 = 0$ are: $m_1 = -4$ and $m_2 = -2$ (two real roots)
2. $m_1$ and $m_2$ (real and repeated)
   For example, the roots of $m^2 + 2m + 1 = 0$ are: $m_1 = m_2 = -1$ (two roots are the same)
3. $m_1$ and $m_2$ (a pair of complex conjugates)
   For example, the roots of $m^2 + 4m + 13 = 0$ are: $m_1 = -2 + 3j$; $m_2 = -2 - 3j$ (a pair of complex conjugates)
4. $m_1$ and $m_2$ (two imaginary numbers)
   For example, the roots of $m^2 + 25 = 0$ are: $m_1 = 5j$; $m_2 = -5j$ (two imaginary numbers)

To return to the problem at hand, that is, to solve the differential equation of (1.21), the characteristic equation is set up as indicated in equation

(1.26) and its roots $m_1$ and $m_2$ are calculated. The component $y_1(t)$ is stated in equation (1.28).

The component of the output $y_1(t)$ is the output of the system with no input. It is the *source-free* solution of the output. It depends only on the system parameters and initial conditions. In a *stable system* this component will reduce to zero as time increases. For this reason the input-free component $y_1(t)$ is called the *transient component* of the output signal.

$$m^2 + 4m + 3 = 0 \qquad (m+3)(m+1) \qquad (1.26)$$

$$m_1 = -3 \quad \text{and} \quad m_2 = -1 \qquad\qquad (1.27)$$

$$y_1(t) = Ae^{m_1 t} + Be^{m_2 t}$$

$$y_1(t) = Ae^{-3t} + Be^{-t} \qquad\qquad (1.28)$$

In equation (1.28) $A$ and $B$ are constants. Note that this component reduces to zero as $t$ approaches infinity. This is a mandatory condition for all stable systems. Suppose one of the roots of the $m$-equation were positive. In this case, $y_1(t)$ would continue to increase with time. A system with an ever-increasing transient component will sooner or later fail. In such a case the system is said to be *unstable*.

In order to find $y_2(t)$, the input is put back into the equation. Thus the component $y_2(t)$ is the output due to the input. This component follows the input and is called the *steady-state component* of the output signal. The steady-state component depends on the input as well as the physical system itself.

The signal $y_2(t)$ satisfies equation (1.21). The left-hand side of the equation contains the function, its first derivative, and its second derivative as specified by equation (1.21). The right-hand side is the input signal, in our case a constant. We assume combinations of functions as $y_2(t)$ so as to satisfy equation (1.21). One can assume combinations of all possible func-

TABLE 1.1    Various forms of $y_1(t)$

| Roots of $m$-equation | Form of $y_1(t)$ |
| --- | --- |
| $m_1$ and $m_2$ (real) | $Ae^{m_1 t} + Be^{m_2 t}$ |
| $m_1 = m_1 = m$ (and real) | $e^{mt}(At + B)$ |
| $m_1$ and $m_2$ (complex conjugates)* | $e^{at}(A \sin bt + B \cos bt)$ |
| $m_1$ and $m_2$ (imaginary numbers)** | $A \sin bt + B \cos bt$ |

*The roots $m_1$ and $m_2$ are a pair of complex conjugates such that $m_1 = a + bj$ and $m_2 = a - bj$.
**The roots $m_1$ and $m_2$ are imaginary numbers such that $m_1 = jb$ and $m_2 = -jb$.

tions, but most of them will be found to be zero. Yet, recognizing that the left-hand side contains only constants, we can safely assume that

$$y_2(t) = A_1 t^2 + A_2 t + A_3 \qquad (1.29)$$

The combination of these three functions are the only possible ones that might yield constants in the function, its derivative, and its second derivative.

$$\frac{dy_2}{dt} = 2A_1 t + A_2 \qquad (1.30)$$

$$\frac{d^2 y_2}{dt^2} = 2A_1 \qquad (1.31)$$

Substituting these functions in equation (1.21), we obtain

$$2A_1 + 8A_1 t + 4A_2 + 3A_1 t^2 + 3A_2 t + 3A_3 = 0t^2 + 0t + 1 \qquad (1.32)$$

Comparing coefficients, we have

$$2A_1 + 4A_2 + 3A_3 = 1 \qquad (1.33)$$

$$8A_1 + 3A_2 = 0 \qquad (1.34)$$

$$3A_1 = 0 \qquad (1.35)$$

Solving for $A_1$, $A_2$, and $A_3$, the results are

$$A_1 = 0, \quad A_2 = 0 \quad \text{and } A_3 = \tfrac{1}{3} \qquad (1.36)$$

Hence, the steady-state solution is

$$y_2(t) = \tfrac{1}{3} \qquad (1.37)$$

Note that when the input function is a constant, it is required only to let $y_2(t) = A_3$, as $A_1$ and $A_2$ will be zeros in most cases. Assuming additional terms for the function, however, will not lead to incorrect results. If a term that is required is not included, the result will be wrong. It can be proven that $A_1$ and $A_2$ are always zero if the differential equation contains the $y(t)$ term. The complete solution of the output is given as

$$y(t) = Ae^{-3t} + Be^{-t} + \tfrac{1}{3} \qquad (1.38)$$

The constants $A$ and $B$ are now found using the initial conditions.

$$Y(0) = A + B + \tfrac{1}{3} = 0 \qquad (1.39)$$

$$\frac{dy}{dt} = -3Ae^{-3t} - Be^{-t} \qquad (1.40)$$

$$Y'(0) = -3A - B = 0 \qquad (1.41)$$

From equations (1.39) and (1.41), we have

$$A = \tfrac{1}{6} \quad \text{and} \quad B = -\tfrac{1}{2} \qquad (1.42)$$

The required solution of $y(t)$ is expressed as

$$y(t) = \tfrac{1}{3} + \tfrac{1}{6}e^{-3t} - \tfrac{1}{2}e^{-t} \tag{1.43}$$

A response curve for $y(t)$ is given in Figure 1.13, where three individual curves are drawn for each component and then graphically added together. Note also that for the exponential function of the form $e^{at}$, the time constant is $1/a$.

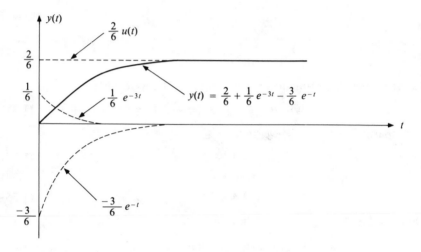

FIGURE 1.13. Response curve of $y(t) = (\tfrac{1}{3} + \tfrac{1}{6}e^{-3t} - \tfrac{1}{2}e^{-t})u(t)$

---

### Example 1.6

Solve the following differential equation:

$$\frac{d^2x}{dt^2} + 4\frac{dx}{dt} + 5x = 10u(t)$$

$$X(0) = 2 \qquad X'(0) = -1$$

*Solution.*    The output is $x(t)$ and the input is $10u(t)$.

$$x(t) = x_1(t) + x_2(t)$$

In order to find $x_1(t)$, the input is replaced by zero, and the roots of $m$-equation are found.

$$m^2 + 4m + 5 = 0$$

$$m_1 = -2 + 1j, \; m_2 = -2 - 1j$$

The transient component is expressed as

$$x_1(t) = e^{-2t}(A \cos t + B \sin t)$$

To find the steady-state component, the input is placed back in the equation and the output function is assumed to be

$$x_2(t) = A$$

$$\frac{dx_2}{dt} = 0$$

$$\frac{d^2x_2}{dt^2} = 0$$

$$5A = 10 \quad \text{or} \quad A = 2$$

The steady-state component of the output is given by the form

$$x_2(t) = 2$$

The output $x(t)$ is given by the form

$$x(t) = 2 + e^{-2t}(A \cos t + B \sin t)$$

Differentiating with respect to $t$, we obtain

*Uses: $\frac{dy}{dx}$ of sin + cos, of $\frac{dy}{dx}$ of Ln, + product rule*

$$\frac{dx(t)}{dt} = e^{-2t}(-A \sin t + B \cos t) - 2e^{-2t}(A \cos t + B \sin t)$$

Substituting initial conditions, we have

$$2 = 2 + (A + 0) \qquad \text{or } A = 0$$
$$-1 = (0 + B) - 2(A + 0) \qquad \text{or } B = -1$$

The output $x(t)$ thus becomes

$$x(t) = 2 - e^{-2t} \sin t$$

An approximate time-domain response curve is shown in Figure 1.14.

The output $x(t)$ is made up of a step function of two units and an exponentially multiplied sine wave. The amplitude of the sine wave is $-e^{-2t}$. In order to draw a sine wave, the positive and negative amplitudes must be drawn first. The sine wave swings within the positive and negative amplitudes, in our case, within $-e^{-2t}$ and $e^{-2t}$. This sine wave is now shifted by two units.

---

## Problems

**1.8**  For the following differential equations both initial conditions are zeros. Solve for the output signal and draw the approximate time-response curve for each.

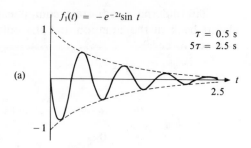

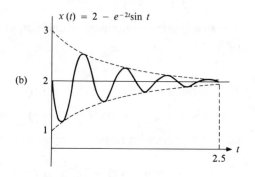

FIGURE 1.14. Response curves for Example 1.6: (a) $f_1(t) =$ $-e^{-2t} \sin t$. (b) $x(t) = 2 - e^{-2t} \sin t$.

(a) $d^2y/dt^2 + dy/dt + y = 10$     (b) $d^2p/dt^2 - dp/dt + p = 1$

(c) $d^2x/dt^2 + 2\,dx/dt + x = 1$     (d) $d^2z/dt^2 + 4\,dz/dt + z = 1$

(e) $d^2y/dt^2 + 16y = 10$        (f) $d^2y/dt^2 = 20$

(g) $d^2y/dt^2 + 10\,dy/dt = 16$     (h) $d^2x/dt^2 - 16 = 20$

(i) $dx/dt + 20x = 1$           (j) $dx/dt = 2$

**1.9**   For the differential equations of Problem 1.8, the initial conditions are $Y(0) = 1$ and $Y'(0) = -1$ (if needed). Solve for the output signal and draw an approximate time-domain response curve for each.

## 1.9 Summary

This chapter has investigated analog signals and systems and defined the system parameters. A mathematical description of a physical system, in general, is an integro-differential equation, which, for LTI systems, can be reduced to an ordinary, linear differential equation. The classical method of solving a differential equation is used in this chapter, with particular emphasis placed on the two components of the system outputs—the transient and steady-state components. Examples of solutions of differential equations are deliberately kept simple. Only second-order equations with simple input functions are investigated. The examples were kept simple in the interest of saving time. The procedure for solving a complicated tenth-order differential equation is the same as the one we investigated, but the mathematical manipulations are time-consuming. This is the best reason to look for another method of solving differential equations.

## Key Terms

Define the following terms:

signal

LTI system

superposition theorem

delayed causal signal

driving function

rate of rate function

exponential function

system

unit step

analog system

transient

parameter

rate function

time response

linear system

eternal signal

causal signal

impulse function

steady state

stability

initial condition

# CHAPTER 2

# Laplace Transformation

## 2.1 Introduction

It has been established that (1) the relationship between the input variable and the output variable can be mathematically expressed by an integro-differential equation, and (2) finding the output involves solving the integro-differential equation or the modified differential equation. The French mathematician Pierre Simon Marquis de Laplace (1749–1827) developed a mathematical method of solving differential equations by algebraic techniques. His method of solving differential equations is now known as Laplace transformation. The British physicist Oliver Heaviside (1850–1925) is credited with expanding on Laplace's method and introducing it in circuit analysis and design.

## 2.2 Transforms

Whenever one changes something from one set of conditions to another set, a transformation has taken place. For some forms of analysis, it may be easier to make the required operation in a transformed domain rather than in the original domain. The result obtained in the transformed domain can be inversely transformed to the original set of conditions. For example, if one wants to add two decimal numbers using a computer, the computer transforms the decimal numbers to binary numbers, adds them to obtain the result in binary number, and then inversely transforms the result to a decimal number.

Another demonstration of the process of transformation is the logarithm. For example, it is assumed that multiplication is a more difficult mathematical operation than addition. In order to ease that task, a logarithm is used. The logarithmic operation multiplies two numbers through addition. The logarithmic technique is illustrated in Figure 2.1(a). The general scheme of the transform/inverse transform operation is shown in Figure 2.1(b).

The necessity of the transformation technique is dictated by the ease with which the required operation can be performed on the transformed quantities. Generally, the classical method of solving a differential equation is difficult and very time-consuming even for skilled mathematicians. The Laplace transform technique, however, simplifies solving a differential equation to solving an algebraic equation. Compared to solving differential equa-

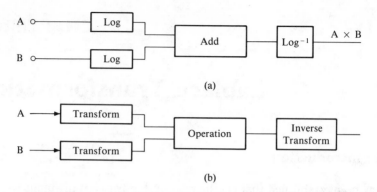

FIGURE 2.1. (a) Logarithmic and inverse logarithmic transformation to multiply A and B using only addition. (b) Transform/inverse transform operation.

tions, solving an algebraic equation seems easy. It is based primarily on this premise that we justify Laplace transformation.

We have seen that nearly every signal used as an input of a system can be expressed as the sum of exponential functions. As long as the system is linear, the output will be the sum of all the output components caused by the various input components, each of which is an exponential function. For an exponential input, the output will be the same exponential function but with a different coefficient. The reason for this is that an exponential function and its differentiation contain the same exponential function, as evidenced in equation (2.2).

$$f(t) = e^{st} \tag{2.1}$$

$$\frac{df(t)}{dt} = se^{st} \tag{2.2}$$

$$\frac{d^2f(t)}{dt^2} = s^2e^{st} \tag{2.3}$$

$$\frac{d^nf(t)}{dt^n} = s^ne^{st} \tag{2.4}$$

In equations (2.1), (2.2), (2.3), and (2.4) the exponential term $e^{st}$ remains the same. In a differential equation the exponential term occurs on both sides of the equation, leaving only the coefficient terms to deal with.

## 2.3  Laplace Transforms

Laplace transformation converts a causal signal from the time domain form to the *Laplace domain* form. The Laplace domain is the frequency domain and the new transform variable is the complex frequency $s$.

$$f(t) \leftrightarrow F(s) \tag{2.5}$$

The variable $s$ in the Laplace domain is the complex frequency, which is expressed as

$$s = \sigma + j\omega \qquad (2.6)$$

where $\sigma$ is the real part of the complex frequency and $\omega$ the imaginary part. A Laplace transform obtained for a causal signal implies a boundary condition of $t = 0$ and $t = $ infinity.

The Laplace transformation is defined as

$$F(s) = \mathcal{L}[f(t)u(t)] = \int_0^\infty f(t)e^{-st}\, dt \qquad (2.7)$$

In equation (2.7) $F(s)$ is the Laplace transform of $f(t)u(t)$. Note the convention that the functions of time are to be written in lowercase letters and the functions of frequency in uppercase letters. If $m(t)$ is a signal in the time domain, its Laplace transform is $M(s)$.

The symbol $\mathcal{L}$ should be read as "the Laplace transform of" and the symbol $\mathcal{L}^{-1}$ should be read as "the inverse Laplace transform of."

$$\mathcal{L}[m(t)] = M(s) \qquad (2.8)$$
$$\mathcal{L}^{-1}[M(s)] = m(t) \qquad (2.9)$$

Note the boundary conditions implied in the integration limits of the defining equation. A note of caution: Laplace transformation applies only to causal functions, and although not recommended, boundary conditions are sometimes omitted, leaving it to be assumed that the signals are causal functions.

Since Laplace transformation is defined as an integration, some basic rules of integration are applicable to Laplace transformation as well. Equation (2.10) is an example of the rule of integration that states: The integration of a sum is the same as the sum of integration.

$$\mathcal{L}[f_1(t) + f_2(t)] = \mathcal{L}[f_1(t)] + \mathcal{L}[f_2(t)] \qquad (2.10)$$
$$\mathcal{L}^{-1}[F_1(s) + F_2(s)] = \mathcal{L}^{-1}[F_1(s)] + \mathcal{L}^{-1}[F_2(s)] \qquad (2.11)$$

But the Laplace transform of $f_1(t)f_2(t)$ is **not** $\mathcal{L}[f_1(t)] \times \mathcal{L}[f_2(t)]$, since the integration of a product function is not the same as the product of the integration of individual functions.

From a strictly mathematical point of view, it is possible to transform a function other than time to another variable, but it is not likely to have any physical relation to the transform, as we have in Laplace transformation — namely, time domain versus frequency domain. Some of the most common Laplace transforms of interest will be discussed in the following sections.

## Unit Step Signal

A *unit step* is a very important signal. In electric systems, a unit step is a dc signal. A unit step signal is defined as

$$u(t) = 1 \quad \text{for} \quad t \geq 0$$
$$u(t) = 0 \quad \text{for} \quad t < 0$$

A unit step is a defined causal signal that is used as a multiplicant to indicate causality of other signals. The time-domain response of a unit step function was given in Figure 1.1(b).

For a unit step signal,

$$f(t) = u(t)$$

Substituting $f(t)$ in the defining equation (2.7) of Laplace transformation, we have

$$F(s) = \int_0^\infty e^{-st} \, dt \qquad (2.12)$$

$$= \frac{e^{-st}}{-s} \Big|_0^\infty$$

$$= \frac{-1}{s} (0 - 1)$$

The Laplace transform of a unit step signal is stated by

$$F(s) = \mathcal{L}[u(t)] = \frac{1}{s} \qquad (2.13)$$

**Exponential Signal**

The decaying and growing exponential signals were described in section 1.4. For a decaying exponential signal

$$f(t) = e^{-at}u(t)$$

Substituting this function in equation (2.7), we have

$$F(s) = \int_0^\infty e^{-at}e^{-st} \, dt \qquad (2.14)$$

$$= \int_0^\infty e^{-(s+a)t} \, dt$$

$$= \frac{-1}{s+a} (e^{-(s+a)t}) \Big|_0^\infty$$

$$= \frac{-1}{s+a} (0 - 1) = \frac{1}{s+a}$$

The Laplace transformation of a decaying exponential signal is expressed as

$$F(s) = \mathcal{L}[e^{-at}u(t)] = \frac{1}{s+a} \qquad (2.15)$$

The Laplace transform of the unit step signal can also be obtained by setting the coefficient of the exponent of the exponential function, $a = 0$

$$F(s) = \mathcal{L}[e^{-0t}u(t)] = \mathcal{L}[u(t)] = \frac{1}{s+0} = \frac{1}{s}$$

If the coefficient of the exponent is positive, such that $f(t) = e^{|a|t}u(t)$, then its Laplace transform is expressed as

$$F(s) = \mathcal{L}[e^{at}u(t)] = \frac{1}{s-a} \qquad (2.16)$$

## Unit Ramp Signal

A *unit ramp* signal is a proportional function. The function $f(t)$ is proportional to time $t$. The time-domain response curve of a unit ramp signal is a straight line passing through the origin. A unit ramp indicates a unity slope. Triangular waveforms are made up of segmented ramp signals. For a unit ramp signal

$$f(t) = tu(t) \qquad (2.17)$$

$$F(s) = \mathcal{L}[tu(t)] = \int_0^\infty te^{-st}\, dt \qquad (2.18)$$

The integration required in this case contains products of two functions of time. The technique of integrating product functions can be expressed as

$$\int v\, du = vu - \int u\, dv \qquad (2.19)$$

Let $\quad v = t$

and $\quad du = e^{-st}\, dt$

$\quad dv = dt$

$\quad u = \dfrac{e^{-st}}{-s}$

Now, the required integral is derived from

$$\int te^{-st}\, dt = t\,\frac{e^{-st}}{-s} - \int \frac{e^{-st}}{-s}\, dt$$

$$= \frac{te^{-st}}{s} - \frac{e^{-st}}{s^2}$$

Applying the integration limits results in

$$\left((0-0) - \left(0 - \frac{1}{s^2}\right)\right) = \frac{1}{s^2}$$

The Laplace transform of a unit ramp signal is expressed as

$$F(s) = \mathcal{L}[tu(t)] = \frac{1}{s^2} \tag{2.20}$$

## Sine Wave Signal

The sine wave function is discussed in detail in section 1.5. A sine wave signal is given by

$$f(t) = \sin \omega t u(t)$$

From Euler's identity, however, we have

$$\sin \omega t = \frac{e^{j\omega t} - e^{-j\omega t}}{2j}$$

Substituting this function in equation (2.7), we have

$$F(s) = \mathcal{L}[\sin \omega t u(t)] = \int_0^\infty \sin \omega t e^{-st} \, dt \tag{2.21}$$

*Review*

$$= \int_0^\infty \frac{e^{j\omega t} - e^{-j\omega t}}{2j} e^{-st} \, dt$$

$$= \frac{1}{2j} \int_0^\infty (e^{-(s-j\omega)t} - e^{-(s+j\omega)t}) \, dt$$

$$= \frac{1}{2j} \left( \frac{-1}{s-j\omega} e^{-(s-j\omega)t} + \frac{1}{s+j\omega} e^{-(s+j\omega)t} \right) \Big|_0^\infty$$

$$= \frac{1}{2j} \left( \frac{-1}{s-j\omega}(0-1) + \frac{1}{s+j\omega}(0-1) \right)$$

$$= \frac{(s+j\omega) - (s-j\omega)}{2j(s-j\omega)(s+j\omega)} = \frac{1}{2j} \frac{s+j\omega - s + j\omega}{s^2 + \omega^2}$$

$$= \frac{\omega}{s^2 + \omega^2}$$

The Laplace transform of a sine wave signal is expressed as

$$F(s) = \mathcal{L}[\sin \omega t u(t)] = \frac{\omega}{s^2 + \omega^2} \tag{2.22}$$

## Cosine Signal

The Laplace transform of a cosine function can be derived as

$$F(s) = \mathcal{L}[\cos \omega t u(t)] = \frac{s}{s^2 + \omega^2} \tag{2.23}$$

## Higher Order Signals

The signal indicated by equation (2.24) is an $n$th order function.

$$f(t) = t^n u(t) \tag{2.24}$$

The Laplace transform of an $n$th order function is expressed as

$$F(s) = \mathcal{L}[t^n u(t)] = \frac{n!}{s^{n+1}} \tag{2.25}$$

where $n! = 1 \times 2 \times 3 \times 4 \times 5 \times \ldots \times n$ (factorial $n$).

## Impulse Function

Impulse function can be considered as a rectangular pulse of width $a$ units and height of $1/a$ units, with the value of $a$ approaching zero. The area under the curve is always unity. A unit pulse is a single pulse with infinite amplitude and zero pulse width.

$$\delta(t) = \lim_{a \to 0} \frac{1}{a} \left( u(t) - u(t - a) \right) \tag{2.26}$$

The Laplace transform of a unit impulse is expressed as

$$F(s) = \mathcal{L}[\delta(t)] = 1 \tag{2.27}$$

---

### Example 2.1      *Study*

Find the Laplace transform of the causal function

$$f(t) = \sin\left(4t + \frac{\pi}{4}\right)$$

*Solution.*      $f(t) = \sin 4t \cos\dfrac{\pi}{4} + \cos 4t \sin\dfrac{\pi}{4}$

$$= 0.707 \sin 4t + 0.707 \cos 4t$$

$$F(s) = 0.707 \left( \frac{4}{s^2 + 16} + \frac{s}{s^2 + 16} \right)$$

$$F(s) = \frac{0.707(s + 4)}{s^2 + 16}$$

---

### Example 2.2      *Study*

Find the inverse Laplace transform of

$$F(s) = \frac{3s - 6}{s^2 + 16}$$

*Solution.*    The given function can be split into two functions as

$$F(s) = \frac{3s}{s^2 + 4^2} - \frac{6}{s^2 + 4^2}$$

The inverse Laplace transform can be recognized in the general form for cosine and sine functions. Constants are adjusted to match the proper form of the transform equations.

$$F(s) = 3\,\frac{s}{s^2 + 4^2} - \frac{6}{4}\,\frac{4}{s^2 + 4^2}$$

The inverse Laplace transform is given as

$$f(t) = (3 \cos 4t - \tfrac{6}{4} \sin 4t)u(t)$$

---

**Example 2.3**

Find the Laplace transform of $f(t) = 20$

*Solution.*    The question is not very clear. Although no boundary condition is given, the signal is assumed to be causal, in which case the answer is

$$F(s) = \frac{20}{s}$$

---

**Problems**

HW
Evans

(2.1)  Find the Laplace transforms of the following causal functions.

(a)  $20\delta(t)$

(b)  $30t$

(c)  $\frac{1}{16}t^6$

(d)  $\sin 400t$

(e)  $\cos 4t$

(f)  $23\delta(t) + 3t^3 + 2t^2 - t - 7$

(g)  $12e^{-5t}$

(h)  $20e^{27t}$

(i)  $\sin\left(9t - \frac{\pi}{3}\right)$

$\frac{1}{16} \quad \frac{6\,!}{s^{(7)}} \quad \frac{400}{s^2 + 400^2}$

TABLE 2.1   Some causal signals and their Laplace transforms

| Number | Name | $f(t)$ | Waveform | $F(s)$ |
|--------|------|--------|----------|--------|
| 1 | Impulse | $\delta(t)$ | | 1 |
| 2 | Step | $u(t)$ | | $\dfrac{1}{s}$ |
| 3a | Exponential | $e^{-at}u(t)$ | | $\dfrac{1}{s + a}$ |
| 3b | | $e^{at}u(t)$ | | $\dfrac{1}{s - a}$ |
| 4a | Sinusoidal | $\sin \omega t\, u(t)$ | | $\dfrac{\omega}{s^2 + \omega^2}$ |
| 4b | | $\cos \omega t\, u(t)$ | | $\dfrac{s}{s^2 + \omega^2}$ |
| 5 | Ramp | $t\, u(t)$ | | $\dfrac{1}{s^2}$ |
| 6 | Higher order | $t^n u(t)$ | | $\dfrac{n!}{s^{(n+1)}}$ |

(j) $\cos\left(4t + \dfrac{\pi}{4}\right)$

(k)  $\sin 4t - 4\cos 2t + e^{-2t}$

(l)  $e^{4t} + 10$

(m)  $4t^4 + 3t^3 - 2t^2 - 4t + 12 + \delta(t)$

(n)  $e^{-t}e^{4t}$

**2.2**  Find the inverse Laplace transforms of the following functions of $s$.

(a) 20

(b) $\dfrac{4}{s}$

(c) $\dfrac{20}{4}$

(d) $\dfrac{4}{s} - \dfrac{6}{s + 4}$

(e) $\dfrac{4s + 8}{s^2 + 81}$

(f) $\dfrac{20}{s - 8}$

(g) $\dfrac{40}{s^2 + 25} - \dfrac{4s}{s^2 + 81}$

(h)* $\dfrac{-4s + 5}{s + 8}$

(i)  $1 - \dfrac{4}{s}$

(j)* $\dfrac{6s^2 + 20s + 8}{s^2 + 4}$

(k) $\dfrac{7s - 9}{s^2 + 36}$

(l)* $\dfrac{s + 8}{s - 8}$

*[**Hint**: Divide the numerator by the denominator.]

**2.3**  Derive the Laplace transform of

(a) $\cos \omega t u(t)$

(b) $0.5t^2 u(t)$

---

## 2.4  Partial Fraction Expansion

The Laplace transform of a signal can be represented as a fraction. In equation (2.28), $N(s)$ stands for the numerator as a function of $s$ and $D(s)$ the denominator as a function of $s$.

$$F(s) = \frac{N(s)}{D(s)} \qquad (2.28)$$

Very often, the highest power of $s$ in the numerator function is equal to or less than the highest power of $s$ in the denominator function. Equation

(2.29) is an example of Laplace transform of a signal. The highest power of $s$ in the numerator and denominator are 2 and 3, respectively.

$$F(s) = \frac{s^2 + 3s + 60}{s(s + 3)(s - 5)} \tag{2.29}$$

In order to find the inverse transform, it is often required to split the function as a sum of simpler functions. To this end we need to use *partial fraction expansion*. Partial fraction expansion expands a fraction as a sum of several fractions. Equation (2.30) illustrates a partial fraction expansion.

$$\frac{3s + 6}{s(s + 1)} = \frac{A}{s} + \frac{B}{s + 1} \tag{2.30}$$

The fraction that is to be expanded is $(3s + 6)/s(s + 1)$. It is important to make sure that this fraction is a *proper fraction*. A proper fraction means that the highest power of the variable in the numerator of the fraction is less than that (the highest power of the variable) in the denominator. In equation (2.30) the fraction that is to be expanded is in fact a proper fraction. If an *improper fraction* is to be expanded, then the fraction must be made proper by repeated division, as illustrated in Example 2.4.

---

**Example 2.4**

Make the given fraction a proper fraction.

$$F(s) = \frac{s^2 + 10s + 20}{s^2 + 5s + 15}$$

*Solution.*  The given fraction is not a proper fraction. The highest power of $s$ in the numerator is 2, the same as that in the denominator. In order to obtain the proper fraction, the numerator is divided by the denominator until a remainder is obtained that has as its highest power of the variable at least the value of one less than in the denominator.

$$
\begin{array}{r}
1 \phantom{aaaaaaaaaa} \\
s^2 + 5s + 15 \overline{\big)\, s^2 + 10s + 20} \\
\underline{s^2 + \phantom{0}5s + 15} \\
5s + 5 \phantom{aa}
\end{array}
$$

$$F(s) = 1 + \frac{5s + 5}{s^2 + 5s + 15}$$

The new fraction is now a proper fraction. The original function is made up by the sum of the dividend and the proper fraction.

---

The form of the partial fraction expansion depends only on the denominator of the function. Various forms of expansion are described in the cases that follow, always assuming the function is a proper fraction.

**Case 1.** Denominator containing products of first-order functions.

$$F(s) = \frac{N(s)}{(s - P_1)(s - P_2)(s - P_3)} \tag{2.31}$$

The function $F(s)$ is expanded to

$$F(s) = \frac{A}{s - P_1} + \frac{B}{s - P_2} + \frac{C}{s - P_3} \tag{2.32}$$

$A$, $B$, and $C$ are constants that are to be solved.

**Case 2.** Denominators containing perfect powers.

$$F(s) = \frac{N(s)}{(s - 1)(s - 2)^2(s - 3)^3} \tag{2.33}$$

Equation (2.34) is the expansion of $F(s)$.

$$\tag{2.34}$$

$$F(s) = \frac{A}{s - 1} + \frac{B}{s - 2} + \frac{C}{(s - 2)^2} + \frac{D}{s - 3} + \frac{E}{(s - 3)^2} + \frac{F}{(s - 3)^3}$$

**Case 3.** Denominators containing higher powers.

$$F(s) = \frac{N(s)}{(s - 1)(s - 2)^2(4s^2 + 2s + 5)} \tag{2.35}$$

$F(s)$ of equation (2.35) is expanded to

$$F(s) = \frac{A}{s - 1} + \frac{B}{s - 2} + \frac{C}{(s - 2)^2} + \frac{Ds + F}{4s^2 + 2s + 5} \quad \tag{2.36}$$

For higher power terms, numerators containing one less term than the denominator—namely, the highest power term—are added with unknown constants.

---

## Problems

**2.4** State the expansions for the following functions of $s$.

(a) $\dfrac{s^2 + 3s + 20}{(s + 10)(s + 2)} = \dfrac{s^2 + 3s + 20}{s^2 + 12s + 20} = 1 + \dfrac{-9s}{s + 10} + \dfrac{-9s}{s + 2}$

(b) $\dfrac{20s^2 - 8s + 9}{s(s+1)}$ $= \dfrac{20s^2 - 8s + 9}{s^2 + s} = 20 + \dfrac{-9s + 9}{s} + \dfrac{-9s+9}{s+1}$

$\rightarrow = (20) + \left(-9 + \dfrac{9}{s}\right) + \left(-9 + \dfrac{8}{s+1}\right)$

(c) $\dfrac{s}{(s+1)(s+3)}$ $= \dfrac{s}{s+1} + \dfrac{s}{s+3} = \left(1 + \dfrac{-1}{s+1}\right) + \left(1 + \dfrac{-3}{s+3}\right) \leftarrow$

(d) $\dfrac{9s + 2}{s(s^2 + 9)}$

(e) $\dfrac{s^2 + 3s + 8}{(s+1)^2(s-3)}$

(f) $\dfrac{10}{(s+1)(s+3)^2}$

(g) $\dfrac{20s + 9}{(s+1)(s-3)^2(s^2 - 4s + 4)}$

(h) $\dfrac{8s - 6}{(s^2 - 9)^3}$

(i) $\dfrac{20s^2 + 100}{(s+1)(s+2)(s+6)}$

(j) $\dfrac{s}{s + 100}$

(k) $\dfrac{4s}{s(s^2 + 4s + 4)}$

(l) $\dfrac{4}{s(s^2 + 4s + 4)}$

(m) $\dfrac{s^2}{s(s^2 + 4s + 4)}$

(n) $\dfrac{s^2 + 4}{s(s^2 + 4s + 4)}$

## 2.5   Cover-up Rule

When the denominator of a proper fraction contains the product of two or more first-order functions, a simple technique – the cover-up rule – can be used to evaluate the numerator constants. These constants are called *residues*. Consider the following function:

$$F(s) = \frac{s^2 + 3s + 9}{s(s + 10)(s + 20)} \tag{2.37}$$

The function $F(s)$ is a proper fraction, and is expanded as

$$\frac{s^2 + 3s + 9}{s(s + 10)(s + 20)} = \frac{A}{s} + \frac{B}{s + 10} + \frac{C}{s + 20} \tag{2.38}$$

The denominator factors $s$, $(s + 10)$, and $(s + 20)$ are first-order functions of $s$, and $A$, $B$, and $C$ are the residues. In order to find $A$, both sides of the equation (2.38) are multiplied by $s$.

$$\frac{s^2 + 3s + 9}{(s + 10)(s + 20)} = A + \frac{Bs}{s + 10} + \frac{Cs}{s + 20} \tag{2.39}$$

Now, if we set $s = 0$, the right-hand side of the equation will be simply $A$.

$$A = \frac{s^2 + 3s + 9}{(s + 10)(s + 20)} \bigg|_{s=0} \tag{2.40}$$

In order to evaluate $B$, multiply both sides of equation (2.38) by $(s + 10)$, and let $s$ equal $-10$.

$$\frac{s^2 + 3s + 9}{s(s + 20)} = \frac{A(s + 10)}{s} + B + \frac{C(s + 10)}{s + 20} \tag{2.41}$$

$$B = \frac{s^2 + 3s + 9}{s(s + 20)} \bigg|_{s=-10} \tag{2.42}$$

$$C = \frac{s^2 + 3s + 9}{s(s + 20)} \bigg|_{s=-20} \tag{2.43}$$

As a technique, the cover-up rule can be formulated as follows: In order to find the residue of a simple factor of the form $(s + P_1)$, cover up (ignore) the $s + P_1$ factor of the denominator, and let $s = -P_1$ for the leftover fraction. The resulting value is the required residue.

---

**Example 2.5**

Find the inverse Laplace transform and draw an approximate time-domain response curve of

$$F(s) = \frac{s^2 + 3s + 9}{s(s + 10)(s + 20)}$$

*Solution.*    The function $F(s)$ given is a proper fraction. It is expanded as

$$\frac{s^2 + 3s + 9}{s(s + 10)(s + 20)} = \frac{A}{s} + \frac{B}{s + 10} + \frac{C}{s + 20}$$

To find $A$, cover up $s$ and let $s = 0$

*Cover up Rule* $A = \dfrac{0 + 0 + 9}{(0 + 10)(0 + 20)} = \dfrac{9}{200} = 0.045$

To find $B$, cover up $s + 10$ and let $s = -10$.

$B = \dfrac{100 - 30 + 9}{(-10)(-10 + 20)} = \dfrac{-79}{100} = -0.79$

To find $C$, cover up $s + 20$ and let $s = -20$

$C = \dfrac{400 - 60 + 9}{(-20)(-20 + 10)} = \dfrac{349}{200} = 1.745$

The required partial fraction expansion is

$$F(s) = \frac{0.045}{s} - \frac{0.79}{s + 10} + \frac{1.745}{s + 20}$$

The inverse Laplace transform of $F(s)$ is given as

$$f(t) = (0.045 - 0.79e^{-10t} + 1.745e^{-20t})u(t)$$

where $f(t)$ is made up of three signals, a step, and two exponential functions. The time constant of $e^{-10t}$ is $1/10$ s and for $e^{-20t}$ is $1/20$ s. In Figure 2.2 these three functions are graphically added to obtain the approximate time-domain response curve of $f(t)$.

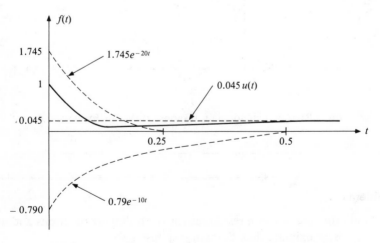

FIGURE 2.2. Response curve for $f(t)$ of Example 2.5

**Example 2.6**

Find $\mathcal{L}^{-1}[F(s)] = \mathcal{L}^{-1}\left[\dfrac{(s+10)(s+1)}{s(s-4)}\right]$

*Solution.*    The function $F(s)$ given is not a proper fraction. Dividing the numerator by the denominator, we obtain

$$F(s) = 1 + \frac{15s+10}{s(s-4)}$$

$$= 1 + \frac{A}{s} + \frac{B}{s-4}$$

The constants $A$ and $B$ are found by the cover-up rule.

$$A = -2.5, \qquad B = 17.5$$

$$F(s) = 1 - \frac{2.5}{s} + \frac{17.5}{s-4}$$

$$f(t) = \delta(t) - 2.5u(t) + 17.5e^{4t}u(t)$$

The time-domain response curve is given in Figure 2.3.

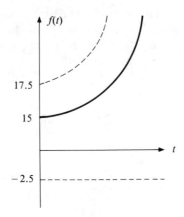

FIGURE 2.3. Time-domain response curve for Example 2.6

**Problems**

**2.5**  Find the time-domain responses for the following functions and draw their approximate time-domain response curves.

(a)  $\dfrac{(s+4)(s^2-8s+9)}{s(s+2)(s-8)(s+10)(s-10)}$

(b) $\dfrac{179}{s(s+20)}$

(c) $\dfrac{4s^3 - 5s^2 + 22s - 10}{s(s+4)(s-6)(s+6)}$

(d) $\dfrac{s}{s+240}$

(e) $\dfrac{2s-10}{s(s-200)(s+20)}$

(f) $\dfrac{(s-1)}{s(s-49)(s+25)}$

(g) $\dfrac{s^3}{s(s+1)(s-2)(s-5)(s+4)}$

(h) $\dfrac{s-2}{s+100}$

(i) $\dfrac{(s+1)^2}{s(s+6)(s-6)}$

(j) $\dfrac{s^2(s-4)}{(s+4)(s-1)(s+1)(s+5)}$

(k) $\dfrac{4}{s^2-16}$

(l) $\dfrac{s}{s^2-16}$

**2.6**  Prove:

$$\mathcal{L}\Big[\sinh \omega t\Big] = \frac{\omega}{(s^2 - \omega^2)}$$

and

$$\mathcal{L}\Big[\cosh \omega t\Big] = \frac{s}{(s^2 - \omega^2)}$$

[**Hint:** $s^2 - \omega^2 = (s+\omega)(s-\omega)$]

$$\cosh \omega t = \frac{(e^{\omega t} + e^{-\omega t})}{2}$$

$$\sinh \omega t = \frac{(e^{\omega t} - e^{-\omega t})}{2}$$

## 2.6  Coefficient Comparison Method

The cover-up rule is a simple technique to find the residues for simple denominator factors of the form $(s + P_1)$. The same technique is valid for the evaluation of the numerator constant $A$ of the expansion $A/(s + P_1)^n$, where $n$ is the highest exponent. The solution of constants involving other types of expansion forms requires a much more general approach. The *coefficient comparison method* is applicable to any form of expansion. However, the computation will be facilitated if any constant that can be found by the cover-up rule is found first.

Partial fraction expansion is stated as an equation. One side of the equation is a proper fraction and the other side is the sum of several fractions (written according to the format described in section 2.5). If the right-hand side of the equation is rationalized with a common denominator that is the same as the denominator of the proper fraction of the left-hand side, both numerators, one at the left and the other at the right, will be the same. Consider the partial fraction expansion

$$\frac{3s + 8}{s^2(s + 1)(s^2 + 4)} = \frac{A}{s} + \frac{B}{s^2} + \frac{C}{s + 1} + \frac{Ds + E}{s^2 + 4} \tag{2.44}$$

The constants $A$, $D$, and $E$ cannot be found by using the cover-up rule. The right-hand side of equation (2.44) is rationalized with a common denominator that matches the denominator of the left-hand side. Since the denominators of both sides of equations are the same, the numerators will also be the same.

$$3s + 8 = As(s + 1)(s^2 + 4) + B(s + 1)(s^2 + 4) \tag{2.45}$$
$$+ Cs^2(s^2 + 4) + (Ds + E)s^2(s + 1)$$

Now the coefficients of various powers of $s$ are compared to solve all the constants.

---

**Example 2.7**

Find the inverse Laplace transform of

$$F(s) = \frac{3s + 8}{s^2(s + 1)(s^2 + 4)}$$

*Solution.*   The partial fraction expansion of the given function is given by equation (2.44). The constants $B$ and $C$ are evaluated by the cover-up rule.

$$B = \frac{0 + 8}{(0 + 1)(0 + 4)} = 2$$

$$C = \frac{-3 + 8}{1(1 + 4)} = 1$$

The numerator of the left-hand side is

$$0s^4 + 0s^3 + 0s^2 + 3s + 8$$

The rationalized numerator of the right-hand side is

$$As(s + 1)(s^2 + 4) + B(s + 1)(s^2 + 4) + Cs^2(s^2 + 4)$$
$$+ (Ds + E)s^2(s + 1)$$

*multiply each term & compare to the original numerator when*

The expression is expanded and the coefficients of various powers of $s$ are collected using a standard tabular format, which will take the following form:

$$s^4 \mid A + C + D = 0 \qquad (a)$$
$$s^3 \mid A + B + D + E = 0 \qquad (b)$$
$$s^2 \mid 4A + B + 4C + E = 0 \qquad (c)$$
$$s^1 \mid 4A + 4B = 3 \qquad (d)$$
$$s^0 \mid 4B = 8 \qquad (e)$$

*setting up*

From equation (e), $B = 2$. Substituting $B$ in (d), $A = -5/4$. From (a), $D = \frac{1}{4}$. From (b), $E = -1$. Use equation (c) for a check:

$$-5 + 2 + 4 - 1 = 0$$

The expanded function is

$$F(s) = \frac{-1.25}{s} + \frac{2}{s^2} + \frac{1}{s + 1} + \frac{0.25s}{s^2 + 4} + \frac{-1}{s^2 + 4}$$

*Remember To Use Tables*

The inverse Laplace transform is

$$f(t) = (-1.25 + 2t + e^{-t} + 0.25 \cos 2t - 0.5 \sin 2t)u(t)$$

## Problems

**2.7**  Find the unknown constants of the partial fraction expanded functions of Problem 2.4.

## 2.7  Summary

This chapter has investigated Laplace transforms of some commonly used signals. Laplace transformation converts signals from the time domain to the complex frequency domain. As is the case with all transforms, inverse transformation is required to convert the signal back to the time domain. Unlike most other transforms, a Laplace transform has measurable physical characteristics in the transformed domain. This makes it possible to analyze the systems in the frequency domain without converting the signal back to the time domain, leaving us with two related, but separate modes of system analysis; namely, time-domain analysis and frequency-domain analysis. Laplace and inverse Laplace transformations are *uniquely corresponding*. This is not usually true for other transforms.

## Key Terms

Define the following terms:

logarithmic transform

$F(s)$

cover-up rule

transformation

$f(t)$

unit ramp

$n$th-order function

unit impulse

partial fraction expansion

residue

sinusoidal

proper fraction

uniquely corresponding

CHAPTER **3**

# Properties of Laplace Transformation

## 3.1 Introduction

In this chapter a few properties of Laplace transformation are explored. These properties, together with the transforms of the commonly used signals discussed in Chapter 2, can be used to solve differential equations, which are mathematical descriptions of physical systems. The section covering delayed signals and the Laplace transformation of periodic signals will yield irrational functions that are rather difficult to handle using algebraic methods. However, they will form the basis of another type of transformation, namely, Z-transformation. A few other properties of Laplace transformation are included for the sake of completeness of the coverage, although they are of minor importance in network analysis and design.

## 3.2 Exponential Multiplier

When a time function $f(t)$ is multiplied by an exponential function in the time domain, the result is a frequency shift in the frequency domain.
    If

$$\mathcal{L}[f(t)] = F(s)$$

then

$$\mathcal{L}[f(t)e^{at}] = F(s - a) \tag{3.1}$$

The time function is $f(t)$ and $e^{at}$ is the exponential function with which $f(t)$ is multiplied. The Laplace transform of the product function $f(t)e^{at}$ is $F(s - a)$. In words, $F(s - a)$ means a function of $(s - a)$ rather than $s$. It is obtained by replacing all the $s$ terms in $F(s)$ by $(s - a)$.

$$\text{Proof.} \quad \mathcal{L}[f(t)e^{at}] = \int_0^\infty f(t)e^{at}e^{-st}\, dt \tag{3.2}$$

$$= \int_0^\infty f(t)e^{-(s-a)t}\, dt$$

Compare equation (3.2) with (3.3):

$$\mathcal{L}[f(t)] = \int_0^\infty f(t)e^{-st}\, dt = F(s) \tag{3.3}$$

$$\mathcal{L}[f(t)e^{at}] = F(s-a) \tag{3.4}$$

Equation (3.4) reveals that exponential multiplication in the time domain produces a frequency shift in the frequency domain. This result is called the *frequency shifting* property.

---

**Example 3.1**

Find the Laplace transform of the following causal signal:

$$f(t) = e^{-3t}\sin 4t - e^{4t}t^6 + e^{-4t}\cos 8t$$

*Solution.*

$$F(s) = \frac{4}{(s+3)^2 + 16} - \frac{6!}{(s-4)^7} + \frac{s+4}{(s+4)^2 + 64}$$

Initially, the exponential multiplier is ignored and the Laplace transform of the remaining function is found. Then all the $s$ terms of the transform are replaced by $(s-a)$, where $a$ is the coefficient of the exponent of the exponential multiplier.

---

**Example 3.2**

Find the inverse Laplace transform of

$$F(s) = \frac{10}{(s+10)^2}$$

*Solution.* In the frequency domain, $s$ is replaced by $(s+10)$. This indicates an exponential multiplier of $e^{-10t}$. The inverse Laplace transform of $10/s^2$ is $10t$. The required inverse Laplace transform of this example is

$$f(t) = 10te^{-10t}u(t)$$

---

**Example 3.3**

Find the inverse Laplace transform of

$$F(s) = \frac{s}{s^2 + 10s + 29}$$

and draw a time-domain response curve.

*Solution.* The denominator is a quadratic expression. If the roots of the quadratic are real, it can be expressed as a product of two linear functions of $s$. Here the discriminant of the quadratic term $[b^2 < 4ac]$ is less than zero, and therefore, the roots are a pair of complex numbers.

$$s^2 + 10s + 25 + 4 = (s + 5)^2 + 4$$

When $s$ is replaced by $s + 5$, an exponential multiplier function is implied. In order for the function to be an exponential multiplier function, it is necessary to replace all $s$ terms by $s + 5$. The given $F(s)$ is thus corrected:

$$F(s) = \frac{(s + 5) - 5}{(s + 5)^2 + 4}$$

$$= \frac{(s + 5)}{(s + 5)^2 + 2^2} - \frac{5}{2} \frac{2}{(s + 5)^2 + 2^2}$$

$$f(t) = e^{-5t}(\cos 2t - 2.5 \sin 2t)u(t)$$

$\cos 2t - 2.5 \sin 2t$ can be combined to a sine wave with a phase angle. From equations (1.12), (1.13), and (1.14)

$$f(t) = Ae^{-5t}(\sin 2t - \phi)u(t)$$

where $A = (1^2 + (-2.5)^2)^{0.5} = 7.25^{0.5}$, and
$\qquad \phi = \arctan(-1/-2.5) \qquad$ (third quadrant)

When $t = 0$, $f(0) = 1$
When $t = \infty$, $f(\infty) = 0$

The time-domain response curve is given in Figure 3.1.

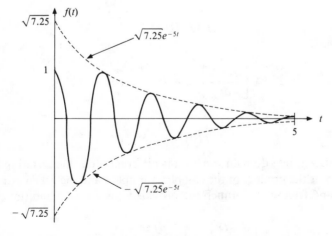

FIGURE 3.1. Response curve for Example 3.3.

## Problems

**3.1** Find the Laplace transforms of the following causal functions:

(a) $t^2 e^{-3t}$  (b) $e^{-4t} \cos 4t$  (c) $e^{-t} \sin 20t$

(d) $e^{4t} t^4$  (e) $e^{-5t} e^{5t}$  (f) $e^{-t}$

(g) $\delta(t) e^{-4t}$  (h) $e^6 \sin 4t$  (i) $e$

**3.2** Find the inverse Laplace transforms of the following:

(a) $\dfrac{s}{(s+3)^2}$  (b) $\dfrac{s}{s^2 + 3s + 8}$  (c) $\dfrac{1}{s^2 + s + 1}$

(d) $\dfrac{1}{s^2 + 4s + 1}$  (e) $\dfrac{1}{(s+4)^6}$  (f) $\dfrac{s+3}{s^2 + s + 1}$

(g) $\dfrac{1}{s^2 + 2s + 1}$  (h) $\dfrac{9s - 4}{s^2 + 2s + 1}$  (i) $\dfrac{6s + 8}{s^2 + 4s + 3}$

(j) $\dfrac{10s^2}{s^2 + 10s + 100}$  (k) $\dfrac{20s}{s^2 + 10s + 100}$  (l) $\dfrac{9(s^2 + 100)}{s^2 + 10s + 100}$

## 3.3 Time Differentiation

When a signal in the time domain is differentiated, its Laplace transform is multiplied by the frequency variable in the frequency domain.

If

$$\mathcal{L}[f(t)] = F(s)$$

then

$$\mathcal{L}\left[\frac{df(t)}{dt}\right] = sF(s) - f(0) \tag{3.5}$$

where

$$f(0) = f(t)|_{t=0}$$

*Notes:* When a time-domain function is differentiated, the resulting Laplace transform is the product of the complex variable $s$ and the Laplace transform of the undifferentiated function, provided the initial condition is zero.

*Proof.*

$$\mathcal{L}\left[\frac{df(t)}{dt}\right] = \int_0^\infty \frac{df(t)}{dt} e^{-st} \, dt \tag{3.6}$$

Let
$$u = e^{-st}$$

and
$$dv = \frac{df(t)}{dt} \, dt$$

$$du = -se^{-st} \, dt$$
$$v = f(t)$$

The required integral as stated by equation (3.6) is

$$e^{-st}f(t)\big|_0^\infty - \int_0^\infty f(t)(-s)e^{-st} \, dt$$

$$= (0 - f(0)) + s \int_0^\infty f(t)e^{-st} \, dt$$

$$= sF(s) - f(0)$$

The result can be extended for higher order differentiation as

$$\mathcal{L}\left[\frac{d^n f(t)}{dt^n}\right] = s^n F(s) - s^{n-1}f(0) - s^{n-2}f(0)^{-1}\ldots f(0)^{-(n-1)} \qquad (3.7)$$

where

$$f(0)^{-n} = \frac{d^n f(t)}{dt^n}\bigg|_{t=0}$$

---

**Example 3.4**

The Laplace transform of $\sin \omega t$ is given as

$$F(s) = \frac{\omega}{s^2 + \omega^2}$$

Using the time differentiation property, prove that the Laplace transform of $\cos \omega t$ is

$$\frac{s}{s^2 + \omega^2}$$

*Solution.*  
$$\frac{d(\sin \omega t)}{dt} = \omega(\cos \omega t)$$

or

$$\cos \omega t = \frac{1}{\omega} \frac{d(\sin \omega t)}{dt}$$

Taking Laplace transformation on both sides of the equation, we obtain

$$\mathcal{L}[\cos \omega t \, u(t)] = \frac{1}{\omega}\left(s\frac{\omega}{s^2 + \omega^2} - f(0)\right)$$

$$f(0) = \sin \omega t|_{t=0} = 0$$

$$\mathcal{L}[\cos \omega t \, u(t)] = \frac{s}{s^2 + \omega^2}$$

**Example 3.5**

Find the Laplace transform of $dx/dt$, where

$$x(t) = (t^2 + \sin 4t + 8)u(t)$$

*Solution.* The required Laplace transform of the equation above is:

$$F(s) = sX(s) - X(0)$$

$$X(0) = x(t)_{t=0} = 0 + 0 + 8 = 8$$

$$X(s) = \mathcal{L}[x(t)] = \frac{2}{s^3} + \frac{4}{s^2 + 16} + \frac{8}{s}$$

Therefore,

$$F(s) = \frac{2}{s^2} + \frac{4s}{s^2 + 16} + 8 - 8 = \frac{2}{s^2} + \frac{4s}{s^2 + 16}$$

*Check.* $\qquad f(t) = \dfrac{dx}{dt} = [2t + 4\cos 4t]u(t)$

Therefore,

$$F(s) = \frac{2}{s^2} + \frac{4s}{s^2 + 16}$$

**Example 3.6**

Find the Laplace transform of

$$\frac{d^2y}{dt^2} - 4\frac{dy}{dt} + 9y(t)$$

The initial conditions are $Y(0) = 1$ unit and $Y(0)' = 2$ units.

*Solution.* The $y(t)$ is a variable and a function of $t$. Its Laplace transform is the variable $Y(s)$, which is a function of $s$.

$$F(s) = s^2Y(s) - 1s - 2 - 4(sY(s) - 1) + 9Y(s)$$
$$= s^2Y(s) - 4sY(s) + 9Y(s) - s + 2$$
$$= Y(s)(s^2 - 4s + 9) - s + 2$$

**Problems**

**3.3**  The Laplace transform of cos $\omega t$ is given as

$$\frac{s}{s^2 + \omega^2}$$

Using the property of time differentiation, prove that the Laplace transform of sin $\omega t$ is

$$\frac{\omega}{s^2 + \omega^2}$$

**3.4**  Find the Laplace transforms of the following causal signals:

(a) $d^4y/dt^4$   where $y(t) = 2t^3 + \sin 2t + 1$

(b) $d^2x/dt^2 + 2dx/dt + 8x(t)$   where $x(t) = 3 \sin 4t$

(c) $d^6p/dt^6 - p(t)$   where all initial conditions are zero

(d) $d(e^{-3t} \sin 4t)/dt$

(e) $d(e^{3t} \cos 2t)/dt$

(f) $d(e^{-4t}t^2)/dt$

(g) $e^{-4t}d(t^2)/dt$

## 3.4  Time Integration

When a signal in the time domain is integrated, its Laplace transform is divided by the frequency variable in the frequency domain.

If

$$\mathcal{L}[f(t)] = F(s) \tag{3.8}$$

then

$$\mathcal{L}\left[\int f(t)\ dt\right] = \frac{F(s)}{s} + \frac{f(0)^1}{s} \tag{3.9}$$

where

$$f(0)^1 = \int f(t)\ dt|_{t=0}$$

*Proof.*  $\mathcal{L}\left[\int f(t)\ dt\right] = \int_0^\infty \int f(t)\ dt\ e^{-st}\ dt \tag{3.10}$

Let $\quad u = \int f(t) \, dt$

and $\quad dv = e^{-st} \, dt$

$$du = f(t) \, dt$$

$$v = \frac{e^{-st}}{-s}$$

The required integral is

$$\left( \int f(t) \, dt \, \frac{e^{-st}}{-s} \right) \Bigg|_0^\infty + \frac{1}{s} \int_0^\infty f(t) e^{-st} \, dt = \left( 0 + \frac{1}{s} f(0)^1 \right) + \frac{1}{s} F(s)$$

$$= \frac{F(s)}{s} + \frac{f(0)^1}{s}$$

Assuming the initial condition is zero, the Laplace transform of a time-domain function is simply divided by the complex frequency $s$, when the time function is integrated. Compare this rule with that for differentiation: $sF(s)$ for differentiation and $F(s)/s$ for integration. The initial conditions will, of course, have some effect and are to be included as stated in respective equations.

---

**Example 3.7**

Find the Laplace transform of

$$\int \sin 4t \, u(t) \, dt$$

*Solution.*    The required transformation is

$$\frac{4}{s(s^2 + 16)} + \frac{f(0)^1}{s}$$

$$f(0)^1 = \int \sin 4t \, dt \, \Bigg|_{t=0} = \frac{-\cos 4t}{4} \Bigg|_{t=0} = \frac{-1}{4} (1) = -0.25$$

$$\mathcal{L} \left[ \int \sin 4t \, dt \right] = \frac{4}{s(s^2 + 16)} - \frac{0.25}{s} = \frac{-0.25s}{s^2 + 16}$$

---

**Example 3.8**

Find the Laplace transform of $y(t)$. Assume all the initial conditions are zero. The following integro-differential equation is given:

$$4 \frac{dy}{dt} + 16 \int y \, dt + 12y(t) = 8u(t)$$

*Solution.*   Laplace transformation is applied to both sides of the equation. The variable $y(t)$ is transformed to variable $Y(s)$ in the frequency domain. The objective is to find $Y(s)$.

$$4sY(s) + \frac{16Y(s)}{s} + 12Y(s) = \frac{8}{s}$$

$$Y(s)\left(4s + \frac{16}{s} + 12\right) = \frac{8}{s}$$

$$Y(s)\left(\frac{4s^2 + 12s + 16}{s}\right) = \frac{8}{s}$$

$$Y(s) = \frac{8}{4s^2 + 12s + 16} = \frac{2}{s^2 + 3s + 4}$$

$Y(s)$ is the required Laplace transform.

---

## Example 3.9

Find the inverse transform $Y(s)$ of Example 3.8.

*Solution.*   The denominator of the function is quadratic. It cannot be split into two factors since the roots of the quadratic are not real. The first two terms of the quadratic are matched to two terms of a perfect square function. Proper correction is made for the remaining term.

$$s^2 + 3s + 4 = (s + 1.5)^2 + 1.75$$

The denominator indicates an exponentially multiplied sinusoidal function. Inspection of the numerator indicates a sine function. The numerator is corrected for the proper format of the sine function.

$$Y(s) = \frac{\frac{2}{(1.75)^{0.5}}(1.75)^{0.5}}{(s + 1.5)^2 + [(1.75)^{0.5}]^2} = 1.5\frac{1.32}{(s + 1.5)^2 + 1.32^2}$$

$$y(t) = 1.5e^{-1.5t}\sin 1.32t\ u(t)$$

---

## Example 3.10

Draw a time-domain response curve for $y(t)$ of Example 3.9.

*Solution.*   The function $y(t)$ is a sine wave of frequency 1.32 rad/s. Its amplitude is a decaying exponential function. The sine wave will swing between positive and negative amplitudes.

These amplitudes form an envelope for the sine wave. The time-domain response curve is shown in Figure 3.2.

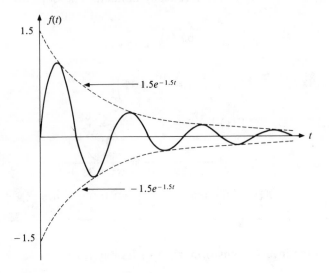

FIGURE 3.2. Time-domain response of Example 3.10

## Problems

**3.5**  Solve the integro-differential equations below for both of the following: all initial conditions are zero; and $Y(0) = -1$, $Y(0)^1 = -5$.

(a) $10 = 10y + 34 \int y \, dt + dy/dt$

(b) $100 = 6y + 5 \int y \, dt + dy/dt$

(c) $\sin 2t = 3y + 10 \int y \, dt + dy/dt$

(d) $e^{-t} \sin t = y + \int y \, dt + dy/dt$

## 3.5  Differential Equations

At the outset, it was stated that using Laplace transformation would make it easy to solve differential equations. In Examples 3.8, 3.9, and 3.10, we have actually solved an integro-differential equation using Laplace transformation. We used the classical method of solving differential equations in section 1.7 for unit step inputs. Other inputs were ignored because of the complications involved. Solutions of differential equations with other inputs, such as exponential and ramp functions, are not much more complicated if they are solved using Laplace transformation. The general plan of attack can be summarized as follows:

*Solution Steps*

1. Identify the input signal and the output variable.
2. Take Laplace transformation on both sides of the equation. The input is known and therefore so is its transform. The output variable is unknown and is transformed as the unknown variable as a function of $s$.
3. Solve for the output variable, and manipulate the expression in proper form for the inverse Laplace transformation.
4. Take the inverse Laplace transformation of the output variable to obtain the output in the time domain.

The required number of initial conditions should be provided to properly transform the differentiation (and integration) terms of the system equation.

---

**Example 3.11**

Solve the following differential equation:

$$\frac{d^2y}{dt^2} + \frac{dy}{dt} + y(t) = 1u(t)$$

The initial conditions are $Y'(0) = 0.5$ unit and $Y(0) = 1$ unit. A block diagram of the system represented by this differential equation is shown in Figure 3.3.

*Solution.*   For this solution, we will follow the four steps summarized above.

1. The input is 1 unit step and the output is $y(t)$.

$u(t)$ ——————▶ [ ] ——————▶ $y(t)$

FIGURE 3.3. Block diagram of system represented by differential equations of Example 3.11

2. The Laplace transform of the input is $1/s$. The transform of the output variable $y(t)$ is $Y(s)$. The Laplace transform is expressed as

$$s^2 Y(s) - sY(0) - Y'(0) + sY(s) - Y(0) + Y(s) = \frac{1}{s}$$

Substituting values for the initial conditions and collecting $Y(s)$ terms, we have

$$Y(s)(s^2 + s + 1) = \frac{1}{s} + 1s + 0.5 + 1$$

$$= \frac{s^2 + 1.5s + 1}{s}$$

3. Solving $Y(s)$ and expanding by partial fractions, we obtain

$$Y(s) = \frac{s^2 + 1.5s + 1}{s(s^2 + s + 1)} = \frac{A}{s} + \frac{Bs + C}{s^2 + s + 1}$$

$$= \frac{A(s^2 + s + 1) + (Bs + C)s}{s(s^2 + s + 1)}$$

The numerator $N(s)$ is:

*Use Cover Rule*

$$s^2 \mid A + B = 1$$
$$s^1 \mid A + C = 1.5$$
$$s^0 \mid A = 1$$

From the three equations above we can solve for the three unknowns:

$$A = 1, B = 0, C = 0.5$$

$$Y(s) = \frac{1}{s} + \frac{0.5}{s^2 + s + 1} = \frac{1}{s} + \frac{0.5}{(0.75)^{0.5}} \frac{(0.75)^{0.5}}{(s + 0.5)^2 + 0.75}$$

*Refer to Tables* 4. The inverse transform is taken for $F(s)$.

$$y(t) = 1 - \frac{0.5}{0.87} e^{-0.5t} \sin 0.87t \, u(t)$$

The output when time approaches zero is evaluated as:

$$y(0) = \lim_{t \to 0} y(t), \quad y(0) = 1$$

The output when time approaches infinity is given by:

$$y(\infty) = \lim_{t \to \infty} y(t), \quad y(\infty) = 1$$

The time-domain response curve is given in Figure 3.4.

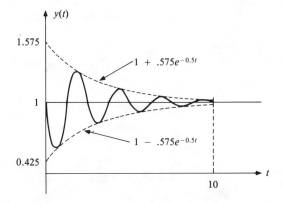

FIGURE 3.4. Time-domain response curve for $f(t)$ of
Example 3.11

The transient response of a second-order differential equation is highly
dependent on the middle term of the differential equation. In equations
(3.11) through (3.15), for instance, $f(t)$ is the input of the system. The term
may be a unit step, a sine wave, an exponential, or any other commonly used
input signal. In all the differential equations listed, the first and the last
terms remain the same, and only the middle term is changed.

$$\frac{d^2y}{dt^2} + 20\frac{dy}{dt} + 100y = f(t) \tag{3.11}$$

$$\frac{d^2y}{dt^2} + 25\frac{dy}{dt} + 100y = f(t) \tag{3.12}$$

$$\frac{d^2y}{dt^2} + 12\frac{dy}{dt} + 100y = f(t) \tag{3.13}$$

$$\frac{d^2y}{dt^2} + 100y = f(t) \tag{3.14}$$

$$\frac{d^2y}{dt^2} - 8\frac{dy}{dt} + 100y = f(t) \tag{3.15}$$

The solutions of these equations will reveal that the transient components of the output depend on the middle term. If the transient component
of the output is a multiple of $e^{at}$, where $a$ is positive, the system will be
unstable, since no system can sustain an ever-increasing output component.
In Examples 3.12 through 3.16, each of the listed differential equations are
solved assuming initial conditions are zero and a unit step input.

---

**Example 3.12**
   Solve $y(t)$ of equation (3.11). Assume that $f(t) = 1u(t)$ and the initial conditions are $Y(0) = 0$ and $Y'(0) = 0$.

*Solution.* $s^2Y(s) + 20sY(s) + 100Y(s) = \dfrac{1}{s}$

$$Y(s) = \frac{1}{s(s^2 + 20s + 100)} = \frac{1}{s(s+10)^2}$$

$$Y(s) = \frac{A}{s} + \frac{B}{s+10} + \frac{C}{(s+10)^2}$$

$A$ and $C$ are found by the cover-up rule, where $A = 0.01$ and $C = -0.1$.

Comparing numerators, after making the denominators of both sides of the equations the same, we have

$$s^2 \mid A + B = 0$$
$$s^1 \mid 20A + 10B + C = 0$$
$$s^0 \mid 100A = 1$$

Since

$$A + B = 0 \quad \text{or} \quad B = -A = -0.01$$

*Check.* $20A + 10B + C = 0, \qquad 0.2 - 0.1 - 0.1 = 0$

$$Y(s) = \frac{0.01}{s} - \left( \frac{0.01}{(s+10)} + \frac{0.1}{(s+10)^2} \right)$$

---

$$y(t) = 0.01u(t) - e^{-10t}(0.01 + 0.1t)u(t)$$

---

The output component $0.01u(t)$ follows the input which is $1u(t)$. This part of the output is the steady-state component of $y(t)$. The second term, $e^{-10t}(0.01 + 0.1t)$, is independent of the input. It is the transient component of $y(t)$. This component decays to zero as time approaches infinity. Therefore, the system defined by the differential equation of Example 3.10 is a stable system.

---

## Example 3.13

Solve $y(t)$ of equation (3.12). Assume that $f(t) = 1u(t)$ and the initial conditions are $Y(0) = 0$ and $Y'(0) = 0$.

*Solution.* $s^2Y(s) + 25sY(s) + 100Y(s) = \dfrac{1}{s}$

$$Y(s) = \frac{1}{s(s^2 + 25s + 100)}$$

The quadratic term of the denominator can be factored.

$$Y(s) = \frac{1}{s(s + 20)(s + 5)} = \frac{A}{s} + \frac{B}{s + 5} + \frac{C}{s + 20}$$

$A$, $B$, and $C$ can be found by the cover-up rule: $A = 0.01$, $B = -0.01333$, and $C = 0.00333$

$$Y(s) = \frac{0.01}{s} - \frac{0.01333}{s + 5} + \frac{0.00333}{s + 20}$$

$$y(t) = 0.01u(t) + (0.00333e^{-20t} - 0.0133e^{-5t})u(t)$$

The steady-state component is $0.01u(t)$ and the transient component is $(0.00333e^{-20t} - 0.0133e^{-5t})$. The system is stable since the transient component eventually decays to zero.

## Example 3.14

Solve $y(t)$ of equation (3.13). Assume that $f(t) = 1u(t)$ and the initial conditions are $Y(0) = 0$ and $Y'(0) = 0$.

*Solution.*    $s^2Y(s) + 12sY(s) + 100Y(s) = \dfrac{1}{s}$

$$Y(s) = \frac{1}{s(s^2 + 12s + 100)}$$

The quadratic cannot be factored into simple factors.

$$Y(s) = \frac{A}{s} + \frac{Bs + C}{s^2 + 12s + 100}$$

By the cover-up rule, $A = 0.001$. Comparing coefficients, we have

$$s^2 \;|\; A + B = 0 \tag{a}$$
$$s^1 \;|\; 12A + C = 0 \tag{b}$$
$$s^0 \;|\; 100A = 1 \tag{c}$$

From (a), $B = -A = -0.01$.

From (b), $C = -12A = -0.12$.

$$Y(s) = \frac{0.01}{s} - \frac{0.01s + 0.12}{(s + 6)^2 + 64} = \frac{0.01}{s} - \frac{0.01(s + 6) + 0.06}{(s + 6)^2 + 8^2}$$

$$y(t) = 0.01u(t) - e^{-6t}(0.01 \cos 8t + 0.0075 \sin 8t)u(t)$$

Here again, $0.01u(t)$ is the steady-state component and $-e^{-6t}(0.01 \cos 8t + 0.0075 \sin 8t)$ the transient component. Since the transient component decays to zero after a long time, the system is stable.

**Example 3.15**

Solve $y(t)$ of equation (3.14). Assume that $f(t) = 1u(t)$ and the initial conditions are zero.

*Solution.*
$$s^2Y(s) + 100Y(s) = \frac{1}{s}$$

$$Y(s) = \frac{1}{s(s^2 + 100)} = \frac{A}{s} + \frac{Bs + C}{s^2 + 100}$$

Comparing coefficients, we have

$$1 = (A + B)s^2 + Cs + 100A$$
$$A = 0.01, \, B = -0.01, \text{ and } C = 0$$

$$Y(s) = \frac{0.01}{s} - \frac{0.01s}{s^2 + 100}$$

$$y(t) = 0.01(1 - \cos 10t)u(t)$$

As before, $0.01u(t)$ is the steady-state component and the source-free component is $-0.01 \cos 10t$. The so-called transient component is neither a growing function nor a decaying function. The system is said to be *marginally stable.* An example of a marginally stable system is an *oscillator.*

**Example 3.16**

Solve $y(t)$ of equation (3.15). Assume that $f(t) = 1u(t)$ and the initial conditions are $Y(0) = 0$ and $Y'(0) = 0$.

*Solution.*
$$s^2Y(s) + 8sY(s) + 100Y(s) = \frac{1}{s}$$

$$Y(s) = \frac{1}{s(s^2 - 8s + 100)} = \frac{A}{s} + \frac{Bs + C}{s^2 - 8s + 100}$$

Comparing coefficients, we have

$$s^2 \bigg| A + B = 0$$
$$s^1 \bigg| -8A + C = 0$$
$$s^0 \bigg| 100A = 1$$

From the equations above we can solve for the three unknowns:

$$A = 0.01, \ B = -A = -0.01, \text{ and } C = 8A = 0.08$$

$$Y(s) = \frac{0.01}{s} - \frac{0.01s - 0.08}{(s-4)^2 + 84}$$

$$= \frac{0.01}{s} - \frac{0.01(s+4) - 0.04 - 0.08}{(s-4)^2 + 84}$$

$$= \frac{0.01}{s} - \frac{0.01(s-4)}{(s-4)^2 + 84} + \frac{0.12}{84^{0.5}} \frac{84^{0.5}}{(s-4)^2 + 84}$$

$$y(t) = 0.01u(t) - e^{4t}\left(0.01 \cos 9.3t + \frac{0.12}{9.3} \sin 9.3t\right)u(t)$$

As before, the steady-state component of the output is $0.01u(t)$. The so-called transient component in this case is a growing, exponentially multiplied function. A system with such a transient component is unstable.

The initial conditions of Examples 3.12 through 3.16 were zeros. If they exist, they can be considered as additional inputs due to stored energy in elements such as capacitors and inductors. These additional inputs are lumped with the system input, as observed in Example 3.11.

**Example 3.17**

Solve the following differential equation:

$$d^2y + 4dy + 3y = 2e^{-2t}$$

The initial conditions are $Y(0) = 1$ unit and $Y'(0) = 2$ units.

*Solution.*

$$s^2Y(s) - s - 2 + 4(sY(s) - 1) + 3Y(s) = \frac{2}{s+4}$$

$$Y(s)(s^2 + 4s + 3) - s - 10 = \frac{2}{s+4}$$

$$Y(s)(s^2 + 4s + 3) = \frac{2}{s+4} + s + 10 = \frac{s^2 + 14s + 42}{(s+4)}$$

$$Y(s) = \frac{s^2 + 14s + 42}{(s^2 + 4s + 3)(s+4)} = \frac{s^2 + 14s + 42}{(s+1)(s+3)(s+4)}$$

$$= \frac{A}{(s+1)} + \frac{B}{(s+3)} + \frac{C}{(s+4)}$$

$A$, $B$, and $C$ can be found by the cover-up rule.

$$A = \frac{1 - 14 + 42}{(2)(3)} = \frac{29}{6}$$

$$B = \frac{9 - 42 + 42}{(-2)(1)} = \frac{-9}{2}$$

$$C = \frac{16 - 56 + 42}{(-3)(-1)} = \frac{2}{3}$$

$$Y(s) = \frac{29}{6}\frac{1}{s+1} - \frac{9}{2}\frac{1}{s+3} + \frac{2}{3}\frac{1}{s+4}$$

$$y(t) = \left(\frac{29}{6}e^{-t} - \frac{9}{2}e^{-3t} + \frac{2}{3}e^{-4t}\right)u(t)$$

---

## Problems

**3.6** Draw the time-domain response curves for $y(t)$ of equations (3.11) through (3.15).

**3.7** Solve the differential equations (3.11) through (3.15) with initial conditions that are zero and $f(t)$ as listed below:

(a) $e^{-2t}u(t)$                    (b) $\delta(t)$

(c) $\sin 4t\, u(t)$                    (d) $2t\, u(t)$

**3.8** Do Problem 3.7, where the initial conditions are $Y(0) = 1$ unit and $Y'(0) = 0.8$ unit.

**3.9** Solve the following integro-differential equations. All initial conditions are zero.

(a) $di/dt + 0.1 \int i\, dt + 4i(t) = 10u(t)$

(b) $dp/dt + 6 \int p\, dt + 12p(t) = \delta(t)$

(c) $9 dx/dt - 3 \int x \, dt + 10x(t) = e^{-2t}u(t)$

**3.10** Solve the following differential equations. All initial conditions are zero.

(a) $y'' - y' - 6y = \delta(t)$        (b) $y'' + 2y' + y = t \, e^{-t}u(t)$

(c) $x'' + 4x' + 5x = e^{-t}u(t)$        (d) $z'' = 100 \sin 10t \, u(t)$

**3.11** Do all parts of Problem 1.8 using Laplace transformation and compare with the results obtained by the classical method.

---

## 3.6 Delayed Functions

If $f(t)u(t)$ is a causal function, then $f(t - T)u(t - T)$ is a shifted and delayed causal function. $T$ is the time delay as well as the time shift. In section 1.3, delayed causal functions were presented. An item of special interest in this section is the delayed and shifted function where the time shift equals the time delay. We will call such a function a *truly delayed function*. It can be said that $u(t - T)$ is a delayed unit step with a time delay of $T$. It is used as a multiplicant to indicate a causal function. It can also be said that $f(t - T)$ is a time-domain function, time shifted by $T$. Note that the time shift must be equal to the time delay in order for the function to be a truly delayed function. If such is not the case, we must first correct the time-domain function to a truly delayed function. For example, if the time-domain function is $tu(t - 1)$, it is a ramp function with a 1 s delay. However, if the function is not shifted, it can be corrected as $(t - 1)u(t - 1) + u(t - 1)$, which is a truly delayed causal function. In this section, the Laplace transformation of a delayed function is investigated.

$$f(t - T)u(t - T) = 0 \qquad \text{for} \quad t < T \quad \text{and} \qquad (3.16)$$
$$= f(t - T) \qquad \text{for} \quad t > T$$

$$F(s) = \mathcal{L}[f(t - T)u(t - T)] = \int_0^T 0 \, dt + \int_T^\infty f(t - T)e^{-st} \, dt \quad (3.17)$$

Let $t - T = x$, $dt = dx$ and

when $t = T$, $x = 0$
when $t = \infty$, $x = \infty$

$$F(s) = \int_0^\infty f(x)e^{-s(x+T)} \, dx = e^{-sT}\int_0^\infty f(x)e^{-sx} \, dx$$

$$= e^{-sT}\int_0^\infty f(t)e^{-st} \, dt = e^{-sT}F(s)$$

$$\mathcal{L}[f(t - T)u(t - T)] = e^{-sT}F(s) \qquad (3.18)$$

When a function $f(t)$ is delayed in the time domain, it is multiplied by an exponential function in the frequency domain. This property is known as *time shifting*. Compare this property with that of frequency shifting, which is evidenced by exponential multiplication in the time domain.

---

### Example 3.18

Prove that the Laplace transform of a unit impulse is 1.

*Solution.*   A unit impulse is defined as

$$\delta(t) = \lim_{a \to 0} \frac{1}{a} (u(t) - u(t - a)) \tag{3.19}$$

A unit impulse function is given in Figure 3.5.

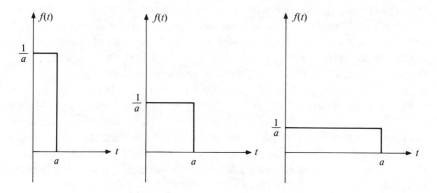

FIGURE 3.5. A unit impulse function

$$\mathcal{L}[\delta(t)] = \lim_{a \to 0} \frac{1}{a} \left( \frac{1}{s} - \frac{1}{s} e^{-as} \right) = \frac{0}{0}$$

The required function $F(s)$ is indeterminate. Using the l'Hospital rule, we find

$$F(s) = \lim_{a \to 0} \frac{\dfrac{d(1 - e^{-sa})}{da}}{\dfrac{das}{da}} = \frac{(0 + s)}{s} = 1$$

---

### Example 3.19

Find the Laplace transformation of the following functions:

(a) $\sin 4t\, u(t)$                                    (b) $\sin 4(t - 1)u(t)$

(c) $\sin 4t\, u(t-1)$ 　　　　　　　　(d) $\sin 4(t-1)u(t-1)$

*Solution.* 　(a) $F(s) = 4/(s^2 + 16)$
　　　　　(b) The function is not a delayed function.

$$\sin(A - B) = \sin A \cos B - \cos A \sin B$$

$$f(t) = (\sin 4t \cos 4 - \cos 4t \sin 4)u(t)$$

$\cos 4$ and $\sin 4$ are constants.

$$F(s) = \frac{4\cos 4}{s^2 + 16} - \frac{s \sin 4}{s^2 + 16}$$

(c) Although the function is delayed, it is not shifted. For a properly shifted and delayed function, every variable $t$ in $f(t)$ must be delayed by the same amount.

$$\sin 4t = \sin(4(t-1) + 4)$$

$$f(t) = [\sin 4(t-1) \cos 4 + \cos 4(t-1) \sin 4]u(t-1)$$

$$F(s) = e^{-1s}\frac{4\cos 4 + s \sin 4}{s^2 + 16}$$

(d) The following function is a properly delayed function.

$$F(s) = (4e^{-1s})/(s^2 + 16)$$

## Problems

**3.12** Find the Laplace transforms of the following:

(a) $2t\, u(t)$ 　　　　　　　　　(b) $2t\, u(t-1)$

(c) $(t-1)u(t)$ 　　　　　　　　(d) $(t-1)u(t-1)$

(e) $te^{-2t}u(t)$ 　　　　　　　　(f) $te^{-2t}u(t-1)$

(g) $(t-1)e^{-2t}u(t)$ 　　　　　(h) $(t-1)e^{-2t}u(t-1)$

(i) $te^{-2(t-1)}u(t)$ 　　　　　　(j) $(t-1)e^{-2(t-1)}u(t-1)$

**3.13** Find the inverse Laplace transforms of the following:

(a) $\dfrac{se^{-s}}{s+10}$ 　　　　　　　　(b) $\dfrac{e^{-s} + e^{-2s}}{(s+4)(s+2)}$

(c) $\dfrac{e^{-(s-1)}}{(s-1)^2 + 4}$

(d) $\dfrac{e^{-s}}{s^2 + 2s + 6}$

(e) $\dfrac{4e^{-s}}{s^2 + 2s + 10}$

(f) $\dfrac{5e^{-(s-2)}}{s^2 + 4s + 10}$

## 3.7 Truncated Signals

A causal signal starts at $t = 0$ and exists for the entire causal interval of zero and infinity. If the signal starts later and exists for the remainder of the causal interval, it is a delayed causal signal. If a signal exists only during a finite interval, it is a *truncated signal*. A truncated signal can be constructed as the sum of causal and delayed causal functions, as illustrated by Examples 3.18, 3.19, and 3.20.

### Example 3.20

Find the Laplace transform of the single pulse.

*Solution.*  The pulse (see Figure 3.6) is the sum of a step function $u(t)$ and a delayed step function $-u(t - T)$.

$$f(t) = u(t) - u(t - T)$$

$$F(s) = \frac{1}{s} - \frac{1}{s} e^{-Ts} = \frac{1}{s}(1 - e^{-Ts})$$

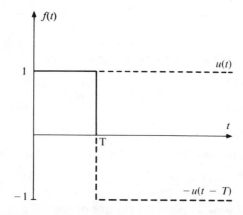

FIGURE 3.6. The single pulse of Example 3.18

**Example 3.21**
Find the Laplace transform of the first half-cycle of sin $\omega t$ (see Figure 3.7(a)).

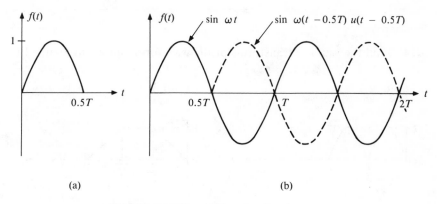

(a)                                (b)

FIGURE 3.7. First half-cycle of a sine wave

*Solution.*   The following solution is illustrated in Figure 3.7(b).

$$f(t) = \sin \omega t\, u(t) + \sin \omega (t - T/2) u(t - T/2)$$

$$F(s) = \frac{\omega}{s^2 + \omega^2}\, (1 + e^{-0.5Ts})$$

**Example 3.22**
Find the Laplace transformation of the waveform shown in Figure 3.8.

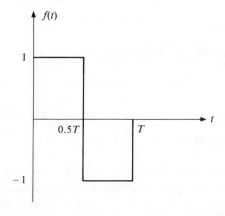

FIGURE 3.8. Waveform of Example 3.20

*Solution.*    $f(t) = u(t) - 2u(t - 0.5T) + u(t - T)$
$$F(s) = (1 - 2e^{-0.5Ts} + e^{-Ts})$$

## Problems

**3.14**    Find the Laplace transforms of the waveforms shown in Figure 3.9.

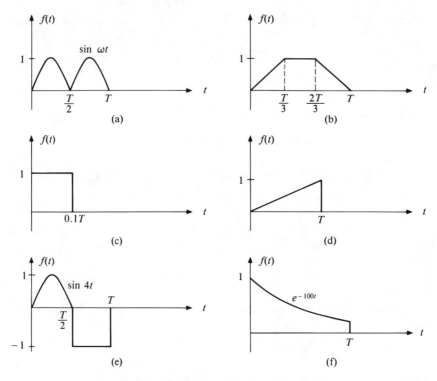

FIGURE 3.9. Waveforms for Problem 3.14

## 3.8  Periodic Signals

A *periodic signal* repeats itself every $T$ seconds. Some periodic signals are *continues* and *analog* that can be defined by a single equation for the entire causal interval. An example of such a periodic signal is $\sin \omega t$. Other periodic signals are *continues* and *discrete*. A square wave is an example of a continues and discrete signal. In this section, the Laplace transform of continues and discrete signals are investigated. Since a periodic signal repeats itself every period, it can be represented as a sum of the functions during the first period and the same functions delayed by whole number periods. In general a periodic waveform $f(t)$ can be represented as

$$f(t) = f_0(t) + f_0(t - T) + f_0(t - 2T) + \ldots + f_0(t - nt) \qquad (3.20)$$

where $f_0(t)$ is the signal during the first period.

$$F(s) = F_0(s) + F_0(s)e^{-Ts} + F_0(s)e^{-2Ts} + F_0(s)e^{-3Ts}$$
$$+ \ldots + F_0(s)e^{-nTs}$$
$$F(s) = F_0(s)(1 + e^{-Ts} + e^{-2Ts} + e^{-3Ts} + \ldots + e^{-nTs}) \qquad (3.21)$$

$1 + e^{-Ts} + e^{-2Ts} + e^{-3Ts} + \ldots + e^{-nTs}$ is of the form:

$$1 + x + x^2 + x^3 + x^4 + \ldots + x^n = \frac{1}{1 - x} \text{ for } 0 < x < 1$$

$$F(s) = \frac{F_0(s)}{(1 - e^{-Ts})} \qquad (3.22)$$

where $F_0(s)$ is the Laplace transform of the signal during the first period.

---

**Example 3.23**

Find the Laplace transform of the half-wave rectified signal of Figure 3.10.

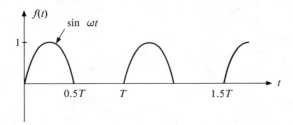

FIGURE 3.10. Half-wave rectified signal for Example 3.21

*Solution.* $f(t) = \sin \omega t\, u(t) + \sin \omega(t - 0.5T)u(t - 0.5T)$

$$F_0(s) = \frac{\omega}{s^2 + \omega^2}(1 + e^{-0.5Ts})$$

$$F(s) = \frac{F_0(s)}{1 - e^{-Ts}} = \frac{\omega}{s^2 + \omega^2}\frac{1 + e^{-0.5Ts}}{1 - e^{-Ts}}$$

---

## Example 3.24

Find $F(s)$ of the waveform of Figure 3.11.

*Solution.*   $f(t) = u(t) - 2u(t - 0.5T) + u(t - T)$ (for one period)

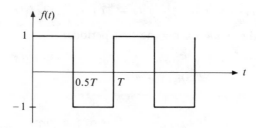

FIGURE 3.11. Square wave of Example 3.22

$$F_0(s) = (1 - 2e^{-0.5Ts} + e^{-Ts})/s$$

$$F(s) = \frac{1 - 2e^{-0.5Ts} + e^{-Ts}}{s(1 - e^{-Ts})}$$

The function $F(s)$ is not a rational function due to the existence of $e^{-Ts}$ for the Laplace transformation of delayed functions. In order to make $F(s)$ rational, another transform is performed using a complex variable $Z$ instead of $s$. The new transform is called $Z$-transformation.

## Problems

**3.15**   Find the Laplace transforms of the waveforms of Figure 3.12.

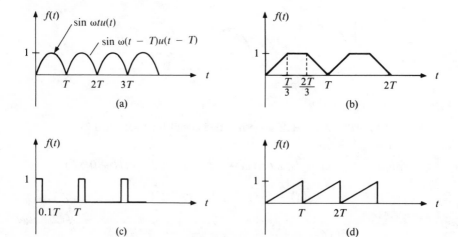

FIGURE 3.12. Waveforms for Problem 3.15

## 3.9   Other Properties of Laplace Transformation

In this section four more properties of Laplace transformation are investigated. These additional properties lead to Laplace transformation of more complicated time-domain signals. Some of the signals are mathematically significant, but not that important in a practical sense with respect to network analysis and design. These properties are included here to ensure the completeness of the coverage of Laplace transformation. They are as follows:

1. frequency-domain integration
2. frequency-domain differentiation
3. initial value theorem, and
4. final value theorem

### Frequency-Domain Integration

If

$$\mathcal{L}^{-1}[F(s)] = f(t) \tag{3.23}$$

then

$$\mathcal{L}^{-1}\left[\int_0^\infty F(s) \, ds\right] = \frac{f(t)}{t} \tag{3.24}$$

Compare the effects of integration in the time domain and in the frequency domain. Integration of functions in the time domain causes frequency division in the frequency domain. A similar effect occurs when functions in the frequency domain are integrated.

*Proof.*  $\displaystyle \int_s^\infty F(s) \, ds = \int_s^\infty \int_0^\infty f(t)e^{-st} \, dt \, ds$

$$= \int_0^\infty \int_s^\infty f(t)e^{-st} \, ds \, dt$$

$$= \int_0^\infty \left. \frac{f(t)e^{-st}}{-t} \right|_s dt$$

$$= \int_0^\infty \frac{f(t)}{t} e^{-st} \, dt = \mathcal{L}\left[\frac{f(t)}{t}\right]$$

or

$$\mathcal{L}^{-1}\left[\int_s^\infty F(s) \, ds\right] = \frac{f(t)}{t}$$

### Example 3.25

Find the Laplace transform of

$$\frac{\sin 4t}{t}$$

*Solution.* $$\mathcal{L}[\sin 4t] = \frac{4}{s^2 + 16}$$

The required function is divided by $t$. It means that $F(s)$ is integrated between the limits of $s$ and infinity.

$$\mathcal{L}\left[\frac{\sin 4t}{t}\right] = \int_s^\infty \frac{4}{s^2 + 16} \, ds = \arctan(s/4)\Big|_s^\infty$$

$$= (\pi/2) - \arctan(s/4)$$

$$= \text{arcCot}(s/4)$$

## Frequency-Domain Differentiation

If

$$\mathcal{L}^{-1}[F(s)] = f(t)$$

then,

$$\mathcal{L}^{-1}\left[\frac{dF(s)}{ds}\right] = -tf(t) \tag{3.25}$$

Compare this property with that of time differentiation.

*Proof.* $$\frac{dF(s)}{ds} = \frac{d\int_0^\infty [f(t)e^{-st} \, dt]}{ds} \tag{3.26}$$

$$= \int_0^\infty \frac{d(f(t)e^{-st})}{ds} \, dt$$

$$= \int_0^\infty -tf(t)e^{-st} \, dt$$

$$= \mathcal{L}[-tf(t)] \quad \text{or} \quad \mathcal{L}^{-1}\left[\frac{dF(s)}{ds}\right] = -tf(t)$$

## Example 3.26

Find the Laplace transform of $-t \sin t \, u(t)$.

*Solution.* $$\mathcal{L}[\sin t \, u(t)] = \frac{1}{s^2 + 1}$$

$$\mathcal{L}[-t \sin t \, u(t)] = \frac{d}{ds}\left(\frac{1}{s^2 + 1}\right) = \frac{d(s^2 + 1)^{-1}}{ds}$$

$$= -1(s^2 + 1)^{-2}2s = \frac{(-2s)}{(s^2 + 1)^2}$$

**Initial Value Theorem**

The initial value of a function $f(t)$ is its magnitude when $t = 0$. It is defined as

$$f(0) = \lim_{t \to 0} f(t) \tag{3.27}$$

If the function is known in the frequency domain, equation (3.27) requires us to find the inverse Laplace transform of $F(s)$ before evaluating the initial value. The initial value theorem will enable us to find the initial value without having to change $F(s)$ to $f(t)$. According to the initial value theorem, the initial value is given as

$$f(0) = \lim_{t \to 0} f(t) = \lim_{s \to \infty} sF(s) \tag{3.28}$$

*Proof.*  From the property of differentiation, we have

$$\mathcal{L}\left[\frac{df(t)}{dt}\right] = sF(s) - f(0) = \int_0^\infty \frac{df(t)}{dt} e^{-st}\, dt$$

$$f(0) = sF(s) - \frac{df(t)}{dt} e^{-st}\, dt \tag{3.29}$$

When $s \to \infty$, equation (3.29) becomes

$$f(0) = \lim_{s \to \infty} sF(s)$$

**Final Value Theorem**

The final value is defined as

$$f(\infty) = \lim_{t \to \infty} f(t) = \lim_{s \to 0} sF(s) \tag{3.30}$$

*Proof.*    $$sF(s) = f(0) + \int_0^\infty \frac{df(t)}{dt} e^{-st}\, dt \tag{3.31}$$

$$\lim_{s \to 0} sF(s) = f(0) + \int_0^\infty \frac{df(t)}{dt}\, dt = f(0) + f(t)\big|_0^\infty$$

$$= f(0) + f(\infty) - f(0) = f(\infty)$$

---

**Example 3.27**

The steady-state error (SSE) of a unity feedback system (see Figure 3.13) is given by

$$\text{SSE} = \lim_{t \to \infty} e(t)$$

where $e(t)$ is the error signal.

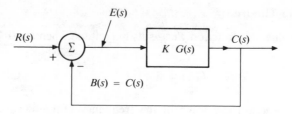

FIGURE 3.13. Unity feedback system

The Laplace transform of $e(t)$ is $E(s)$ and is expressed as

$$E(s) = \frac{R(s)}{1 + KG(s)}$$

$$R(s) = \mathcal{L}[r(t)]$$

where $r(t)$ is the input signal.

If $KG(s) = 100/s(0.001s + 1)$, find the steady-state errors for inputs of (a) unit step $u(t)$, (b) unit ramp $tu(t)$, and (c) unit acceleration $0.5t\ u(t)$.

*Solution.*   The steady-state error

$$= \lim_{s \to 0} sE(s) \quad \text{(Final Value Theorem)}$$

$$= \lim_{s \to 0} \frac{sR(s)}{1 + \dfrac{100}{s(0.001s + 1)}}$$

(a)  $R(s) = \dfrac{1}{s}$, SSE $= \dfrac{1}{0 + 100/0} = 0$

(b)  $R(s) = \dfrac{1}{s^2}$, SSE $= \dfrac{1}{0 + 100} = 0.01$

(c)  $R(s) = \dfrac{1}{s^3}$, SSE $= \dfrac{1}{0 + 0} = \infty$

## Problems

**3.16**   Find the Laplace transforms of the following causal functions:

(a)  $(\cos 8t)/t$                    (b)  $t \cos 8t$

(c)  $e^{-3t}/t$                         (d)  $te^{-2t} \sin 4t$

(e)  $(t - 1)e^{-2t} \sin 4(t - 1)u(t - 1)$    (f)  $(e^{-2t} \sin 4t)/t$

**3.17**  Find the inverse Laplace transforms of the following functions:

(a) $\ln \dfrac{s + 3}{s - 4}$

(b) $\ln \dfrac{s + 4}{s(s - 2)(s + 3)}$

**3.18**  Find the initial and final values of the following functions:

(a) $\dfrac{4s^2 + 6s + 2}{s(s + 7)(s - 4)}$

(b) $\dfrac{\sin t}{t}$

TABLE 3.1  Some properties of Laplace transformations

| Properties | $f(t)$ | $F(s)$ |
|---|---|---|
| Exponential multiplier | $f(t)e^{at} u(t)$ | $F(s - a)$ |
| Time differentiation | $[df(t)/dt] u(t)$ | $sF(s) - f(0)$ |
| | | $f(0) = f(t)\|_{t=0}$ |
| Higher order differentiation | $d^2 f(t)/dt^2$ | $s^2 F(s) - sf(0) - f(0)^{-1}$ |
| Time integration | $\int f(t)\ dt\ u(t)$ | $(F(s) + f(0)^1)/s$ |
| | | $f(0)^1 = \int f(t)\ dt\|_{t=0}$ |
| Time delay | $f(t - T_o)u(t - T_o)$ | $F(s)e^{-sT_o}$ |
| Initial value theorem | $\lim_{t \to 0} f(t)$ | $\lim_{s \to \infty} sF(s)$ |
| Final value theorem | $\lim_{t \to \infty} f(t)$ | $\lim_{s \to 0} sF(s)$ |
| Frequency differentiation | $-tf(t)u(t)$ | $dF(s)/ds$ |
| Frequency integration | $[f(t)/t] u(t)$ | $\displaystyle\int_s^\infty F(s)\ ds$ |

## 3.10  Summary

The properties of Laplace transformation discussed in this chapter together with the transforms of signals covered in Chapter 2 will enable us to obtain Laplace and inverse Laplace transforms of all the signals encountered in linear time-invariant systems. The properties of integration and differentiation in the time-domain form the basis of the method of solving differential equations. The property of time-delayed functions is used to obtain Laplace transforms of *continues* and *discrete* signals. It also forms the basis for Z-transformation. The integration and differentiation in the frequency domain lead to Laplace and inverse Laplace transforms of even more functions. Initial and final value theorems are useful in evaluating important system parameters such as steady-state error.

## Key Terms

Define the following terms:

| | |
|---|---|
| exponential multiplier | continues analog signals |
| frequency shifting | continues discrete signals |
| truncated signals | $f(0)$ |
| $f'(0)$ | $f(0)^1$ |
| $f_0(t)$ | $F_0(s)$ |
| initial value theorem | final value theorem |
| l'Hospital rule | Z-transformation |
| rational function | |

# CHAPTER 4

# Transfer Functions

## 4.1 Introduction

In a linear time-invariant system, the relationship between the output signal and input signal can be mathematically described by an integro-differential equation. In the frequency domain, this relationship will become an algebraic equation as a function of the complex frequency $s$. The *transfer function* is the ratio of the output signal and input signal, both expressed in the frequency domain. In this respect, the transfer function is similar to *gain*. As a matter of fact, gain is a transfer function. All transfer functions need not be gains, however. Gains imply that the output and input are of the same kind, such as output voltage and input voltage for voltage gain or output current and input current for current gain. The transfer functions do not have any such restrictions.

## 4.2 Transfer Function

The transfer function is defined as the ratio of the Laplace transform of the output signal and the Laplace transform of the input signal. The initial conditions are arbitrarily assumed to be zero. If they do exist, they are to be lumped with the input signal.

If $R(s)$ is the Laplace transform of the input signal $r(t)$, and, $C(s)$ is the Laplace transform of the output signal $c(t)$, then the transfer function is $G(s)$, expressed as

$$G(s) = \frac{C(s)}{R(s)} \tag{4.1}$$

Finding the transfer function can be performed in four steps:

1. Identify the input and output. Represent them in a simple block diagram, as in Figure 4.1(b).
2. Write down the system equation or equations describing the system.
3. Take Laplace transformation of the system equation or equations. All initial conditions must be zero.
4. Rearrange the equation or equations to solve for the transfer function.

**Example 4.1**

Find the transfer function relating the voltage across the inductance $V_o(t)$ and the input $V_a(t)$ of Figure 4.1(a).

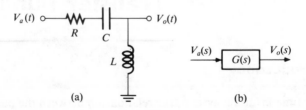

(a)                                    (b)

FIGURE 4.1. (a) Network for Example 4.1. (b) Block diagram representation of the required transfer function.

*Solution.*

1. The input variable is $V_a(t)$ and output variable is $V_o(t)$. The block diagram is shown in Figure 4.1(b).
2. The equations (4.2) and (4.3) describing the system are

$$V_a(t) = L\frac{di}{dt} + \frac{1}{C}\int i\,dt + Ri(t) \tag{4.2}$$

$$V_o(t) = L\frac{di}{dt} \tag{4.3}$$

3. Laplace transformation is applied to both sides of equations (4.2) and (4.3). The three variables, $V_a(t)$, $i(t)$, and $V_o(t)$, are transformed as $V_a(s)$, $I(s)$, and $V_o(s)$, respectively.

$$V_a(s) = L[sI(s) - I(0)] + \frac{1}{Cs}[I(s) + I(0)^1] + RI(s) \tag{4.4}$$

$$V_o(s) = L[sI(s) - I(0)] \tag{4.5}$$

All initial conditions are set to zero. The equations (4.4) and (4.5) are simplified to (4.6) and (4.7), respectively.

$$V_a(s) = I(s)\left(sL + \frac{1}{Cs} + R\right) \tag{4.6}$$

$$V_o(s) = sLI(s) \tag{4.7}$$

4. We have two equations (4.6) and (4.7) containing three variables. The required transfer function contains two variables. The unwanted variable $I(s)$ must be eliminated between the two equations. Therefore, we obtain

$$I(s) = \frac{V_o(s)}{sL} \tag{4.8}$$

$$V_a(s) = \frac{V_o(s)}{sL}\left(sL + \frac{1}{Cs} + R\right) \tag{4.9}$$

$$G(s) = \frac{V_o(s)}{V_a(s)} = \frac{sL}{sL + 1/Cs + R}$$

$$G(s) = \frac{s^2LC}{s^2LC + sRC + 1} \tag{4.10}$$

If the objective is to find the output, it can be found by rearranging equation (4.1) as

$$C(s) = G(s)R(s) \tag{4.11}$$

The output in the time domain is the inverse Laplace transform of $C(s)$.

$$c(t) = \mathcal{L}^{-1}[C(s)] \tag{4.12}$$

**Problems**

**4.1**  Find the transfer function relating the voltage across the capacitor and the input voltage of Figure 4.1.

**4.2**  Find the transfer function relating the voltage across the resistor and the input voltage of Figure 4.1.

**4.3**  For the circuit of Figure 4.1, assume $V_a(t) = 10$ V dc, $C = 1$ F, $L = 1$ H and $R = 1$ $\Omega$. Find the following:

(a) voltage across capacitor          (b) voltage across resistor

(c) voltage across the inductor

**4.4**  Solve Problem 4.3 if the resistance is changed to each of the following:

(a) 2 $\Omega$                    (b) 0 $\Omega$                    (c) 4 $\Omega$

**4.5**  Draw time-domain response curves for the output voltages of Problems 4.3 and 4.4.

## 4.3  Transfer Function Forms

The transfer function must be presented in one of three acceptable forms: *polynomial*, *factored*, and *time constant*. The intended application will dictate which one of the three forms to use.

### Polynomial Form

The transfer function in polynomial form is expressed as a ratio of the functions of $s$, where both numerator and denominator are expressed in decreasing powers of $s$:

$$G(s) = \frac{N(s)}{D(s)} \tag{4.13}$$

where $N(s)$ is the numerator, $D(s)$ the denominator, and both are functions of $s$. The numerator usually contains a constant multiplier. The coefficient of the term that has the highest power is made unity for both the numerator and denominator polynomials.

$$G(s) = \frac{K(s^n + a_1 s^{n-1} + \ldots + a_n)}{(s^m + b_1 s^{m-1} + \ldots + b_m)} \tag{4.14}$$

### Factored Form

In factored form, the numerator and denominator polynomials are factored in the form

$$G(s) = \frac{K(s + Z_1)(s + Z_2) \ldots (s + Z_n)}{(s + P_1)(s + P_2) \ldots (s + P_m)} \tag{4.15}$$

The numerator, as well as the denominator, may contain any number of first-order and quadratic polynomial factors. This form for transfer function is sometimes called *pole-zero* (P-Z) form. Poles and zeros will be discussed in section 4.4.

### Time-Constant Form

The time-constant form is obtained by rearranging the factors of the numerator and denominator of the transfer function with the unity coefficient for the lowest power of $s$, most often the coefficient of $s^0$.

$$G(s) = \frac{K(\tau_1 s + 1)(\tau_2 s + 1) \ldots (\tau_n s + 1)}{(\tau_a s + 1)(\tau_b s + 1) \ldots (\tau_m s + 1)} \tag{4.16}$$

The coefficient of $s$ in the time-constant form will always be a time constant. Since $s$ is frequency and $\tau$ is time, $\tau s$ is a dimensionless constant. As it should be, since $\tau s$ is added to one, another dimensionless constant.

---

### Example 4.2

Express the given transfer function in all three acceptable forms.

$$G(s) = \frac{100(s + 10)(0.2s + 5)}{s^2(2s^2 + 20s + 10)}$$

*Solution.*

**Polynomial form:**

$$G(s) = \frac{100(0.2s^2 + 5s + 2s + 50)}{2s^4 + 20s^3 + 10s^2}$$

$$= \frac{100(0.2)}{2} \frac{(s^2 + 35s + 250)}{(s^4 + 10s^3 + 5s^2)}$$

$$= \frac{10(s^2 + 35s + 250)}{s^4 + 10s^3 + 5s^2}$$

**Factored form:** The highest power of $s$ within each factor must have a unity coefficient in this form.

$$G(s) = \frac{10(s + 10)(s + 25)}{s^2(s^2 + 10s + 5)}$$

The quadratic term $s^2 + 10s + 5$ can be factored. However, quadratic factors are acceptable in both factored and time constant forms.

**Time-constant form:** In the time-constant form, the coefficient of the lowest power of $s$, very often $s^0$, is made unity. $= 1$

$$G(s) = \frac{10 \times 10 \times 25}{5} \frac{(0.1s + 1)(0.4s + 1)}{s^2(0.2s^2 + 2s + 1)}$$

---

## Problems

**4.6**  Change the following to the P-Z form.

(a) $\dfrac{20(0.1s + 1)(0.01s + 1)}{(0.8s + 1)(0.6s + 1)}$

(b) $\dfrac{80(0.3s + 1)}{s(8s + 20)(20s + 10)}$

(c) $\dfrac{(8s + 800)(s^2 + 2s - 20)}{s^2(0.2s + 6)^2(10s + 1)}$

(d) $\dfrac{10(0.5s^2 + 6s + 20)}{s^2(0.001s^2 + 2s + 100)}$

**4.7**  Express the following transfer functions in the time-constant form.

(a) $\dfrac{20s(s + 10)(s + 6)}{(s + 20)^4}$

(b) $\dfrac{2(s^2 + 2s + 3)}{s(s + 20)(s - 20)}$

(c) $\dfrac{0.56(s + 10)}{0.4s + 6}$

(d) $\dfrac{1}{s(s + 2)(s - 7)}$

(e) $\dfrac{1,000,000}{s^2 + 1000s + 1,000,000}$

(f) $\dfrac{10(s^2 + 1000)}{s^2 + 20s + 1000}$

(g) $\dfrac{200s}{s^2 + 100s + 1{,}000{,}000}$

(h) $\dfrac{10s^2}{(s + 100)(s + 200)}$

(i) $\dfrac{R_3(R_2Cs + 1)}{R_1R_2Cs + R_3R_2Cs + R_1 + R_2 + R_3}$

## 4.4  Poles and Zeros

*Zeros* are those values of the variable $s$ that make the transfer function zero. They are the roots of $N(s) = 0$ where $N(s)$ is the numerator of the transfer function. Zeros can be real, imaginary, or complex. Imaginary and complex zeros are the roots of quadratic factors of the numerator. The very nature of the roots of quadratic equations demands that they be complex conjugate pairs, if they are complex at all.

$$N(s) = (s + Z_1)(s + Z_2)(s + Z_3)\ldots(s + Z_n) \qquad (4.17)$$

The values $-Z_1$, $-Z_2$, $-Z_3$, etc., are the zeros.

*Poles* are those values of the variable $s$ that make the transfer function infinity. They are the roots of $D(s) = 0$ where $D(s)$ is the denominator of the transfer function.

$$D(s) = (s + P_1)(s + P_2)(s + P_3)\ldots(s + P_m) \qquad (4.18)$$

In (4.18) $-P_1$, $-P_2$, $-P_3$, etc., are the poles. Again, if there are complex poles, they must exist as complex conjugate pairs. The response, $G(s)$ versus $s$ (shown in Figure 4.2), may suggest why the name pole came about. Notice the sharply rising values of the graphical presentation.

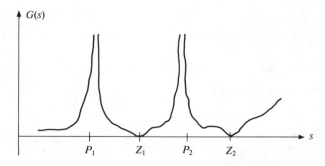

FIGURE 4.2. Transfer function response of $G(s)$

**Example 4.3**

Find the finite zeros and poles of the expression

$$G(s) = \frac{20(s + 40)(s^2 + 4s + 5)}{s^2(s - 20)(s + 50)^2}$$

*Solution.*   The poles are the roots of $D(s) = 0$ where $D(s)$ is the denominator of the transfer function. It is easy to identify them when the transfer function is expressed in P-Z form. Similarly, zeros are the roots of $N(s) = 0$ where $N(s)$ is the numerator of the transfer function.

Poles are: 0, 0, 20, $-50$, and $-50$

Zeros are: $-40$, $-2 + j$, and $-2 - j$

Note that the two double poles are obtained as repeated roots and the pair of complex conjugate zeros are obtained as the roots of the quadratic factor. The poles and zeros play very important roles in the stability as well as the frequency response of the system. It may be helpful to draw a map of the pole-zero distribution of a system. Poles and zeros are mapped on a complex plane. A pole is identified by the symbol $\otimes$ and a zero by the symbol $\odot$. The constant part of the transfer function is placed in a square box, as indicated in Figure 4.3, which is a pole-zero map of Example 4.3.

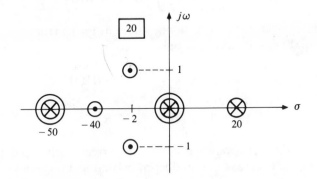

FIGURE 4.3. Pole-zero map of Example 4.3

**Problems**

**4.8**   List the poles and zeros, and draw pole-zero maps for the transfer functions of Problems 4.6 and 4.7.

## 4.5 Impedance in Frequency Domain

The four steps in finding the Laplace transform of a physical system are listed in section 4.2. However, step 3 can be eliminated for electric networks by converting the electric parameters and signals to the frequency domain. For example, consider the network of Figure 4.4(a). It is an *LRC* network with input voltage $V_a(t)$ and current $i(t)$.

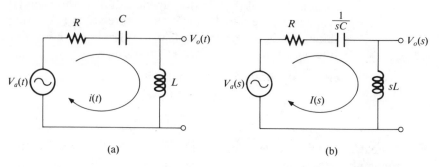

FIGURE 4.4. (a) *LRC* network in the time domain. (b) *LRC* network in the frequency domain.

Equation (4.19) is the integro-differential equation describing the relationship between the system variables $V_a(t)$ and $i(t)$.

$$V_a(t) = L \frac{di}{dt} + \left(\frac{1}{C}\right) \int i(t) \, dt + Ri(t) \qquad (4.19)$$

Taking Laplace transformation on both sides of the equation and keeping all initial conditions at zero, we obtain

$$V_a(s) = sLI(s) + \left(\frac{1}{Cs}\right) I(s) + RI(s) \qquad (4.20)$$

$$V_a(s) = I(s) \left(sL + \frac{1}{Cs} + R\right) \qquad (4.21)$$

where $V_a(s)$ is the input voltage and $I(s)$ the current, both in the frequency domain. Voltage is always the product of current and impedance.

$$V(s) = I(s)Z(s) \qquad (4.22)$$

where $Z(s)$ is the impedance of the network in the frequency domain, we have

$$Z(s) = sL + \frac{1}{Cs} + R \qquad (4.23)$$

Hence, in the frequency domain $sL$ is the impedance of inductor $L$, $(1/sC)$ is the impedance of capacitor $C$, and $R$ is the impedance of resistor R. In

Figure 4.4(b), the network of Figure 4.4(a) is represented in the frequency domain. The networks in the frequency domain obey all network laws and theorems. For example, the voltage divider rule can be used to find the voltage across the inductor.

$$V_o(s) = \frac{sL}{R + sL + 1/sC} \, V_a(s) \tag{4.24}$$

$$\frac{V_o(s)}{V_a(s)} = \frac{s^2 CL}{s^2 LC + RCs + 1} \tag{4.25}$$

Equation (4.25) is the same as that obtained in Example 4.1. In Example 4.1, we used step 3 of the procedures for finding transfer functions (see page 82). Here we simply used the voltage divider rule.

---

### Problems

**4.9**  Do Problems 4.3 and 4.4 using impedances in the Laplace domain.

---

## 4.6   Electric Networks

A transfer function is the ratio of the output signal and the input signal. Very often, but not always, transfer functions of electric networks are voltage gains; i.e., a ratio of output voltage $V_o(s)$ and input voltage $V_i(s)$. We will identify the transfer function $V_o(s)/V_i(s)$ by the notation $A(s)$. Both passive and active networks are investigated. Operational amplifiers (op-amps) are used as the active device for active networks. However, any other active device such as a bipolar transistor or field effect transistor (FET) can be used instead.

### Passive Network

A network that does not contain an active device that is capable of a power gain is a passive network. Transistors and operational amplifiers are two examples of active devices. These devices need biasing to ensure proper operation. Their capability of a power gain is derived from the biasing sources (power supplies). Note that a passive network may produce a voltage gain or a current gain, but never a power gain. As an example, a step-up transformer is a passive device since it does not require biasing. The ratio of the output voltage and the input voltage is greater than one. However, the ratio of the output power and the input power will never be greater than one. The generalized topology of a passive network is shown in Figure 4.5(a). The transfer function $A(s)$ is given as

$$A(s) = \frac{Z_2(s)}{Z_1(s) + Z_2(s)} \tag{4.26}$$

## Inverting Network

An inverting network is one in which the output voltage is 180° out of phase with the input voltage. We are specifically interested in the inverting network using an operational amplifier as the active device. An inverting amplifier network is shown in Figure 4.5(b). The transfer function for an inverting network is expressed as

$$A(s) = -\frac{Z_f(s)}{Z_i(s)} \tag{4.27}$$

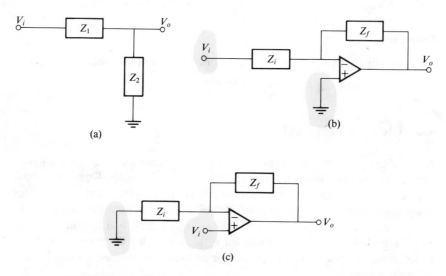

(a)

(b)

(c)

FIGURE 4.5. (a) Passive network. (b) Inverting amplifier. (c) Noninverting amplifier.

## Noninverting Network

A noninverting network is one in which the output voltage and the input voltage are in phase. The basic topology of a noninverting network is given in Figure 4.5(c). The transfer function is expressed as

$$A(s) = 1 + \frac{Z_f(s)}{Z_i(s)} \tag{4.28}$$

If more than one input is applied, the superposition theorem can be used to find the output.

## Example 4.4

Find the output of the network of Figure 4.6(a). The operational amplifier is biased such that its saturation voltage $V_{sat} = \pm 10$ V.

*Solution.* When more than one input is applied to a linear system, the superposition theorem can be used to find the output. The amplifier represented in Figure 4.6(a) has four inputs, each of which contributes an output component.

$$V_o = V_{o1} + V_{o2} + V_{o3} + V_{o4}$$

where $V_o$ is the output voltage; $V_{o1}$ is the output contributed by $V_1$; $V_{o2}$ is the output contributed by $V_2$; and so on.

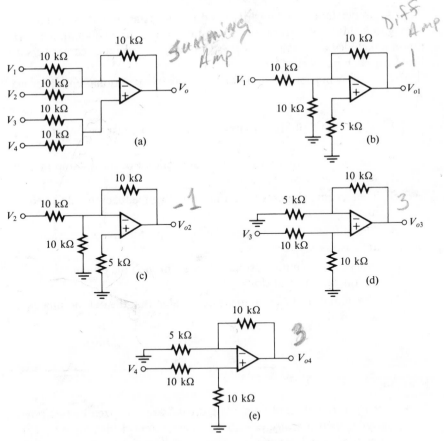

FIGURE 4.6. (a) Network for Example 4.4. (b), (c), (d), and (e) Equivalent networks for individual inputs.

In order to find $V_{o1}$, all inputs other than $V_1$ are grounded, and the gain $A_1$ and the output component $V_{o1}$ are calculated. To find the individual gains $A_1$, $A_2$, $A_3$, and $A_4$, the networks were redrawn as shown in Figure 4.6(b) through 4.6(e).

$$V_o = A_1 V_1 + A_2 V_2 + A_3 V_3 + A_4 V_4$$

$$A_1 = -1, A_2 = -1, A_3 = 1.5, \text{ and } A_4 = 1.5$$

$$A_o = 1.5(V_3 + V_4) - (V_1 + V_2)$$

An understanding of inverting and noninverting amplifiers is assumed throughout this book. Problem 4.9 contains several basic op-amp networks that are included as a revision of these amplifiers. The required answers are listed for each network.

The following list contains some aspects of operational amplifier networks.

1. The output of the op-amp in saturation must be either $V_{sat}$ or $-V_{sat}$.
2. For linear operation of the network, output of the op-amp must be within the range $V_{sat}$ and $-V_{sat}$.
3. The op-amp requires that a net negative feedback be obtained for linear operation.
4. The differential input of the op-amp, for linear operation, is approximately zero.
5. Practically no input current can pass through the op-amp under linear operating conditions.
6. The output of the op-amp is near ideal in that the output impedance is negligible.

## Problems

**4.10** The operational amplifiers of Figure 4.7 are energized by two power supplies such that $V_{sat} = \pm 10$ V. Assume almost ideal op-amp characteristics. Find the output voltage for each of the circuits. The twenty-two op-amp diagrams of Figure 4.7 are presented in two parts. The first part is on page 93, the second part is on page 94.

_Study_

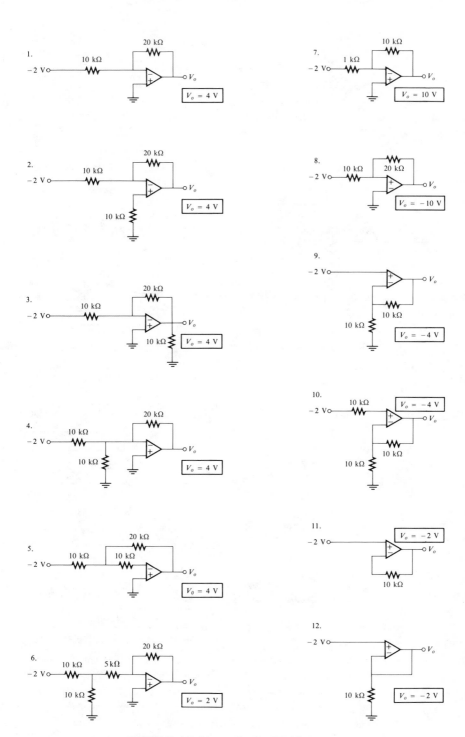

FIGURE 4.7. Networks for Problem 4.10

stady

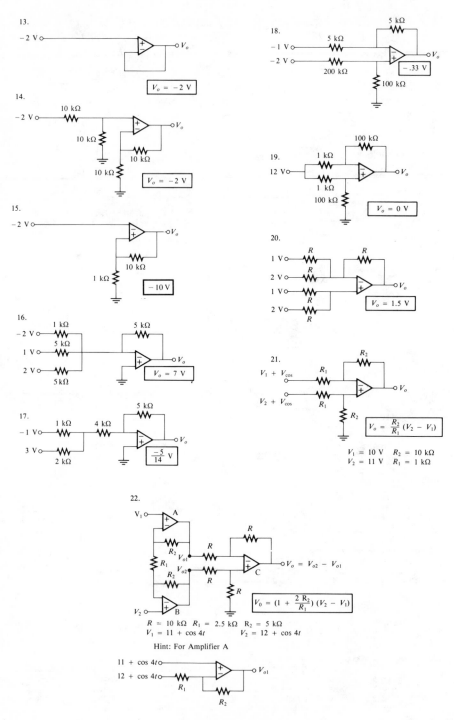

13.

$V_o = -2 \text{ V}$

14.

10 kΩ

10 kΩ

10 kΩ

10 kΩ

$V_o = -2 \text{ V}$

15.

10 kΩ

1 kΩ

$-10 \text{ V}$

16.

1 kΩ

5 kΩ

5 kΩ

2 V

5 kΩ

$V_o = 7 \text{ V}$

17.

5 kΩ

1 kΩ  4 kΩ

2 kΩ

$\dfrac{-5}{14} \text{ V}$

18.

5 kΩ

5 kΩ

200 kΩ

100 kΩ

$-.33 \text{ V}$

19.

100 kΩ

1 kΩ

12 V

1 kΩ

100 kΩ

$V_o = 0 \text{ V}$

20.

R          R

1 V

R

2 V

1 V

R

2 V

R

$V_o = 1.5 \text{ V}$

21.

$R_2$

$V_1 + V_{\cos}$   $R_1$

$V_2 + V_{\cos}$   $R_1$

$R_2$

$V_o = \dfrac{R_2}{R_1}(V_2 - V_1)$

$V_1 = 10 \text{ V} \quad R_2 = 10 \text{ k}\Omega$
$V_2 = 11 \text{ V} \quad R_1 = 1 \text{ k}\Omega$

22.

$V_1$  A

$R_2$  $V_{o1}$

$R_1$

$R_2$  $V_{o2}$

R

R

R

R

$V_o = V_{o2} - V_{o1}$

C

$V_2$  B

$V_o = \left(1 + \dfrac{2R_2}{R_1}\right)(V_2 - V_1)$

$R = 10 \text{ k}\Omega \quad R_1 = 2.5 \text{ k}\Omega \quad R_2 = 5 \text{ k}\Omega$
$V_1 = 11 + \cos 4t \qquad V_2 = 12 + \cos 4t$

Hint: For Amplifier A

$11 + \cos 4t$

$12 + \cos 4t$

$V_{o1}$

$R_1$

$R_2$

FIGURE 4.7. *continued*

94

## 4.7  First-Order Networks

The number of poles of a transfer function must be equal to the number of zeros. This does not mean, however, that the number of finite poles is equal to the number of finite zeros. The unbalanced number of poles or zeros are at infinity. If $n_p$ is the number of finite poles, and $n_z$ the number of finite zeros, and if $n_p > n_z$, then the number of zeros at infinity is $n_p - n_z$.

$n_p$ finite poles and no pole at infinity.

$n_z$ finite zeros and $n_p - n_z$ zeros at infinity.

In most of the practical systems, $n_p$ is larger than $n_z$. If $n_p > n_z$, then there are no poles at infinity. If the transfer function $A(s)$ of a network has only one pole, it is a first-order network. The single pole can be finite or at infinity. There are three possibilities:

1. one finite pole, no finite zero
2. one finite pole, one finite zero
3. no finite pole, one finite zero.

Although the third possibility is not very common, it can be implemented. A good example of such a system is the differentiator network. Depending on the pole-zero distribution and the intended use, the networks are known by names such as low-, high-, and all-pass filters, integrators, differentiators, lead and lag circuits, compensation networks and many more. In this section we will investigate some of these networks and we will classify them later, in Chapter 7.

---

**Example 4.5**

Find the transfer functions of the three networks shown in Figure 4.8. Draw pole-zero maps for each.

*Solution.*

1. The network is a passive circuit. Its transfer function is given as

$$A(s) = \frac{Z_2(s)}{Z_1(s) + Z_2(s)}$$

$$= \frac{sL}{R + sL}$$

The transfer function is now changed to the time-constant form.

$$A(s) = \frac{sL/R}{sL/R + 1}$$

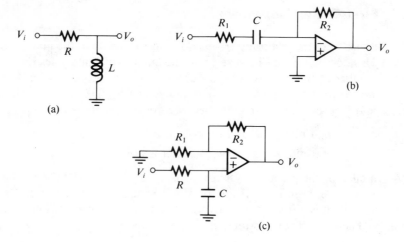

FIGURE 4.8. (a), (b), and (c) Networks for Example 4.5

$$= \frac{\tau s}{\tau s + 1}$$

where the time constant $\tau = L/R$.

Dividing the numerator and denominator by $\tau$, the transfer function can be changed to the P-Z form.

$$A(s) = \frac{s}{s + 1/\tau}$$

There is a zero at the origin and a pole at $-1/\tau$. The pole-zero diagram is shown in Figure 4.9(a).

2. The network is an inverting amplifier. Its gain is expressed as

$$A(s) = \frac{-Z_f(s)}{Z_i(s)}$$

$$Z_f(s) = R_2$$

and $\quad Z_i(s) = R_1 + \dfrac{1}{sC} = \dfrac{R_1 Cs + 1}{sC}$

$$A(s) = \frac{R_2 Cs}{R_1 Cs + 1} = \frac{\tau_2 s}{\tau_1 s + 1}$$

where $\tau_1 = R_1 C$ and $\tau_2 = R_2 C$.

The transfer function can be changed to P-Z form by dividing the numerator and denominator by $\tau_1$.

$$A(s) = \frac{s(\tau_2/\tau_1)}{s + 1/\tau_1} = \frac{-(R_2/R_1)s}{s + 1/\tau_1}$$

The pole-zero map is given in Figure 4.9(b).

3. The network is a noninverting amplifier. Its transfer function is

$$A_1(s) = 1 + \frac{Z_f(s)}{Z_i(s)}$$

This gain is for the signal appearing at the positive terminal of the op-amp. The input signal, however, experiences an attenuation by the passive network made up of $R$ and $C$:

$$A(s) = \frac{(1 + R_2/R_1)1/sC}{R + 1/sC}$$

$$= \frac{(1 + R_2/R_1)}{RCs + 1}$$

$$= \frac{K}{\tau s + 1}$$

where $K = 1 + R_2/R_1$ and $\tau = RC$.

Dividing the numerator and denominator by $\tau$, the transfer function is changed to the P-Z form.

$$A(s) = \frac{K/\tau}{s + 1/\tau}$$

There is a pole at $-1/\tau$ and a zero at infinity. The pole-zero map is shown in Figure 4.9(c).

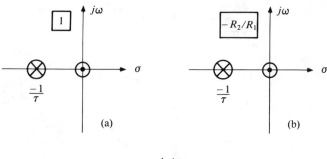

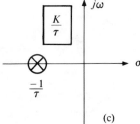

FIGURE 4.9. (a), (b), and (c) Pole-zero maps for network transfer functions of Example 4.5

## Problems

**4.11**   For the networks shown in Figure 4.10 find the transfer functions in both the time-constant and P-Z forms and draw pole-zero maps.

(1)
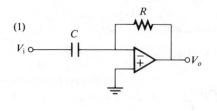

(2)
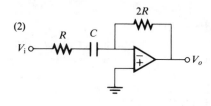

(3)
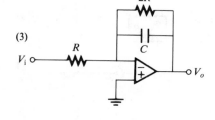

(4)
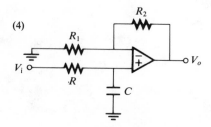

(5)
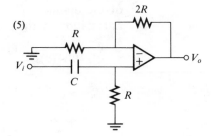

(6)
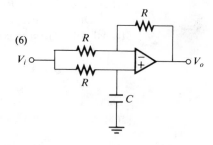

(7)
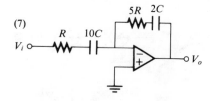

(8)
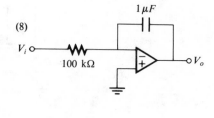

FIGURE 4.10. Networks for Problem 4.11

## 4.8 Step Response of First-Order Systems

The output of a system depends on the input as well as the system itself. The output is made up of two components: a steady-state component which depends on both the system and the input, and a transient component which depends only on the system. The steady-state component usually follows the input; i.e., if the input is a step function, the output component is also a step function. A transient component is usually an exponential or exponentially multiplied function. The transient output component must decay to zero if the system is stable. Otherwise the so-called transient component grows with time, eventually making the system incapable of sustaining the ever-growing output component.

In order to study the transient behavior of a system, it is customary to assume a unit step input and solve for the output.

$$A(s) = \frac{V_o(s)}{V_i(s)}$$

$$V_o(s) = A(s)V_i(s)$$

and

$$V_o(t) = \mathcal{L}^{-1}[V_o(s)]$$

---

**Example 4.6**

The transfer function of a first-order network is expressed as

$$A(s) = \frac{10/\tau}{s + 1/\tau}$$

A unit step input is applied to this network. For $\tau = 0.5$, $\tau = 1$, and $\tau = 5$, find the output voltage $V_o(t)$ and draw time-domain response curves.

*Solution.*   There is one pole at $-1/\tau$ and no finite zero.

$$V_o(s) = A(s)V_i(s), \quad V_i(s) = \frac{1}{s}$$

$$V_o(s) = \frac{10/\tau}{s(s + 1/\tau)} = \frac{A}{s} + \frac{B}{s + 1/\tau}$$

By the cover-up rule, $A = 10$ and $B = -10$.

$$V_o(t) = 10(1 - e^{-t/\tau})u(t)$$

when $\tau = 0.5$

$$V_{o1}(t) = 10(1 - e^{-2t})$$

when $\tau = 1$

$$V_{o2}(t) = 10(1 - e^{-t})$$

when $\tau = 5$

$$V_{o3}(t) = 10(1 - e^{0.2t})$$

The time-domain response curves are shown in Figure 4.11.

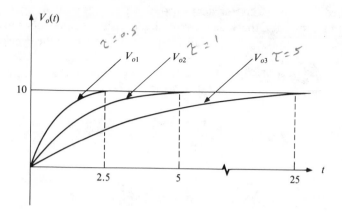

FIGURE 4.11. Response curves for outputs of Example 4.6

For all values of $\tau$, the steady-state component was 10 V and the transient component $-10e^{-t/\tau}$ V. Note that the transient component approaches zero as time $t$ approaches infinity. This is a must condition for system stability. In Example 4.6, suppose the pole is located on the right-hand side of the complex plane. The output of the system can be obtained by simply replacing $\tau$ by $-\tau$.

$$V_o(t) = 10(1 - e^{t/\tau}) \qquad (4.29)$$

Note that the transient component of the output is now $e^{t/\tau}$ and it is an ever-increasing function. The output will keep on increasing until the system cannot satisfy the output demand. If the output is taken from an op-amp, the output will eventually reach $V_{sat}$ and thereafter will remain at $V_{sat}$. In other words, if the system is a bridge and the output is its sag under load, the bridge will eventually collapse. Again suppose the single pole is at the origin, such that $A(s) = 10/s$

$$V_o(s) = \frac{10}{s^2}$$

$$V_o(t) = 10tu(t)$$

The output is also an ever-increasing function. This output does not seem to have the two output components required, namely, the steady-state and the transient. In this case the two components of the output are combined to form a single output function.

---

## Problems

**4.12**  For the networks of Figure 4.12, $R = R_1 = R_2 = 10$ K, $C = 10$ $\mu$F, and $V_i(t) = 1$ V dc. Find $V_o(t)$ and draw approximate time-domain response curves.

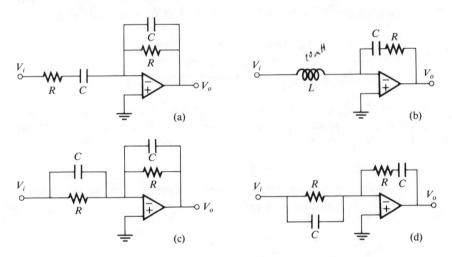

FIGURE 4.12. Networks for Problem 4.14

---

## 4.9  Second-Order Systems

A second-order system has two poles. It may have one, two, or no finite zeros. The poles can be a pair of complex conjugates. Again for the stability of the system, the poles must be located on the left-hand side of the complex plane. If the poles are a pair of imaginary numbers, the system is said to be *marginally stable* or *oscillatory*. (See Example 3.14 for a model of a marginally stable system.)

The transfer function of a second-order system is expressed as

$$A(s) = \frac{N(s)}{s^2 + 2z\omega_n s + \omega_n^2} \tag{4.30}$$

where $N(s)$ is the numerator of the transfer function,
$\qquad$ $z$ is the damping factor, and
$\qquad$ $\omega_n$ is the natural frequency in rad/s.

The numerator may contain one or more of the following terms: $s^0$, $s^1$, or $s^2$.

**Case 1.** Let $z = 1$. The denominator of the transfer function becomes a perfect square $(s + \omega_n)^2$. There are two poles at $-\omega_n$. When $z = 1$, the system is said to be *critically damped*.

**Case 2.** $z > 1$. When $z$ is greater than one, the quadratic expression can be factored as $(s + \omega_1)(s + \omega_2)$. The two poles are at $-\omega_1$ and $-\omega_2$. Under this condition the system is said to be *overdamped*.

**Case 3.** $0 < z < 1$. When $z$ is less than one, the poles of the system are a pair of complex conjugates of the form $(-a + bj)$ and $(-a - bj)$. The system is said to be *underdamped*.

**Case 4.** $z = 0$. When $z$ is zero, the two poles are $j\omega_n$ and $-j\omega_n$. These poles lie on the imaginary axis. This system is marginally stable. A second-order network with zero damping factor will oscillate.

**Case 5.** $z < 0$. When $z$ is negative, the real part of the poles becomes positive. The poles are located at the right-hand side of the complex plane. This system is unstable.

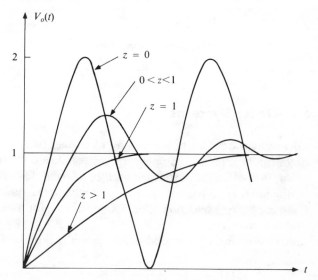

FIGURE 4.13. Typical response curves for second-order systems

Figure 4.13 shows response curves of second-order systems when excited by a unit step input. The transfer function of the system is

$$A(s) = \frac{A_o \omega_n^2}{s^2 + 2z\omega_n s + \omega_n^2} \tag{4.31}$$

144

## Problems

**4.13** In Chapter 3 (page 61), system differential equations are given by equations (3.11), (3.12), (3.13), (3.14), and (3.15). For each of those equations do the following:

(a) Find the transfer function $Y(s)/F(s)$.

(b) Find the poles.

(c) Find $\omega_n$ and $z$.

(d) Classify the system by its damping.

(e) Draw approximate time-domain response curves without making any calculations.

(f) Compare graphs of (e) to those obtained by calculations in Examples 3.10 through 3.14.

**4.14** From the transfer functions $A(s)$ of the networks of Figure 4.12, draw the pole-zero maps.

**4.15** The transfer function of a second-order system is given by

$$A(s) = \frac{144}{s^2 + 24zs + 144}$$

The system is excited by a unit step input.

(a) Find the two poles of the system for the following values of $z$: 1, 0.5, 2, 0, $-1$, $-0.5$, and $-2$; and draw pole-zero maps.

(b) By inspecting the location of poles on the complex plane, determine the stability of the system.

(c) Find the output of the system for all the listed values of $z$ in Problem 4.15(a).

(d) Draw time-domain response curves for the outputs of Problem 4.15(c).

## 4.10   Transient Response of Underdamped Systems

The transient response of an underdamped second-order system is an exponentially decaying sinusoid. In this section, some of the characteristic quantities of this waveform are investigated. Let the transfer function of the second-order system be

$$A(s) = \frac{\omega_n^2}{s^2 + 2z\omega_n s + \omega_n^2} \tag{4.32}$$

### Step Response

Assume a unit step input.

$$V_o(s) = \frac{\omega_n^2}{s(s^2 + 2z\omega_n s + \omega_n^2)} \tag{4.33}$$

$$= \frac{A}{s} + \frac{Bs + C}{s^2 + 2z\omega_n s + \omega_n^2} \tag{4.34}$$

Comparing coefficients of the powers of $s$, we have

$$0s^2 + 0s + \omega_n^2 = (A + B)s^2 + (C + 2z\omega_n A)s + A\omega_n^2$$

$$A + B = 0, \; C + 2z\omega_n A = 0, \text{ and } \omega_n^2 = A\omega_n^2$$

$$A = 1, \; B = -1, \; C = -2z\omega_n$$

$$V_o(s) = \frac{1}{s} - \frac{s + 2z\omega_n}{s^2 + 2z\omega_n s + \omega_n^2} \tag{4.35}$$

$$= \frac{1}{s} - \frac{(s + z\omega_n) + z\omega_n}{(s + z\omega_n)^2 + \omega_n^2 - z^2\omega_n^2}$$

$$V_o(t) = \left(1 - e^{-z\omega_n t}\left(\cos \omega_d t + \frac{z}{a} \sin \omega_d t\right)\right)u(t) \tag{4.36}$$

where

$$a = \sqrt{1 - z^2} \tag{4.37}$$

and

$$\omega_d = a\omega_n \tag{4.38}$$

where $\omega_d$ is the frequency of damped oscillations. If $f_d$ and $T_d$ are the frequency in hertz and the period of the damped oscillations, respectively, then

$$f_d = \frac{\omega_d}{2\pi} \tag{4.39}$$

and

$$T_d = \frac{1}{f_d} \tag{4.40}$$

$$a_1 \sin x + a_2 \cos x = A \sin (x - B)$$
$$\text{where } A = \sqrt{a_1^2 + a_2^2}$$
$$\text{and } B = \arctan(-a_2/a_1)$$

For equation (4.36),

$$a_2 = 1, \qquad a_1 = z/a, \qquad A = 1 + (z/a)^2$$

$$A = \frac{\sqrt{(a^2 + z^2)}}{a} = \frac{\sqrt{(1 - z^2 + z^2)}}{a} = \frac{1}{a} \qquad (4.40A)$$

$$B = \arctan(-a/z)$$

$$V_o(t) = \left(1 - \frac{e^{-z\omega_n t}}{a} \sin (\omega_d t - B)\right) u(t) \qquad (4.41)$$

When $t = 0$

$$V_o(0) = 1 - \frac{\sin (-B)}{a} = 1 + \frac{\sin B}{a} \qquad (4.41A)$$

From equation (4.40A),

$$\tan B = \frac{-a}{z}$$

If $B$ is the angle, $-a$ is the opposite side and $z$ is the adjacent side. Hence, the hypotenuse is 1 as indicated in Figure 4.14(b).

$$\sin B = \frac{-a}{(a^2 + z^2)} = -a \qquad (4.42)$$

From equation (4.41A),

$$V_o(0) = 1 + \frac{-a}{a} = 0$$

when $t$ approaches infinity, $V_o(t)$ approaches $u(t)$. The time-domain response curve of $V_o(t)$ is shown in Figure 4.14(a).

## The Maximum Overshoot

The *maximum overshoot* (M.O.) is the magnitude of the first peak above the steady-state value $1u(t)$. It is a relative value based on a unity steady-state component for the output. It will take one-half of the period of damped oscillation for the output to reach maximum overshoot, as indicated in Figure 4.14(a). Substituting this value for time, the peak level of the output can be calculated.

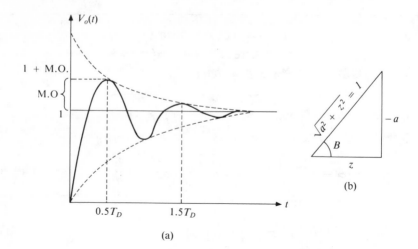

FIGURE 4.14. (a) Time-domain response curve of $V_o(t)$. (b) Right-angled triangle to solve sin $B$.

$$V_o(0.5T_d) = 1 - \frac{e^{-z\omega_n 0.5T_d}}{a} \sin (\omega_d 0.5T_d - B)$$

$$-0.5z\omega_n T_d = -0.5z\omega_n \frac{2\pi}{\omega_d}$$

$$= -\frac{\pi z\omega_n}{a\omega_n} = -\frac{\pi z}{a}$$

$$\sin (0.5\,\omega_d T_d - B) = \sin (\pi - B)$$

Since $(-B)$ is an angle in the second quadrant, $\sin (\pi - B)$ is positive. From equation (4.42), $\sin B = -a$, $\sin (\pi - B) = \sin B = -a$; therefore,

$$V_o(0.5T_d) = 1 + e^{-\pi z/a}$$

The maximum overshoot is

$$\text{M.O.} = e^{-z\pi/a} \tag{4.43}$$

The damped oscillations are due to the transient component of the output. Recall that this component is independent of the input signal. Suppose we have an audio system (second-order or higher) and the frequency of the damped oscillation is 100 Hz. When such a system is switched on and off or the input level is sharply changed, a 100-Hz signal will be audible. The tone will be loud at first and then decay.

The maximum overshoot depends on the damping factor $z$. It is an important criterion in system design. Overshoot is a characteristic of the transient component of a stable underdamped system. The maximum overshoot occurs just after the input level is changed. However, it is independent of the input signal. Suppose a coil is to be designed to carry 2 $A$. If one does not account for the fact that the coil needs to carry $2(1 + \text{M.O.})A$ soon after the input is applied, it is likely that the coil will burn out when the power is applied to it.

### Settling Time

The *settling time* $(T_s)$ is the time taken for the oscillations to settle down within a 5% band of the steady-state component of the output. The amplitude of the damped oscillation is the exponential decay function. The defined band is 0.95 and 1.05, as indicated in Figure 4.15.

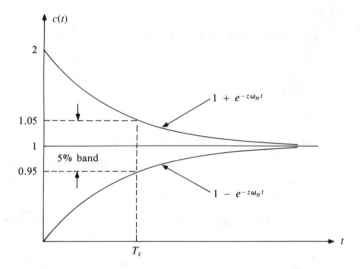

FIGURE 4.15. Settling time for an underdamped second-order system

When the amplitude is 1.05, the time $t = T_s$.

$$1.05 = 1 + e^{-z\omega_n T_s}$$
$$0.05 = e^{-z\omega_n T_s}$$
$$\log_e(0.05) = -z\omega_n T_s$$
$$T_s = \frac{3}{z\omega_n} \tag{4.44}$$

### Example 4.7

A second-order network is excited by 1 V dc. The transfer function of the network is

$$A(s) = \frac{64}{s^2 + 8s + 64}$$

For the equation above, find the following:

(a) $\omega_n$ and $z$

(b) $a$, $\omega_d$, $f_d$, and $T_d$

(c) maximum overshoot

(d) settling time

(e) number of oscillations during settling time

(f) draw an approximate time-domain response curve of $V_o(t)$

*Solution.*

    (a) Compared with the standard transfer function of a second-order system of equation (4.30), $\omega_n = 8$ rad/s and $z = 0.5$

    (b) From equation (4.37), (4.38), and (4.39), $a = 0.867$, $\omega_d = 6.93$ rad/s, and $T_d = 0.93$ s.

    (c) From equation (4.43), maximum overshoot $= 0.16$ V

    (d) From equation (4.44), $T_s = 0.75$ s

    (e) It takes one period for one oscillation. Hence, during $T_s$ seconds, we will have $T_s/T_d$ oscillations. Number of oscillations during settling time $= 0.82$

    (f) The time-domain response curve is shown in Figure 4.16.

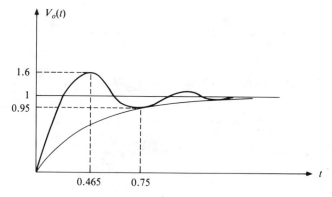

FIGURE 4.16. Time-domain response curve for Example 4.7

A listing of computer programs to calculate the output of a second-order system for a unit step input is given in Appendix B.

$$A(s) = \frac{Cs + D}{s^2 + As + B} \tag{4.45}$$

$$V_o(s) = \frac{Cs + D}{(s^2 + As + B)s} \tag{4.46}$$

## Problems

**4.16**  For Example 4.7, the input voltage is changed to 10 V dc. Do (a) through (f) and compare with the solution of Example 4.7.

**4.17**  The following underdamped second-order systems are driven by unit step inputs. Find the frequency of damped oscillation, settling time, and number of oscillations during settling time and draw the frequency response curve for each of the systems.

(a) $A(s) = \dfrac{10,000}{s^2 + 50s + 10,000}$    (b) $A(s) = \dfrac{10,000}{s^2 + 25s + 10,000}$

(c) $A(s) = \dfrac{10,000}{s^2 + 10s + 10,000}$    (d) $A(s) = \dfrac{10,000}{s^2 + 5s + 10,000}$

(e) $A(s) = \dfrac{100s}{s^2 + 10s + 10,000}$    (f) $A(s) = \dfrac{100s}{s^2 + 5s + 10,000}$

## 4.11  Stability

The output of a system depends on the poles of the transfer function as well as the poles of the input signal. The part of the output contributed by the poles of the transfer function is the so-called transient component of the output. This component, as its name suggests, is supposed to decay to zero after some time. If such is the case, the system is said to be stable. A pole $P_1$ can be positive or negative. It also can be imaginary or complex, provided there is another pole $P_2$ which is a conjugate of $P_1$. The responses due to $P_1$ or a combination of $P_1$ and $P_2$ are given by equations (4.47), (4.48), and (4.49).

1. $P_1$ is real, either positive or negative:

$$\mathcal{L}^{-1}\left[\frac{A}{s - P_1}\right] = Ae^{P_1 t} \tag{4.47}$$

If the pole $P_1$ is negative, the output component decays to zero. If $P_1$ is positive, the output component is an ever-increasing function and the system is unstable.

2. $P_1$ and $P_2$ are two imaginary poles that are conjugates:

$$\frac{A_1}{s - j\omega_n} + \frac{A_2}{s + j\omega_n} = \frac{K_1 s + K_2}{s^2 + \omega_n^2}$$

$$\mathcal{L}^{-1}\left[\frac{Ks + K_2}{s^2 + \omega_n^2}\right] = K \sin (\omega_n t - \phi) \qquad (4.48)$$

This system is said to be marginally stable, or oscillatory. This occurs when a pair of complex poles are located on the imaginary axis.

3. $P_1$ and $P_2$ are a pair of complex conjugates of the form $a + bj$ and $a - bj$:

$$\mathcal{L}^{-1}\left[\frac{A}{s - (a + bj)} + \frac{B}{s - (a - bj)}\right] = Ae^{(a+bj)t} + Be^{(a-bj)t} \qquad (4.49)$$

$$= e^{at}(Ae^{jbt} + Be^{-jbt})$$

$$= Ke^{at}(\sin (bt - \phi))$$

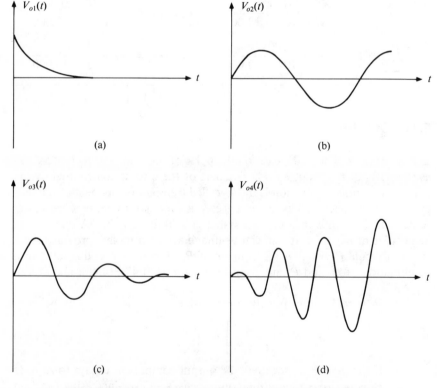

(a)

(b)

(c)

(d)

FIGURE 4.17. Impulse response curves for systems with: (a) Stable pole. (b) Pair of marginally stable poles. (c) Pair of stable and complex poles. (d) Pair of unstable and complex poles.

where $a$ is the real part of the poles. If $a$ is negative, the amplitude of the sinusoid will decay to zero. If $a$ is positive, however, the output component will grow with time, making the system unstable. Typical impulse responses due to a stable and real pole, a pair of stable and complex poles, a pair of marginally stable poles, and a pair of unstable and complex poles are shown in Figure 4.17.

The location of roots on the complex plane determines the stability of the system. If any of the poles lie on the right-half of the plane, the system is unstable. If the system is not unstable and a pair of imaginary poles lie on the $j\omega$ axis, the system is marginally stable. Otherwise, the system is stable. Stable, marginally stable, and unstable poles are illustrated in Figure 4.18.

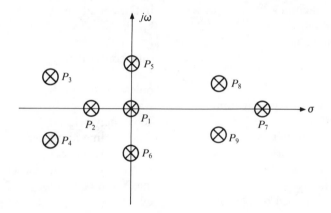

FIGURE 4.18. Pole distribution and stability

The poles $P_1$, $P_2$, $P_3$, and $P_4$ are stable poles, since the real part of each pole is negative. The poles $P_5$ and $P_6$ are marginally stable and lie on the imaginary axis. A network with such poles is an oscillator. The poles $P_7$, $P_8$, and $P_9$ are unstable. The zeros do not directly contribute to stability. The shape of the response depends only on the poles.

## 4.12  Summary

A transfer function relates the output and the input of a system. Since the objective of any physical system is to obtain an output, and we usually need to apply an input for the required response, it is important to know the relationship between what we get (output) and what we give (input). The standard forms in which the transfer functions are to be expressed result from the end use of the transfer function — what we are going to do with it once we have found it. If one is interested to find out how a system responds to frequency, the time-constant form is appropriate. On the other hand, if the time-domain response is required, the transfer function must be expressed in the P-Z form. The location of poles in the complex plane determines the stability of the system. The frequency response of the system depends on poles and zeros. The damping factor and natural frequency refer to second-order systems. The shape of the transient response of a second-order system depends on the damping factor. The frequency of damped oscillations, the damping factor, maximum overshoot, and settling time are very important design parameters of physical systems.

## Key Terms

Define the following terms:

transfer function

system equation

polynomial form

P-Z form

poles

stability

impedance in frequency domain

passive networks

inverting amplifier

first-order networks

damping factor

settling time

period of damped oscillation

critically damped

marginally stable

initial condition

block diagram

factored form

time-constant form

zeros

pole-zero map

stable system

active networks

noninverting amplifier

natural frequency

frequency of damped oscillation

maximum overshoot

overdamped

underdamped

unstable

# CHAPTER 5

# Network Analysis
# and Laplace Transforms

## 5.1 Introduction

In section 4.5, the impedances of electric parameters were derived. A network transformed to the frequency domain obeys all network laws and theorems. In Chapter 4, we have used network laws and theorems to analyze both passive and active networks. In this chapter, more examples of network analysis using various network theorems are presented. The use of a particular network theorem to solve a given problem depends on "economy of effort" and personal preference. The network laws, theorems, and practices, used throughout this book, include:

1. Ohm's law
2. Series and parallel combinations of impedances
3. Series and parallel combinations of admittances
4. Voltage and current divider rules
5. Thevenin's and Norton's theorems
6. Kirchhoff's laws
7. Superposition theorem
8. Delta-wye conversion
9. Loop equations and block diagram reduction

It is assumed that the reader is familiar with all the network theorems and laws listed above except the loop equations and block diagram reduction, which are not traditional methods of network analysis. This technique is used in this chapter because it is a powerful tool for system analysis and design. However, the whole topic of block diagram reduction rightly belongs in a book on control systems, and therefore, only what is required for our limited purpose of circuit analysis and design is presented in this chapter.

## 5.2 Electric Sources

As mentioned in Chapter 1, page 1, the electric system variables are voltage, charge, current, and rate of current. A device that generates any one of these signals is called a *signal source*. A voltage source is the most commonly used signal source in electric systems. The electric outlets in North American homes and work places are an ac voltage source of approximately 120 V (RMS) at 60 Hz. Dry cells or power supplies are available for dc voltages of various magnitudes. An ideal voltage source is one that maintains the same voltage level regardless of the load connected to it. For all practical purposes, the ac and dc sources described earlier can be treated as ideal voltage sources. Otherwise, they are assumed to be in series with an internal impedance. Figure 5.1(a) and (b) are ideal dc and ac sources, respectively. A real dc source is shown in Figure 5.1(c). Ideal and real current sources are shown in Figure 5.1(d) and (e), respectively.

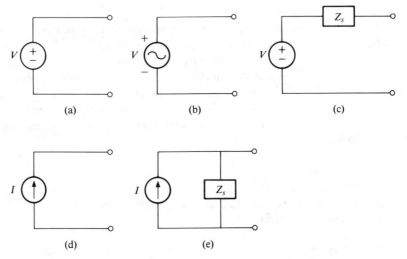

FIGURE 5.1. (a) Ideal dc voltage source. (b) Ideal ac voltage source. (c) Real dc voltage source. (d) Ideal current sources. (e) Real current source.

## 5.3  Energized Parameters

As described in section 1.6, page 14, the three electric parameters are resistance, inductance, and capacitance. Of these three, the inductor and the capacitor are energy-storing elements; while the resistor is an energy-dissipating element. The capacitors and inductors may have some energy stored in them at $t = 0$. The condition of the system output just before $t = 0$ is called the *initial condition*. A nonzero initial condition indicates an energized parameter. An energized parameter is treated as a de-energized parameter that is connected in series with an ideal voltage source or a de-energized parameter connected in parallel with an ideal current source. The former is called the Thevenin model and the latter is called the Norton model, as these two equivalent circuits are derived from Thevenin's theorem and Norton's theorem, respectively. Thevenin's and Norton's theorems are reviewed in Section 5.4. Alternate representations of a charged capacitor are shown in Figure 5.2(b) and (c), and for an energized inductor in Figure 5.2(e) and (f). Figure 5.2(a), (b), and (c) are equivalent circuits of each other, which means that any one of them can be replaced by one of the other two circuits.

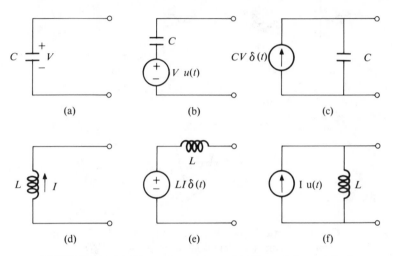

FIGURE 5.2. (a) Charged capacitor. (b) Thevenin's model of (a). (c) Norton's model of (a). (d) Energized inductor. (e) Thevenin's model of (d). (f) Norton's model of (d).

---

## Example 5.1

A 10-$\mu$F capacitor is charged to 5 V and is connected across a de-energized inductor of 100 mH (see Figure 5.3(a)). Find an expression for the output and draw its time-domain response curve.

*Solution.*   In Figure 5.3(b) the charged capacitor is replaced by the voltage source (5 V) in series with the de-energized capacitor. This circuit is an equivalent circuit of Figure 5.3(a). Using the voltage divider rule, we obtain

$$V_o(s) = \frac{5}{s} \frac{sL}{sL + 1/sC} = \frac{sLC}{s^2LC + 1}$$

$$= \frac{5 \times 10^{-6}s}{10^{-6}s^2 + 1} = \frac{5s}{s^2 + 10^6}$$

$V_o(s)$ is the Laplace transform of the output voltage. The signal is inversely transformed for the output in the time domain.

$$V_o(t) = 5 \cos 1000t u(t).$$

The time-domain response curve is shown in Figure 5.3(c).

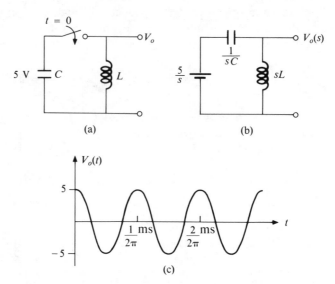

(a)                                    (b)

(c)

FIGURE 5.3. (a) Network for Example 5.1. (b) Thevenin's equivalent circuit. (c) Time-domain response of $V_o(t)$.

---

## Example 5.2

In the network of Figure 5.4(a) the switch S1 is closed for a long time. (The term "long time" is used to indicate that all the transients have been decayed to zero.) Then at $t = 0$, the switch S2 is closed. Find an expression for the output voltage $V_o(t)$ and draw the appropriate time-domain response curve.

*Solution.*   Just before $t = 0$, the steady-state value of the current passing through the inductor is its own initial condition when S2 is closed. Therefore, by Ohm's law, we obtain

$$\frac{100}{s} = (100 + 0.1s)I_o(s)$$

$$I_o(s) = \frac{100}{s(0.1s + 100)} = \frac{1000}{s(s + 1000)}$$

$$= \frac{A}{s} + \frac{B}{(s + 1000)}$$

By the cover-up rule, $A = 1$, $B = -1$

$$I_o(s) = \frac{1}{s} - \frac{1}{s + 100}$$

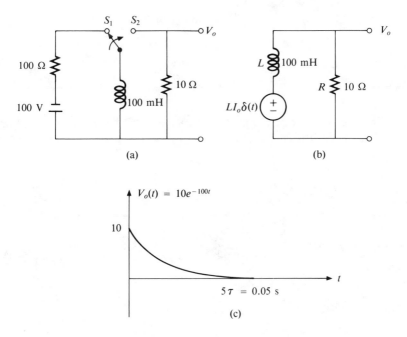

FIGURE 5.4. (a) Network for Example 5.2. (b) Equivalent circuit of (a). (c) Time-domain response curve of $V_o(t)$.

and

$$i_o(t) = (1 - e^{-1000t})u(t)$$

After a long time $(t \to \infty)$, $i_o = 1u(t)$. It is the initial condition for the inductor. The equivalent circuit is shown in Figure 5.4(b).

$$V_o(s) = \frac{Li_o R}{R + sL} = \frac{1}{10 + 0.1s} = \frac{10}{s + 100}$$

In order to obtain the output voltage in the time domain, the inverse transform is taken on $V_o(s)$.

$$V_o(t) = 10e^{-100t}u(t)$$

The time-domain response curve is given in Figure 5.4(c).

## Example 5.3

For Example 5.2, if the switch S1 is closed only for 1 ms, find an expression for $V_o(t)$.

*Solution.*    In Example 5.2, $i_o(t)$ is found to be $(1 - e^{-1000t})u(t)$. The initial condition for the inductor is $i_o(t)$ when $t = 1$ ms.

$$i_o(t) = (1 - e^{-1}) = 0.63 \text{ A instead of 1 A.}$$

Hence

$$V_o(t) = 6.3e^{-100t}u(t)$$

---

**Example 5.4**

For the network of Figure 5.5(a), the switch S1 is opened for a long time. Then it is closed at $t = 0$. Draw the equivalent network.

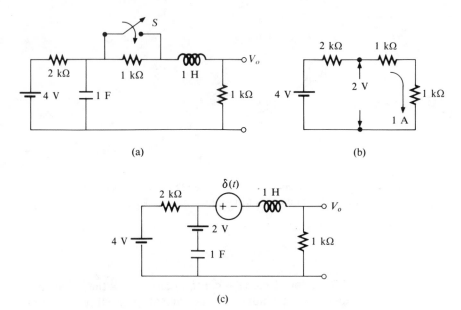

(a)    (b)

(c)

FIGURE 5.5. (a) Network for Example 5.4. (b) Network, a long time after $S$ is open. (c) Equivalent circuit of (a).

*Solution.*    For a dc signal, the capacitor is a short circuit (zero impedance) at $t = 0$, and the impedance increases as the time increases. After a long time the capacitance acts as an open circuit (infinite impedance). The opposite is true for an inductor; that is, after a long time, the inductance behaves as a short circuit. From this network, the voltage across the capacitance is 2 V and the current through the inductor 1 A (see Figure 5.5(b)). The required equivalent circuit is shown in Figure 5.5(c).

---

**Example 5.5**

Find the output voltage $V_o(t)$ when the network of Figure 5.6(a) is excited by the pulse indicated. Draw the time-domain response curve of $V_o(t)$.

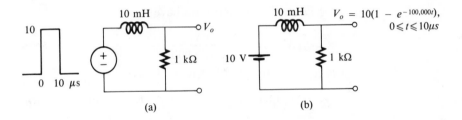

(a)                                    (b)

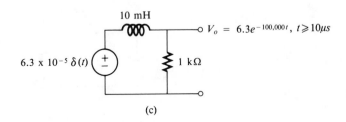

(c)

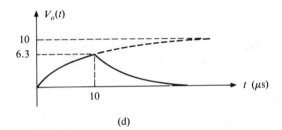

(d)

FIGURE 5.6. (a) Network for Example 5.5. (b) Network model for ON condition. (c) Network model for OFF condition. (d) Time-domain response of $V_o(t)$ and $V_{o1}(t)$.

*Solution.*   The pulse can be considered as a step function switched on for 100 μs and then switched off. The ON condition is illustrated in Figure 5.6(b) and the OFF condition in Figure 5.6(c).

From Figure 5.6(b), we have

$$V_o(s) = \frac{10}{s} \frac{R}{R + sL} = \frac{10R/L}{s(s + R/L)}$$

$$= \frac{10^6}{s(s + 100{,}000)} = \frac{A}{s} + \frac{B}{s + 100{,}000}$$

By the cover-up rule, $A = 10$,   $B = -10$

$$V_o(t) = 10(1 - e^{-100{,}000t})$$

In 10 μs, $V_o(t) = 6.3$ V and the current through the inductor 6.3 mA. This current is the initial condition for the network of Figure 5.6(c).

From Figure 5.6(c), we have

$$V_{o1}(s) = \frac{6.3}{s + 100,000}$$

$$V_{o1}(t) = 6.3e^{-100,000t} \text{ (delayed 10 } \mu s)$$

The time-domain response curve is shown in Figure 5.6(d).

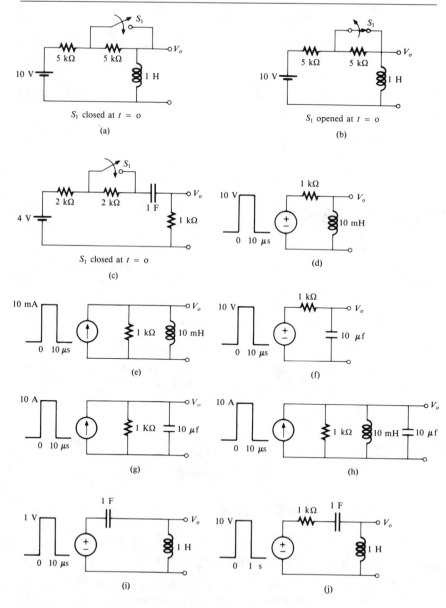

FIGURE 5.7. Networks for Problem 5.1

**Problems**

**5.1**   For the networks of Figure 5.7, find the output voltages and draw their time-domain response curves.

## 5.4 Thevenin and Norton Equivalent Circuits

Any two-terminal network can be represented by an ideal voltage source in series with an impedance or an ideal current source with a parallel admittance. The former is called the Thevenin equivalent circuit and the latter the Norton equivalent circuit. The network of Figure 5.7(a) is made up of interconnected voltage and/or current sources and impedances to the left of terminals A and A', and similar sorts of interconnected components and sources to the right of terminals A and A'. The two parts of the network are illustrated in Figure 5.8(a) as block X and block Y.

The block X can be replaced by a single voltage source $V_{th}$, in series with an impedance $Z_{th}$. As indicated in Figure 5.8(b) $V_{th}$ is the open-circuit voltage across terminals A and A'. One can measure this voltage across the terminals A and A' if the block Y is removed from terminals A and A'. The block Y is called the *load* on the Thevenin (or Norton) circuit. Thus, $V_{th}$ is the voltage across terminals A and A' with the load removed. $Z_{th}$ is the impedance that exists between terminals A and A' after the load (block Y) is removed from the network.

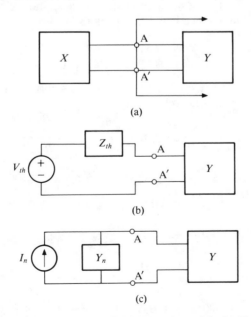

(a)

(b)

(c)

FIGURE 5.8. (a) Two-terminal network model. (b) Thevenin equivalent model. (c) Norton equivalent model.

To find $Z_{th}$, all voltage sources within block X are short-circuited and all current sources open-circuited, and then the equivalent impedance between terminals A and A' is estimated.

For the Norton equivalent circuit, the block X is represented by a current source $I_n$, with a parallel admittance $Y_n$ as indicated in Figure 5.8(c). The short-circuit current is $I_n$. This current passes through a short-circuit between terminals A and A' after the load is removed. The admittance $Y_n$ is related to $Z_{th}$ by the following equation

$$Y_n = \frac{1}{Z_{th}}$$

---

## Example 5.6

Derive the transfer function $V_o(s)/V_i(s)$ of the network in Figure 5.9(a) and find $V_o(t)$ for a unit step input. Draw the time-domain response curve of $V_o(t)$. Let $RC = 0.01$ s.

*Solution.* Applying the Thevenin theorem between terminals A and A', we obtain

$$V_{th} = V_i(s) \frac{1/sC}{R + 1/sC} = \frac{V_i(s)}{RCs + 1}$$

To find $Z_{th}$, the voltage source is short-circuited and the impedance between terminals A and A' is estimated.

$$Z_{th} = \frac{1}{sC} \left\| R = \frac{R}{RCs + 1} \right.$$

The network is now reduced as shown in Figure 5.9(b). Using the voltage divider law,

$$V_o(s) = V_{th} \frac{1/sC}{Z_{th} + R + 1/sC} = \frac{V_i(s)}{RCs + 1} \frac{1/sC}{\dfrac{R}{RCs + 1} + R + 1/sC}$$

$$= V_i(s) \frac{1}{R^2C^2s^2 + 3RCs + 1}$$

$$V_o(s)/V_i(s) = A(s) = \frac{1}{R^2C^2s^2 + 3RCs + 1}$$

and for $RC = 0.01$ s

$$A(s) = \frac{1}{0.0001s^2 + 0.03s + 1} = \frac{10,000}{s^2 + 300s + 10,000}$$

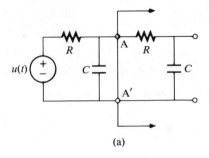

(a)

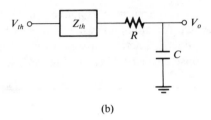

(b)

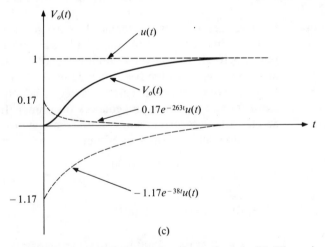

(c)

FIGURE 5.9. (a) Network for Example 5.6. (b) Thevenin equivalent circuit. (c) Time-domain response curve of $V_o(t)$.

The quadratic expression of the denominator can be factored as $(s + 262)(s + 38)$.

$$A(s) = \frac{10,000}{(s + 263)(s + 38)}$$

For a unit step input (1 V dc), $V_i(s) = 1/s$

$$V_o(s) = V_i(s)A(s) = \frac{10,000}{s(s + 38)(s + 263)}$$

$$= \frac{A}{s} + \frac{B}{s + 38} + \frac{C}{s + 263}$$

By the cover-up rule, $A = 1$, $B = -1.17$, and $C = 0.17$:

$$V_o(s) = \frac{1}{s} - \frac{1.17}{s + 38} + \frac{0.17}{s + 263}$$

$$V_o(t) = (1 - 1.17e^{-38t} + 0.17e^{-263t})u(t).$$

The output voltage above is made up of three signals: one step function and two exponential functions. The three component functions are illustrated for the time-domain response curve of $V_o(t)$ in Figure 5.9(c).

## Example 5.7

Find an expression for $V_o(s)$ of the network of Figure 5.10(a).

*Solution.* Both voltage sources are replaced by a Norton model as indicated in Figure 5.10(b), and simplified to the circuit of Figure 5.10(c). The network components of Figure 5.10(a) and (b) are given in the frequency domain. Note also that some network components are expressed as admittances (in siemens) and others as impedances (in ohms). In Figure 5.10(c), the two current sources are combined to one current source and the three admittances to one admittance.

$$I_n(s) = \frac{1}{200}\left(V_i(s) - \frac{1}{s}\right) = \frac{0.005(sV_i(s) - 1)}{s}$$

$$Y_n = 10^{-4}s + 0.005 + 0.005 = \frac{s + 100}{10,000}$$

Note that the admittance of a capacitor is $sC$ and the resultant of three admittances in parallel is their sum. Now the Norton circuit is replaced by a Thevenin circuit as in Figure 5.10(d).

$$V_{th} = \frac{I_n}{Y_n} = \frac{0.005(sV_i(s) - 1)}{0.0001s(s + 100)} = \frac{50(sV_i(s) - 1)}{s(s + 100)}$$

$$Z_{th} = \frac{1}{Y_n} = \frac{10,000}{(s + 100)}$$

From the voltage divider rule, we have

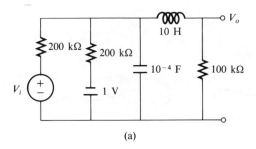

(a)

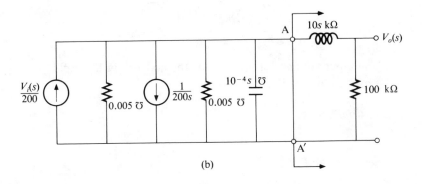

(b)

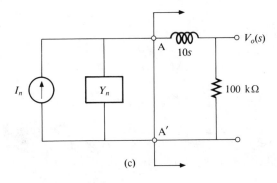

(c)

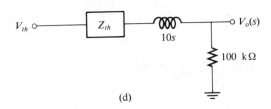

(d)

FIGURE 5.10. (a) Network for Example 5.7. (b) and (c) Norton equation circuit. (d) Thevenin equation circuit.

$$V_o(s) = \frac{5000(sV_i(s) - 1)}{s(s + 100)\left(\dfrac{10{,}000}{(s + 100)} + 10s + 100\right)}$$

$$= \frac{5000(sV_i(s) - 1)}{s(10{,}000 + 10s^2 + 1000s + 100s + 10{,}000)}$$

$$= \frac{500(sV_i(s) - 1)}{s(s^2 + 110s + 2000)}$$

$$V_o(s) = \frac{500(sV_i(s) - 1)}{s(s + 87)(s + 23)}$$

## Example 5.8

If the input voltage $V_i(t)$ is $e^{-t}$ for the network in Example 5.7, find an expression for $V_o(t)$.

*Solution.*   Since

$$V_i(t) = e^{-t}u(t)$$

and

$$V_i(s) = \frac{1}{(s + 1)}$$

$$V_o(s) = \frac{500\left(\dfrac{s}{s + 1} - 1\right)}{s(s + 87)(s + 23)} = \frac{-500}{s(s + 1)(s + 23)(s + 87)}$$

$$= \frac{A}{s} + \frac{B}{s + 1} + \frac{C}{s + 23} + \frac{D}{s + 87}$$

$A$, $B$, $C$, and $D$ are estimated by the cover-up rule: $A = 0.25$, $B = 0.264$, $C = -0.016$, and $D = 0.001$.
The inverse Laplace transform of $V_o(s)$ is $V_o(t)$.

$$V_o(t) = (-0.25 + 0.264e^{-t} - 0.016e^{-23t} - 0.001e^{-87t})u(t)$$

## Problems

**5.2**   Find the transfer function $V_o(s)/V_i(s)$ for the networks of Figure 5.11. Assume $L = 1$ H, $C = 1$ F, and $R = 1$ Ω.

**5.3**   Find the output voltage $V_o(t)$ for each of the networks for Problem 5.2 if the input voltage for each is:

(a) 1 V dc        (b) the unit impulse        (c) $e^{-2t}$        (d) $4t$

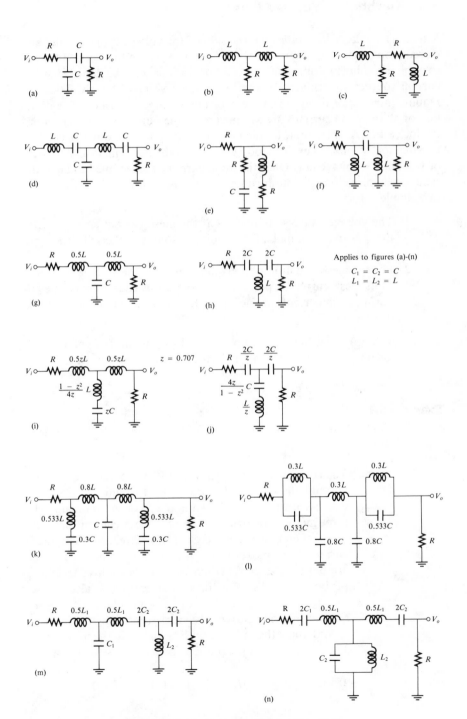

FIGURE 5.11. Networks for Problem 5.2

## 5.5  Kirchhoff's Voltage Law

Kirchhoff's voltage law states that the sum of the voltage drops around any closed loop equals the sum of the source voltages within that loop. In order to apply Kirchhoff's voltage law, several operations must be done. First, all current sources are replaced by their equivalent voltage sources. Then the required number of independent loops or meshes are established. The direction of all the mesh currents are assumed to be the same (for example, counterclockwise). At this point, loop equations can be written down according to Kirchhoff's voltage law. The loop equation is the mathematical statement of Kirchhoff's voltage law. Once the mesh currents are assumed to be in the same cyclic direction, the mesh equations can be written — following these two simple rules:

1. The voltage sources are positive if the mesh current emerges from the positive terminal of the voltage source; otherwise they are negative.
2. For the mesh equation of a given mesh, only the voltage drop due to its mesh current is positive. Voltage drops caused by the neighboring mesh currents are negative. Example 5.9 will illustrate these techniques.

The mesh (loop) equations are set up as stated by Kirchhoff's voltage law. Once equations are set up, they are solved for their mesh currents.

---

**Example 5.9**

Write down all the required mesh equations for the network of Figure 5.12(a).

*Solution.*    The equivalent circuit, shown in Figure 5.12(b), takes into account the energized parameters. In Figure 5.12(c), the equivalent circuit is redrawn in the frequency domain. The three meshes are identified and the mesh currents are indicated assuming a counterclockwise direction. The mesh current $I_1(s)$ passes through two sources, both of which are positive, since $I_1(s)$ emerges at the positive terminals of both sources. The mesh current $I_1(s)$ also passes through two components with a net impedance of $R + sL$. One neighboring current, $I_2(s)$, passes through inductance $L$ and the other, $I_3(s)$, passes through the resistor $R$. Therefore, the loop equation for mesh 1 is written as

$$\frac{10}{s} + 0.5sL = (R + sL)I_1(s) - sL\,I_2(s) - R\,I_3(s)$$

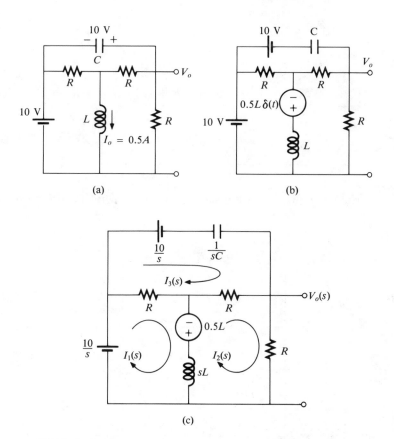

FIGURE 5.12. (a) Network for Example 5.9. (b) Equivalent circuit for (a). (c) Circuit of (b) redrawn in the frequency domain.

For mesh 2, there is only one voltage source and it is negative, since the mesh current $I_2(s)$ emerges at the negative terminal of the voltage source. Thus, its loop equation is written as

$$-0.5L = -sL\, I_1(s) + (2R + sL)I_2(s) - R\, I_3(s)$$

Similarly, for mesh 3

$$\frac{10}{s} = -R\, I_1(s) - R\, I_2(s) + \left(2R + \frac{1}{sC}\right) I_3(s)$$

These three equations now can be written in a simplified shorthand form as

$$
\begin{array}{cccc}
 & I_1(s) & I_2(s) & I_3(s) \\[2mm]
\dfrac{10}{s}+0.5L=(R+sL) & & -sL & -R \\[3mm]
-0.5L= & -sL & +(2R+sL) & -R \\[3mm]
\dfrac{10}{s}= & -R & -R & +\left(2R+\dfrac{1}{s}\right)
\end{array}
$$

## Example 5.10

Write down the three mesh equations for the network of Figure 5.13.

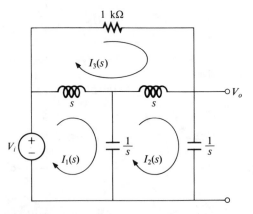

FIGURE 5.13. Network for Example 5.10

*Solution.*   Reasoning in a similar manner as in Example 5.9, the following three equations are written down.

$$
\begin{array}{cccc}
 & I_1(s) & I_2(s) & I_3(s) \\[2mm]
V_i(s)=\left(s+\dfrac{1}{s}\right) & & -\dfrac{1}{s} & -s \\[3mm]
0= & -\dfrac{1}{s} & +\left(\dfrac{2}{s}+s\right) & -s \\[3mm]
0= & -s & -s & +(R+2s)
\end{array}
$$

Once the required equations are written down, it is required to solve the loop currents from the equations.

## Problems

**5.4**  Write down the required loop equations for the networks of Figure 5.11.

## 5.6  Determinants

Consider two linear and independent algebraic equations in two unknowns.

$$a_1 x_1 + b_1 x_2 = c_1 \tag{5.1}$$

$$a_2 x_1 + b_2 x_2 = c_2 \tag{5.2}$$

According to Cramer's rule,

$$x_1 = \frac{\Delta^{x_1}}{\Delta} \tag{5.3}$$

$$x_2 = \frac{\Delta^{x_2}}{\Delta} \tag{5.4}$$

where $\Delta$, $\Delta^{x_1}$, and $\Delta^{x_2}$ are determinants of the equations and are given by

$$\Delta = \begin{vmatrix} a_1 & b_1 \\ a_2 & b_2 \end{vmatrix} = a_1 b_2 - a_2 b_1 \tag{5.5}$$

$$\Delta^{x_1} = \begin{vmatrix} c_1 & b_1 \\ c_2 & b_2 \end{vmatrix} = c_1 b_2 - c_2 b_2 \tag{5.6}$$

$$\Delta^{x_2} = \begin{vmatrix} a_1 & c_1 \\ a_2 & c_2 \end{vmatrix} = a_1 c_2 - a_2 c_1 \tag{5.7}$$

If there were three equations and three unknowns, the equations suggested by (5.3) would still be valid, except that the determinant would be a $3 \times 3$ matrix and its expansion would be more complicated. If more than three equations are to be solved, a computer program may be the easy answer.

## Example 5.11

Find $A(s) = V_o(s)/V_i(s)$ for the network Figure 5.14.

*Solution.*  The two loop equations are formulated as

$$\begin{array}{ccc} & I_1(s) & I_2(s) \\ V_i(s) = & (s+2) & -1 \\ 0 = & -1 & (s+2) \end{array}$$

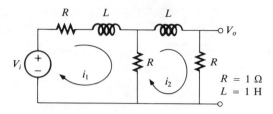

FIGURE 5.14. Network for Example 5.11

$$\Delta = \begin{vmatrix} s+2 & -1 \\ -1 & s+2 \end{vmatrix} = (s+2)^2 - 1 = (s+3)(s+1)$$

$$\Delta^{I_2(s)} = \begin{vmatrix} s+2 & V_i(s) \\ -1 & 0 \end{vmatrix} = V_i(s)$$

$$I_2(s) = \frac{\Delta^{I_2(s)}}{\Delta} = \frac{V_i(s)}{(s+1)(s+3)}$$

$$V_o(s) = I_2(s)1 = \frac{V_i(s)}{(s+1)(s+3)}$$

or

$$A(s) = \frac{1}{(s+1)(s+3)}$$

## Problems

**5.5**  Find $A(s)$ for the networks of Figure 5.11(a) through (j) on page 127.

## 5.7  Block Diagram Reduction

An equation can be illustrated by a block diagram. A set of equations such as the ones obtained as loop equations can be translated into interconnected block diagrams. These block diagrams then can be reduced to a single block. Although it is possible to formulate rules regarding block diagram reductions for many arrangements, most often the task can be accomplished by mere common sense. Rules are derived for block diagram reductions of various formats in this section. These rules are used in manipulating complicated block diagrams to a single block, which is often required in order to find transfer functions of complex systems.

## Transfer Function Blocks in Cascade

When the output of one system is the input of another system, the two systems are said to be in cascade. Two or more transfer function blocks in cascade can be reduced as a single block, as indicated in Figure 5.15.

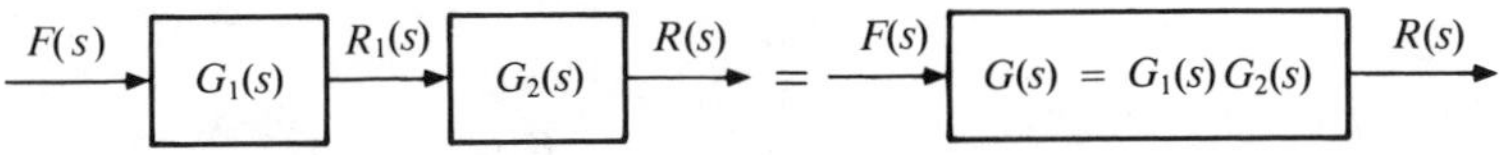

FIGURE 5.15. Reduction of transfer functions in cascade

$$R_1(s) = F(s)G_1(s) \tag{5.8}$$
$$R(s) = R_1(s)G_2(s) \tag{5.9}$$
$$= F(s)G_1(s)G_2(s)$$

or

$$G(s) = \frac{R(s)}{F(s)} = G_1(s)G_2(s) \tag{5.10}$$

Cascaded transfer functions are reduced to a single transfer function as their product.

## Summing Point

A summing point within a system is where two or more signals are algebraically added. Figure 5.16(a) and (b) illustrate two symbols for the summing points. Notice that all inputs must go to the summing point and only one output comes out of it. It is also important to designate the senses (positive or negative) of the inputs on the point.

A summing block with more than two inputs can be split into two summing blocks as shown in Figure 5.16(c) and (d). For Figure 5.16(c)

$$F(s) = F_1(s) + F_3(s) - F_2(s) \tag{5.11}$$

For Figure 5.16(d)

$$F_4(s) = F_1(s) - F_2(s) \tag{5.12}$$
$$F(s) = F_4(s) + F_3(s) \tag{5.13}$$
$$F(s) = F_1(s) + F_3(s) - F_2(s) \tag{5.14}$$

Equation (5.11) for Figure 5.16(c) is identical to equation (5.14) for Figure 5.16(d). Therefore, the two block diagrams are equivalent.

It is possible to move a summing point ahead or behind a transfer function block as illustrated by Figure 5.16(d) and (e).

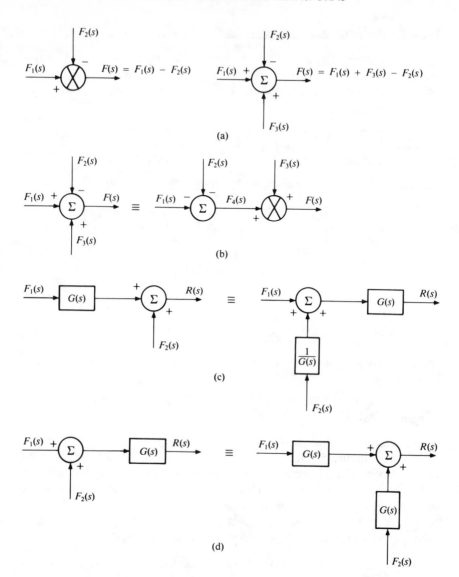

FIGURE 5.16. (a) Two different symbols for summing blocks. (b) Splitting a summing block into two. (c) Moving summing point ahead of transfer function block. (d) Moving summing point behind a transfer function block.

## Pick-off Point

A pick-off point within a system is a point where a signal proceeds along several paths without being attenuated by the paths (see Figure 5.17(a)). The points A and B are the pick-off points. The signals $F(s)$ arriving at point A

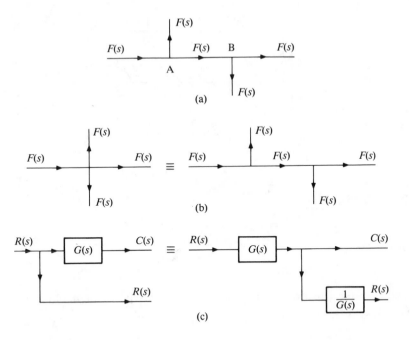

FIGURE 5.17. (a) Pick-off points within a system. (b) Splitting of one pick-off point into two. (c) Moving the pick-off point behind a transfer function block.

proceed along two paths. The signals moving along both paths are the same as the incoming signal $F(s)$. The pick-off point can be split into several pick-off points as shown in Figure 5.17(b). A pick-off point also can be moved ahead or behind a transfer function block as shown in Figure 5.17(c).

### Transfer Function Blocks in Tandem

Two or more transfer function blocks in tandem can be replaced by a single transfer function block. The resultant transfer function is the algebraic sum of the individual summing blocks (see Figure 5.18). The incoming signal $F(s)$ flows into three blocks connected in tandem. The signals proceed from a pick-off point and converge to a summing point.

$$C(s) = F_1(s) + F_2(s) - F_3(s) \qquad (5.15)$$

But,

$$F_1(s) = G_1(s)F(s)$$
$$F_2(s) = G_2(s)F(s)$$

and

$$F_3(s) = G_3(s)F(s)$$

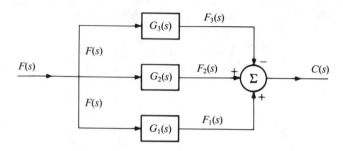

FIGURE 5.18. Tandem system

From (5.15),

$$C(s) = F(s)(G_1(s) + G_2(s) - G_3(s))$$

or

$$C(s)/F(s) = G_1(s) + G_2(s) - G_3(s) \qquad (5.16)$$

The transfer function is the algebraic sum of the tandem block $G_1(s)$, $G_2(s)$, and $G_3(s)$.

### Feedback System

Whenever part of an output is applied back to the input, a feedback is said to occur. The block diagram of a basic feedback system is given in Figure 5.19. Compare this with the tandem blocks of Figure 5.18. Both have a summing point and a pick-off point. Note the locations of the summing and the pick-off points, and the direction of signal flow in both cases. The signal flow for the feedback loop is opposite that of the forward loop.

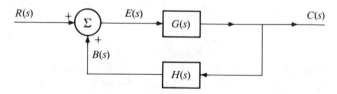

FIGURE 5.19. Simple feedback system

where $G(s)$ is called the forward-loop transfer function.
$H(s)$ is the feedback-loop transfer function.
$G(s)H(s)$ is called the open-loop transfer function.
$C(s)/R(s)$ is the closed-loop transfer function.

The objective is to derive an expression for the closed-loop transfer function. From Figure 5.19, the following three equations can be stated

$$E(s) = R(s) + B(s) \qquad (5.17)$$

$$C(s) = E(s)G(s) \qquad (5.18)$$

$$B(s) = H(s)C(s) \qquad (5.19)$$

These equations contain four variables: $R(s)$, $E(s)$, $C(s)$, and $B(s)$. The closed-loop transfer function contains variables $R(s)$ and $C(s)$. Hence, the variables $E(s)$ and $B(s)$ are unwanted and eliminated between the equations. The resulting equation will contain the variable $C(s)$, the output, and the input $R(s)$.

Substituting $E(s)$ from (5.17) in (5.18), we obtain

$$C(s) = [R(s) + B(s)]G(s) \qquad (5.20)$$

Substituting $B(s)$ from (5.19) in (5.20), we have

$$C(s) = [R(s) + C(s)H(s)]G(s) \qquad (5.21)$$

$$C(s) - C(s)G(s)H(s) = G(s)R(s)$$

$$C(s)[1 - G(s)H(s)] = R(s)G(s)$$

or

$$\frac{C(s)}{R(s)} = \frac{G(s)}{1 - G(s)H(s)} \quad \text{(closed-loop transfer function)} \qquad (5.22)$$

In our derivation, a positive feedback is assumed, in that, the part of the output arriving at the summing point is in phase (without any phase shift) with the system input $R(s)$. If a negative feedback were the case, equation (5.22) would change to

$$\frac{C(s)}{R(s)} = \frac{G(s)}{1 + G(s)H(s)} \qquad (5.23)$$

---

**Example 5.12**

Reduce the block diagram of Figure 5.20 to a single block.

*Solution.*   Recognizing that $G_2(s)$, $G_3(s)$, and a unity gain block (gain 1) are in tandem, they are reduced to a single block as their sum.
Let

$$A = 1 + G_2(s) + G_3(s)$$

$G_1(s)$, $A$, and $G_4(s)$ are in cascade. They are combined as their product.
Let

$$B = AG_1(s)G_4(s)$$

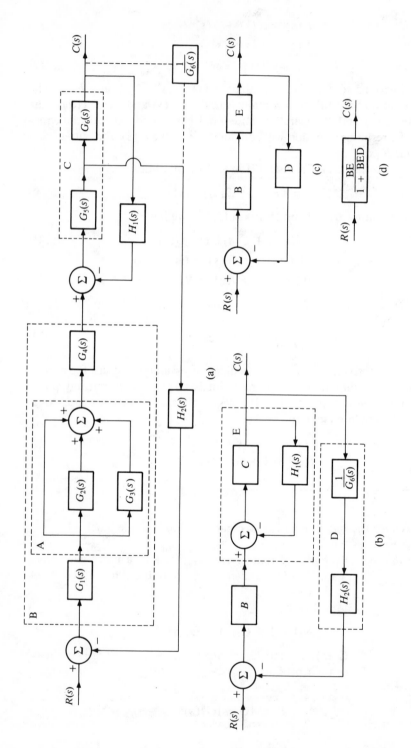

FIGURE 5.20. (a) Block diagram of the system of Example 5.12. (b), (c), and (d) Reduced block diagrams of (a).

The pick-off point is moved behind $G_6(s)$. Now $G_5(s)$ and $G_4(s)$ are in cascade.

Let

$$C = G_5(s)G_6(s)$$

The block diagram is now reduced to that shown in Figure 5.20(b).

Let

$$D = \frac{H_2(s)}{G_6(s)}$$

$$E = \frac{C}{1 + CH(s)} \quad \text{(feedback block)}$$

$$F = BE$$

A negative feedback is now identified where $G(s) = BE$ and $H(s) = D$

$$\frac{C(s)}{R(s)} = \frac{BE}{1 + BED} \quad \text{(the required transfer function)}$$

where $A = 1 + G_2(s) + G_3(s)$
$B = AG_1(s)$
$C = G_5(s)G_6(s)$
$D = H_2(s)/G_6(s)$, and
$E = C/(1 + CH_1(s))$

---

## Example 5.13

Find the transfer function $V_o(s)/V_i(s)$ of the network of Figure 5.21(a).

*Solution.* The loop equations are stated as

$$V_i(s) = \left(2 + 2s + \frac{1}{s}\right)I_1(s) - \frac{1}{s}I_2(s) \qquad (5.24\text{A})$$

$$0 = -\frac{1}{s}I_1(s) + \left(2 + 2s + \frac{1}{s}\right)I_2(s) \qquad (5.24\text{B})$$

Since the current $I_2$ passes through a 2-$\Omega$ resistor, the output voltage is given by

$$V_o(s) = 2I_2(s) \qquad (5.24\text{C})$$

The three equations (5.24A), (5.24B), and (5.24C) are the three system equations. The equation (5.24B) is rewritten as

$$I_1(s) = [sV_i(s) + I_2(s)] \frac{1}{2s^2 + 2s + 1} \tag{5.24D}$$

A block diagram for equation (5.24D) is shown in Figure 5.21(b). From equation (5.24B) we have

$$I_2(s) = I_1(s) \frac{1}{2s^2 + 2s + 1} \tag{5.24E}$$

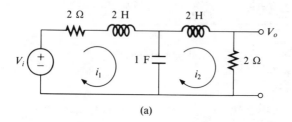

(a)

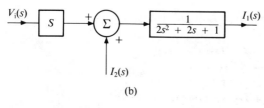

(b)

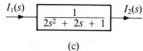

(c)

(d)

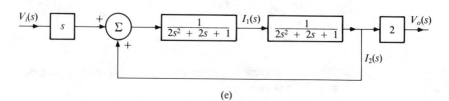

(e)

FIGURE 5.21. (a) Network for Example 5.13. (b), (c), and (d) Block diagrams for equations (5.24D), (5.24E), and (5.24C). (e) The block diagram for the network (a).

A block diagram for equation (5.24E) is given in Figure 5.21(c). A block diagram for equation (5.24C) is shown in Figure 5.21(d). The three block diagrams are combined in Figure 5.21(e). This system block diagram is now reduced to a single block.

$$A(s) = \frac{\dfrac{1}{(2s^2 + 2s + 1)^2}}{1 - \dfrac{1}{(2s^2 + 2s + 1)^2}} \, s$$

$$= \frac{s}{(2s^2 + 2s + 1)^2 - 1} = \frac{s}{(2s^2 + 2s)(2s^2 + 2s + 2)}$$

$$\boxed{a^2 - b^2 = (a + b)(a - b)}$$

$$= \frac{0.5}{(s + 1)(s^2 + s + 1)}$$

## Problems

**5.6** Find the transfer functions of the networks of Figure 5.11, using the block diagram reduction technique.

**5.7** Reduce the block diagrams of Figure 5.22 to single blocks.

**5.8** Find system equations for $X(s)$ in terms of $F_1(s)$ and $F_2(s)$ for the system described by the block diagram of Figure 5.23.

**5.9** Determine the transfer function $C(s)/R(s)$ for the systems of Figure 5.24.

**5.10** Find the value of $G(s)$ to meet the output requirements of the systems of Figure 5.25.

**5.11** All the capacitance and inductance values of the network of Figure 5.21 are divided by 1,000,000. The resistance values are unchanged. Find the transfer function.

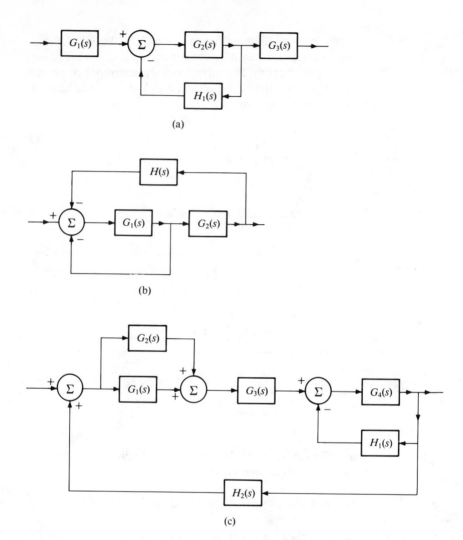

(a)

(b)

(c)

FIGURE 5.22. Block diagrams for Problem 5.7

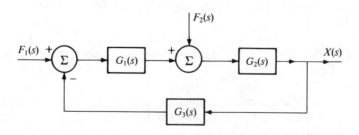

FIGURE 5.23. Block diagram for Problem 5.8

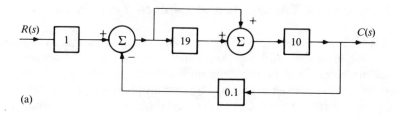

(a)

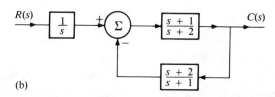

(b)

FIGURE 5.24. Block diagrams for Problem 5.9

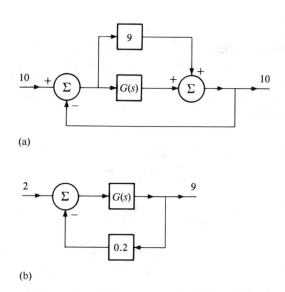

(a)

(b)

FIGURE 5.25. Block diagrams for Problem 5.10

**143**

## 5.8  Network Theorems and Laplace Transformation

In this section, two examples of network analysis using various network theorems are presented. Although some methods are easier than others, personal preference will be the determining factor in selecting a particular method to solve a given problem. The first problem was solved three times using three different methods. The second problem was solved using delta-wye conversion. This method for the second problem was selected simply to provide an example involving delta-wye conversion.

---

**Example 5.14**

(a) Find the transfer function $V_o(s)/V_i(s)$ of the circuit of Figure 5.26(a) using each of the following: (1) Thevenin's theorem, (2) loop equations and determinants, and (3) loop equations and block diagram reduction.

(b) Find $V_o(t)$ for a unit step input.

*Solution.*

(a) **Thevenin's theorem.** The network is redrawn in the frequency domain in Figure 5.26(b). The load $R_2$ is removed from the circuit, as indicated in Figure 5.26(b). The open (output) circuit voltage $V_{th}$ and the short (input) circuit impedance $Z_{th}$ are now estimated.

$$V_{th} = V_i(s) \; \frac{s}{1 + (2/s) + s} = V_i(s) \; \frac{s^2}{s^2 + s + 2} \qquad (5.25A)$$

$$Z_{th} = \left(1 + \frac{2}{s}\right) \Big\| s + \frac{2}{s} \qquad (5.25B)$$

$$= \frac{s(s + 2)}{s^2 + s + 2} + \frac{2}{s}$$

$$= \frac{s^3 + 4s^2 + 2s + 4}{s(s^2 + s + 2)}$$

The resulting network is drawn in Figure 5.26(c).

$$V_o(s) = V_{th} \; \frac{1}{(1 + Z_{th})} \qquad (5.25C)$$

$$= V_i(s) \; \frac{s^2}{(s^2 + s + 2)} \; \frac{1}{1 + \dfrac{s^3 + 4s^2 + 2s + 4}{s(s^2 + s + 2)}}$$

$$\frac{V_o(s)}{V_i(s)} = A(s) = \frac{0.5s^3}{s^3 + 2.5s^2 + 2s + 2} = \frac{0.5s^3}{(s + 2)(s^2 + 0.5s + 1)}$$

**Loop equations and determinants.** The assumed loop currents $I_1(s)$ and $I_2(s)$ are shown in Figure 5.27. The two mesh equations are given by equations (5.26A) and (5.26B).

$$V_i(s) = \left(1 + \frac{2}{s} + s\right) I_1 - sI_2 \qquad (5.26\text{A})$$

$$0 = -sI_1 + \left(1 + \frac{2}{s} + s\right) I_2 \qquad (5.26\text{B})$$

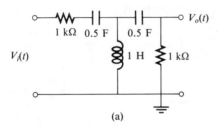

(a)

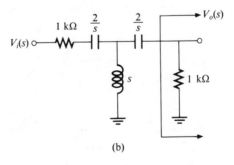

(b)

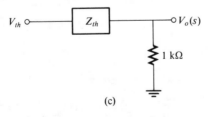

(c)

FIGURE 5.26. Example 5.14

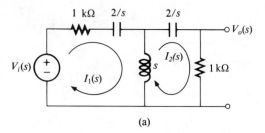

(a)

FIGURE 5.27. Example 5.14 (cont.)

Equations (5.26A) and (5.26B) are restated by equations (5.26C) and (5.26B), respectively.

$$V_i(s) = \frac{s^2 + s + 2}{s} I_1 - sI_2 \qquad (5.26C)$$

$$0 = -sI_1 + \frac{s^2 + s + 2}{s} I_2 \qquad (5.26D)$$

$$\Delta = \begin{vmatrix} \dfrac{s^2 + s + 2}{s} & -s \\[3mm] -s & \dfrac{s^2 + s + 2}{s} \end{vmatrix}$$

$$= \frac{(s^2 + s + 2)^2}{s^2} - s^2$$

$$= \frac{(s^2 + s + 2)^2 - (s^2)^2}{s^2} = \frac{(2s^2 + s + 2)(s + 2)}{s^2}$$

$$\boxed{a^2 - b^2 = (a + b)(a - b)}$$

$$\Delta^{I_2} = \begin{vmatrix} \dfrac{s^2 + s + 2}{s} & V_i \\[3mm] -s & 0 \end{vmatrix}$$

$$= sV_i(s)$$

$$I_2 = \frac{\Delta^{I_2}}{\Delta} = \frac{s^3 V_i(s)}{(s + 2)(2s^2 + s + 2)}$$

$$V_o(s) = I_2 \times 1 \qquad (5.26E)$$

$$A(s) = \frac{V_o(s)}{V_i(s)} = \frac{0.5s^3}{(s + 2)(s^2 + 0.5s + 1)}$$

**Loop equation and block diagram reduction.** The loop equations of (5.26F) and (5.26G) are the rearranged equations of (5.26C) and (5.26D), respectively.

$$I_1 = (V_i + sI_2) \frac{s}{s^2 + s + 2} \tag{5.26F}$$

$$I_2 = I_1 \frac{s^2}{s^2 + s + 2} \tag{5.26G}$$

From equation (5.26F) it is clear that the signal $I_2$ is made up of the amplified sum of two signals, $V_i$ and $sI_2$. The transfer function (gain) is $s/(s^2 + s + 2)$. One of the signals that is to be added is $sI_2$, and is obtained by amplifying $I_2$ by $s$. A block diagram for (5.26F) is shown in Figure 5.28(a).

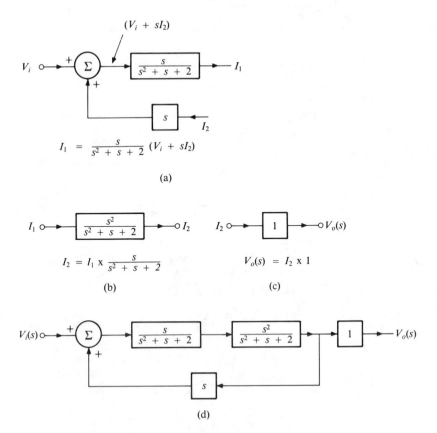

$$I_1 = \frac{s}{s^2 + s + 2} (V_i + sI_2)$$

(a)

$$I_2 = I_1 \times \frac{s}{s^2 + s + 2}$$

(b)

$$V_o(s) = I_2 \times 1$$

(c)

(d)

FIGURE 5.28. Example 5.14 (cont.)

From (5.26G) it is observed that $I_2$ is obtained by amplifying the signal $I_1$ by $s^2/(s^2 + s + 2)$. The block diagram for equation (5.26G) is given in Figure 5.28(b). Likewise, the block diagram for equation (5.26E) is drawn in Figure 5.28(c). The three block diagrams are now combined in Figure 5.28(d) to form the block diagram of the network of Figure 5.26(a). Inspection of the block diagram of Figure 5.28(d) reveals that it is essentially a feedback system with:

$$G(s) = \frac{s}{s^2 + s + 2} \frac{s^2}{s^2 + s + 2}$$

$$= \frac{s^3}{(s^2 + s + 2)^2}$$

and $H(s) = s$, as indicated in Figure 5.29(a).

$$A(s) = \frac{\dfrac{s^3}{(s^2 + s + 2)^2}}{1 - \dfrac{s^4}{(s^2 + s + 2)^2}}$$

$$A(s) = \frac{s^3}{(s^2 + s + 2)^2 - (s^2)^2}$$

$$\boxed{a^2 - b^2 = (a + b)(a - b)}$$

$$= \frac{s^3}{(s^2 + s + 2 + s^2)(s^2 + s + 2 - s^2)}$$

$$= \frac{s^3}{(2s^2 + s + 2)(s + 2)}$$

$$A(s) = \frac{0.5s^3}{(s + 2)(s^2 + 0.5s + 1)}$$

(b) For unit step input $V_i(s) = 1/s$

$$V_o(s) = \frac{0.5s^2}{(s + 2)(s^2 + 0.5s + 1)} = \frac{A}{(s + 2)} + \frac{Bs + C}{s^2 + 0.5s + 1}$$

By the cover-up rule:

$$A = \frac{0.5(-2)^2}{4 - 1 + 1} = 0.5$$

Comparing coefficients of the numerators after making a common denominator, we have

$$s^2 \mid A + B = 0.5$$
$$s^1 \mid 0.5A + 2B + C = 0$$
$$s^0 \mid A = 0$$

$$A + 2C = 0, \ C = -0.25$$
$$A + B = 0.5, \ B = 0$$

Check:   $0.5A + 2B + C = 0$

$$V_o(s) = \frac{0.5}{(s + 2)} - \frac{0.25}{s^2 + 0.5s + 1}$$

$$V_o(t) = \left(0.5e^{-2t} - \frac{0.25}{\sqrt{0.875}} \, e^{-0.25t} \sin \sqrt{0.875} \, t\right) u(t)$$

An approximate time-domain response curve is given in Figure 5.29(b).

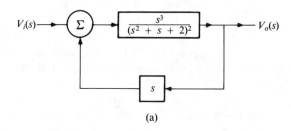

(a)

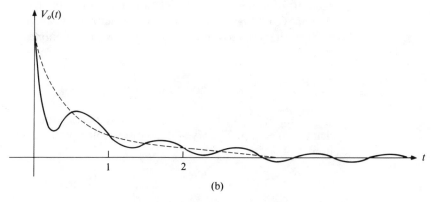

(b)

FIGURE 5.29. Example 5.14 (cont.)

**Example 5.15**

Find the transfer function $V_o(s)/V_i(s)$ of the network of Figure 5.30.

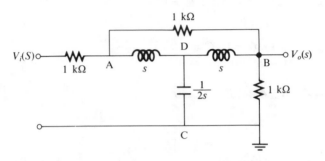

FIGURE 5.30. Network for Example 5.15

*Solution.*   There are several options available. One is to write three loop equations and solve for the output current using any one of the following: (1) simultaneous solutions, (2) determinants, or (3) block diagram reduction.

Another method, however, is to use wye-delta conversion and then find the transfer functions. The wye-delta and delta-wye conversions of impedances are indicated in Figure 5.31(a).

In the wye connection, $Z_{AY}$, $Z_{BY}$, and $Z_{CY}$ are the three impedances, and $Z_{BC}$, $Z_{AC}$, and $Z_{AB}$ are the three impedances in the delta connection. Note the physical connections of impedances with relation to the three points A, B, and C in Figure 5.30. From the network of Figure 5.31(a), the wye section is identified between the points A, B, and C.

$$Z_{AY} = s, \; Z_{BY} = s, \text{ and } Z_{CY} = \frac{1}{2s}$$

The objective is to change the wye connection to a delta connection. The wye-delta conversion equations are used.

$$Z_{BC} = \frac{NR}{Z_{AY}} , \; Z_{AC} = \frac{NR}{Z_{BY}} , \text{ and } Z_{AB} = \frac{NR}{Z_{CY}}$$

$$\text{where} \quad NR = Z_{AY}Z_{BY} + Z_{AY}Z_{CY} + Z_{BY}Z_{CY}$$

$$= s^2 + 0.5 + 0.5 = s^2 + 1$$

$$Z_{BC} = \frac{s^2 + 1}{s}, \; Z_{AC} = \frac{s^2 + 1}{s}, \; \text{and } Z_{AB} = 2s(s^2 + 1)$$

The converted network is shown in Figure 5.31(b). In this network $Z_{AC}$ is parallel with a 1-$\Omega$ resistor, and $Z_{BC}$ is parallel with another 1-$\Omega$ resistor.

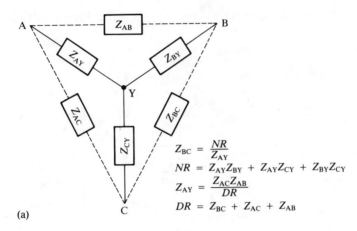

$$Z_{BC} = \frac{NR}{Z_{AY}}$$
$$NR = Z_{AY}Z_{BY} + Z_{AY}Z_{CY} + Z_{BY}Z_{CY}$$
$$Z_{AY} = \frac{Z_{AC}Z_{AB}}{DR}$$
$$DR = Z_{BC} + Z_{AC} + Z_{AB}$$

(a)

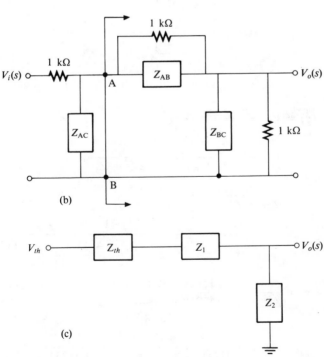

(b)

(c)

FIGURE 5.31. (a) Delta-wye conversion. (b) and (c) Network reductions for Example 5.15.

Let $Z_1 = Z_{AB}\|1$ and $Z_2 = Z_{BC}\|1$. Also, Thevenin's voltage $V_{th}$ and Thevenin's impedance $Z_{th}$ are estimated by removing the network to the left of terminal AB, as the load.

$$V_{th} = V_i(s) \frac{Z_{AC}}{Z_{AC} + 1} \quad \text{and} \quad Z_{th} = Z_{AC}\|1 = Z_2$$

The simplified network is shown in Figure 5.31(c).

$$Z_1 = Z_{AB}\|1 = \frac{2s(s^2 + 1)}{2s(s^2 + 1) + 1}$$

$$= \frac{2s(s^2 + 1)}{2s^3 + 2s + 1}$$

$$Z_2 = Z_{BC}\|1 = \frac{\dfrac{s^2 + 1}{s}}{\dfrac{s^2 + 1}{s} + 1} = \frac{s^2 + 1}{s^2 + s + 1}$$

$$V_{th} = V_i(s) \frac{Z_{AC}}{Z_{AC} + 1} = V_i(s) \frac{s^2 + 1}{s^2 + s + 1}$$

$$Z_{th} = Z_{AC}\|1 = \frac{\dfrac{s^2 + 1}{s}}{\dfrac{s^2 + 1}{s} + 1} = \frac{s^2 + 1}{s^2 + s + 1}$$

$V_o(s)$ is now estimated using the voltage divider rule.

$$V_o(s) = V_{th} \frac{Z_2}{Z_{th} + Z_1 + Z_2}$$

$$= V_{th} \frac{Z_2}{Z_2 + Z_1 + Z_2} = V_{th} \frac{Z_2}{2Z_2 + Z_1}$$

$$= \frac{V_{th}}{2 + Z_1/Z_2}$$

$$= V_i(s) \frac{s^2 + 1}{(s^2 + s + 1)\left(2 + \dfrac{2s(s^2 + 1)(s^2 + s + 1)}{(2s^3 + 2s + 1)(s^2 + 1)}\right)}$$

$$= \frac{(s^2 + 1)(2s^3 + 2s + 1)}{(s^2 + s + 1)(6s^3 + 2s^2 + 6s + 2)}$$

$$(6s + 2)$$

$$A(s) = \frac{V_o(s)}{V_i(s)} = \frac{0.17(s^3 + s + 1)}{(s^2 + s + 1)(s + 0.33)}$$

## 5.9  Summary

In this chapter examples of network analysis are provided using various network laws and theorems and Laplace transformation. The examples are restricted to passive networks since we will be looking at many more active networks in succeeding chapters. No attempt is made in this chapter to present the network laws and theorems in any detailed manner. The reader is expected to be familiar with these topics. Nonetheless, the coverage is meant as a refresher course on those very important tools of network analysis. The loop equations and block diagram reduction method is a nontraditional circuit analysis technique. Yet, in many ways, it is simpler to simultaneously manipulate and visualize the effect of various components on the network performance.

Traditionally, three separate courses in circuit analysis are provided for electronics majors in colleges and universities: one for dc signals, one for ac signals (sinusoidals), and one for pulses (usually, switching circuits). Although the network laws and theorems are fundamental to all three courses, everything else about them seems to be different. With Laplace transform, the approach is always the same. The bonus to using Laplace transforms is that we can analyze not only for dc, ac, and pulse signals, but also for many other signals such as ramp and exponential.

### Key Terms

Define the following terms:

| | |
|---|---|
| Thevenin's theorem | Norton's theorem |
| Kirchhoff's law | block diagram |
| superposition theorem | pick-off point |
| delta-wye conversion | summing point |
| forward-loop transfer function | cascade |
| feedback-loop transfer function | tandem |
| open-loop transfer function | determinants |
| closed-loop transfer function | loop equation |
| mesh | mesh current |
| ideal voltage source | current source |
| energized parameter | Norton's model |
| Thevenin's model | $Z_{th}$ |
| $V_{th}$ | $I_n$ |

# CHAPTER 6

# Steady-State ac Analysis

## 6.1 Introduction

The output of a linear system is made up of two components, the steady-state and the transient. For stable systems, the transient component will decay to zero after some time, leaving only the steady-state component. The steady-state output of a stable system, driven by a sinusoidal input, is another sinusoidal. Both of these sinusoidals, the input and the steady-state output, have the same frequency. However, the amplitudes of these signals may differ. Furthermore, it is likely that the output signal is phase shifted with respect to the input signal. The ratio of the amplitudes of the steady-state component of the output and the input sinusoidal is the magnitude of the gain of the network. This gain is a function of frequency $\omega$. Similarly, the phase shift of the output sinusoidal with respect to that of the input signal is also a function of $\omega$. These two functions, $M(\omega)$ and $\phi(\omega)$ determine the steady-state ac response of electric networks as well as other systems.

## 6.2 Transfer Function and Frequency Response

Suppose a sinusoidal signal $V_i(t)$, given by equation (6.1), is applied to a network at $t = 0$.

$$V_i(t) = A \sin \omega t \tag{6.1}$$

Also assume that the transfer function of the network is given as

$$A(s) = \frac{K(s + Z_1)(s + Z_2)(s + Z_3) \ldots (s + Z_n)}{(s + P_1)(s + P_2)(s + P_3) \ldots (s + P_m)} \tag{6.2}$$

Since the network is stable, all the poles are in the left-hand half-plane.

$$V_i(s) = \frac{\omega}{s^2 + \omega^2} \tag{6.3}$$

The output voltage in the frequency domain is given as

$$V_o(s) = \frac{AK\omega(s + Z_1)(s + Z_2)(s + Z_3) \ldots (s + Z_n)}{(s^2 + \omega^2)(s + P_1)(s + P_2)(s + P_3) \ldots (s + P_m)} \tag{6.4}$$

Equation (6.4) can be expanded into partial fractions as

$$V_o(s) = \underbrace{\frac{K_1 s + K_2}{s^2 + \omega^2}}_{\text{Steady-state}} + \underbrace{\frac{A_1}{s + P_1} + \frac{A_2}{s + P_2} + \cdots \frac{A_n}{s + P_m}}_{\text{Transient}} \qquad (6.5)$$

**Steady-state**      **Transient**
**component**          **component**

For stable systems, all the components except the first will decay to zero after some time. The steady-state component of the output is

$$\textit{study} \longrightarrow \qquad V_o(s)_{ss} = \frac{K_1 s + K_2}{s^2 + \omega^2} \qquad (6.6)$$

where $V_o(s)_{ss}$ is the steady-state component of the output voltage. The constants $K_1$ and $K_2$ depend on the poles and zeros of the network as well as the amplitude of the input. The steady-state output in the time domain is given in (6.7) and (6.8).

$$V_o(t)_{ss} = K_1 \cos \omega t + \frac{K_2}{\omega} \sin \omega t \qquad (6.7)$$

$$= A_o \sin (\omega t - \phi) \qquad (6.8)$$

where $V_o(t)_{ss}$ is the steady-state component of the output in the time domain. A block diagram of the system is illustrated in Figure 6.1.

The following observations of the input and output of steady-state systems can be made:

1. The steady-state output is a sine wave with the same frequency as the input.
2. The amplitude of the output sine wave $A_o$ is dependent on the poles and zeros of the network and are proportional to the amplitude of the input sine wave.
3. The phase shift $\phi(\omega)$ is also dependent on the poles and zeros of the network.

A sin $\omega t$ ⟶ [ Network ] ⟶ $A_o \sin (\omega t - \phi)$

FIGURE 6.1. Block diagram representation of the steady-state input and output of a stable network

4. The magnitude of gain $M(\omega)$ is the ratio of the amplitude of the output sine wave and the amplitude of the input sine wave. $M(\omega)$ is independent of the amplitude of the input sinusoidal, since the output amplitude is proportional to the input amplitude.
5. The phase angle is the phase shift of the output with respect to the input.

The magnitude of gain $M(\omega)$ can be evaluated by letting $s = j\omega$ in the transfer function of the network and then finding its magnitude. Similarly, $\phi(\omega)$ can be found by letting $s = j\omega$ in the transfer function of the network and solving for the phase angle. The technique is as follows: (a) find $A(s)$, (b) substitute $s = j\omega$ and find $A(j\omega)$, and (c) change $A(j\omega)$ to polar form

$$A(j\omega) = M(\omega)\underline{/\phi(\omega)} \tag{6.9}$$

The graph of $M(\omega)$ versus $\omega$ is called the magnitude response curve, and that of $\phi(\omega)$ versus $\omega$ is called the phase response curve. Both are frequency response curves in the sense that the x-axis is the frequency variable $\omega$. However, one curve will convey only partial information (either magnitude or phase). For complete information regarding the frequency response of the system, both magnitude and phase curves are required.

---

**Example 6.1**

Find the magnitude and phase angle as functions of frequency for a network, the transfer function of which is given as

$$A(s) = \frac{100}{(s + 100)}$$

*Solution.*  $A(j\omega) = \dfrac{100}{100 + j\omega}$

$$= \frac{100}{\sqrt{100^2 + \omega^2}\,\underline{/\arctan\,(\omega/100)}}$$

$$= \frac{100}{\sqrt{100^2 + \omega^2}}\,\underline{/-\arctan\,(\omega/100)}$$

$$\boxed{a + bj = \sqrt{a^2 + b^2}\,\underline{/\arctan\,(b/a)}}$$

$$M(\omega) = \frac{100}{\sqrt{10{,}000 + \omega^2}}$$

$$\phi(\omega) = -\arctan\,(\omega/100)$$

**Example 6.2**

Draw the magnitude and phase response curves. The transfer function is given as

$$A(s) = \frac{1}{s^2 + 0.4s + 1}$$

*Solution.*

$$A(j\omega) = \frac{1}{-\omega^2 + 0.4\omega j + 1}$$

$$= \frac{1}{(1 - \omega^2) + j0.4\omega}$$

$$= \frac{1}{\sqrt{(1 - \omega^2)^2 + (0.4\omega)^2}} \underline{/-\arctan (0.4\omega/(1 - \omega^2))}$$

$$M(\omega) = \frac{1}{\sqrt{(1 - \omega^2)^2 + (0.4\omega)^2}} = \frac{1}{\sqrt{1 - 1.84\omega^2 + \omega^4}}$$

$$\phi(\omega) = -\arctan \left[ \frac{0.4\omega}{(1 - \omega^2)} \right]$$

The required data for this solution is compiled and presented in Table 6.1. The magnitude and phase response curves are shown in Figure 6.2.

TABLE 6.1   Data compiled to draw the frequency response curves

| Frequency $\omega$ | Magnitude $M(\omega)$ | Phase $\phi(\omega)$ degree |
|---|---|---|
| 0.01 | 1.0000 | −00.23 |
| 0.02 | 1.0004 | −00.46 |
| 0.05 | 1.0023 | −01.15 |
| 0.10 | 1.0091 | −02.31 |
| 0.20 | 1.0372 | −04.76 |
| 0.50 | 1.2776 | −14.93 |
| 0.60 | 1.4410 | −20.56 |
| 0.80 | 2.0761 | −26.57 |
| 0.90 | 2.4566 | −62.18 |
| 0.95 | 2.5490 | −75.61 |
| 1.0 | 2.2360 | −90.00 |
| 1.1 | 2.0682 | −115.51 |
| 1.5 | 0.7212 | −154.35 |
| 2.0 | 0.3194 | −165.07 |
| 5.0 | 0.0402 | −175.24 |
| 10.0 | 0.0101 | −177.69 |

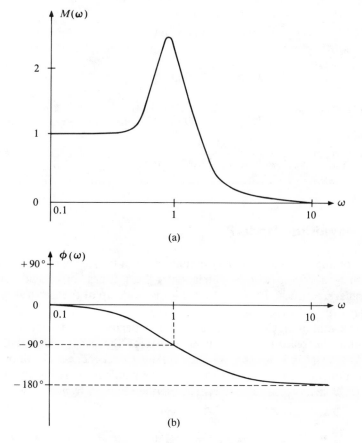

FIGURE 6.2. Magnitude and phase response for Example 6.2:
(a) Magnitude response. (b) Phase response.

The steady-state ac response of a network has two characteristics: the magnitude and the phase. Either one of them, though useful in its own right, contains only part of the steady-state characteristics.

## Problems

**6.1** For the given transfer functions do each of the following: (1) list the poles and zeros of each system, (2) draw the magnitude response curves, (3) draw the phase response curves, and (4) draw the pole-zero maps.

(a) $A(s) = \dfrac{10(s + 1000)}{(s + 100)}$

(b) $A(s) = \dfrac{2(s - 1000)}{(s + 1000)}$

(c) $A(s) = \dfrac{50{,}000{,}000}{s^2 + 2500s + 25{,}000{,}000}$

(d) $A(s) = \dfrac{10{,}000s}{s^2 + 2500s + 25{,}000{,}000}$

(e) $A(s) = \dfrac{2s^2}{s^2 + 2500s + 25{,}000{,}000}$

(f) $A(s) = \dfrac{50{,}000{,}000}{s^2 + 5000s + 25{,}000{,}000}$

## 6.3  Magnitude Bode Plot

Bode plot analysis is simply the examination of a frequency response curve. Since the gain of a network is a function of $(j\omega)$, it has both magnitude and phase characteristics. Thus the Bode plot is made up of two separate plots, the *magnitude Bode plot* and *phase Bode plot*.

The gain of an electric network often depends on the frequency of the network. The reason for this is that two of the electric impedances — *capacitive* $1/sC$ and *inductive* $sL$ — are frequency dependent. The only other electric impedance is *resistance*, and it is independent of frequency. Therefore, for a steady-state ac response, $s$ can be replaced by $j\omega$.

$$s = j\omega = \omega\,\underline{/90^\circ} \tag{6.10A}$$

$$s^2 = -\omega^2 = \omega^2\,\underline{/180^\circ} \tag{6.10B}$$

$$s^3 = -j\omega^3 = \omega^3\,\underline{/270^\circ} \tag{6.10C}$$

$$s^4 = \omega^4 = \omega^4\,\underline{/0^\circ} \tag{6.10D}$$

The magnitude Bode plot is a graph of the magnitude of $A(j\omega)$ in decibels (dB) versus frequency in radians/second (rad/s). It is drawn on semi-log graph paper. Expressing the magnitude of the gain in dB makes it possible to add individual gains to obtain the overall gain in a cascaded system. If the gains were expressed as ratios, the individual gains would have to be multiplied for the resultant gain (see Figure 6.3). Graphical addition is much easier than graphical multiplication.

The use of graphical addition makes it possible to split a complicated function $(j\omega)$ into simpler ones. It also makes it possible to draw the magnitude responses of simple functions, and then to add them graphically to obtain the resultant plot. One only needs to develop the techniques to draw the magnitude response curves for a few simple gain functions to be able to draw the magnitude response curves for functions of any complexity.

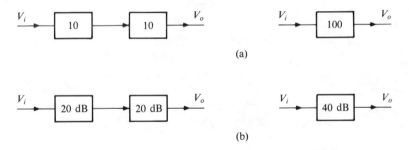

FIGURE 6.3. (a) Individual gains are multiplied when stated as ratio. (b) Individual gains are added when stated in dB.

## 6.4  Transfer Functions of Linear Factors

Transfer functions containing only linear factors and perfect powers of linear factors are given by equation (6.11).

$$A(s) = Ks^n (T_1 s + 1)^m (T_2 s + 1)^p \ldots \qquad (6.11)$$

where $n$, $m$, and $p$ are positive or negative integers.

There are three cases to study:

1. Frequency-independent function of the form $K$
2. Gain function of the form $(\tau s)^n$
3. Gain functions of the form $(\tau s + 1)^n$

**Case 1.**  Frequency-independent functions:

$$A(s) = K \qquad (6.12)$$

$$A(j\omega) = |K| \; \underline{/0° \text{ or } 180°} \qquad (6.13)$$

$$M(\omega) = |K| \qquad (6.14)$$

$$dB = 20 \log |K| \qquad (6.15)$$

where $M(\omega)$ is the magnitude of $A(j\omega)$ and dB is the magnitude $M(\omega)$ expressed in dB. Equation (6.15) is of the form

$$y = mx + b \qquad (6.16)$$

where $m$ is the slope and $b$ the y-axis intercept.

$$dB = 0\omega + 20 \log |K| \qquad (6.17)$$

The slope of the line is zero, and the dB-axis intercept is $20 \log |K|$. The required Bode plot is a straight line with zero slope, crossing the dB axis at $20 \log |K|$. The plot is given in Figure 6.4.

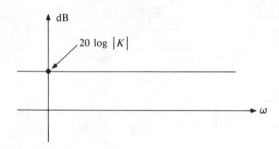

FIGURE 6.4. Magnitude Bode plot for $A(s) = K$

If $K$ is less than one, 20 log $K$ is negative. Note that $K$ is the magnitude of the gain. If the gain is $-10$, the magnitude is $+10$. The magnitude Bode plots of gains of $-10$ and $+10$ are identical. Their phase Bode plots, constant 180° and 0° shifts, respectively, would be different, however.

**Case 2.**    Gain functions of the form $(\tau s)^n$

$$A(s) = (\tau s)^n \tag{6.18}$$

$\tau$ is the coefficient of $s$ and $n$ is the exponent.

$$A(j\omega) = (j\tau\omega)^n \tag{6.19}$$

$$= (\tau\omega\underline{/90°})^n = (\tau\omega)^n \underline{/90°\,n}$$

$$M(\omega) = (\tau\omega)^n \tag{6.20}$$

$$dB = 20n \log (\tau\omega) \tag{6.21}$$

Table 6.2 is a list of $\tau\omega$ and corresponding magnitude of gain in dB. From the table, it can be seen that every *decade* change in frequency produces a $20n$ dB change in magnitude. The Bode plot, therefore, is a straight line with a slope of $20n$ dB/decade. This line crosses the $\omega$-axis at $\tau\omega = 1$ or $\omega = 1/\tau$.

The magnitude Bode plot for $(\tau\omega)^n$ is a straight line with a slope of $20n$ dB/decade crossing $\omega$-axis at $\omega = 1/\tau$.

TABLE 6.2   Change of dB for decade change of $\tau\omega$

| $\tau\omega$ | dB = $20n \log(\tau\omega)$ |
|---|---|
| $\left.\begin{array}{l}0.01\\0.1\end{array}\right\}$ one decade | $\left.\begin{array}{l}-40n\\-20n\end{array}\right\}$ $20n$ dB |
| 1 | 0 |
| 10 | $20n$ |
| 100 | $40n$ |

**Example 6.3**

Draw the magnitude Bode plot for $A(s) = 100/s^2$.

*Solution.*    First $A(s)$ must be rewritten in the form $(\tau s)^n$

$$A(s) = \frac{100}{s^2} = \cfrac{1}{\cfrac{1}{100} s^2} = \cfrac{1}{\left(\cfrac{1}{10} s\right)^2} = (0.1s)^{-2}$$

where $\tau = 0.1$ and $n = -2$. The Bode plot is a straight line with a slope of $-40$ dB/decade and crosses $\omega$-axis at $\omega = 1/0.1$ or $10$ rad/s. The Bode plot is shown in Figure 6.5.

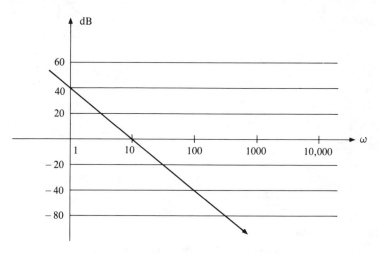

FIGURE 6.5. Magnitude Bode plot of $100/s^2$

**Case 3.**    Gain functions of the form $(\tau s + 1)^n$

The gain functions of the form $(\tau s + 1)^n$ can be divided into the following three regions: (a) $A(j\omega)$, when $\tau\omega \gg 1$ or $\omega \gg 1/\tau$, (b) $A(j\omega)$, when $\tau\omega \ll 1$ or $\omega \ll 1/\tau$, and (c) $A(j\omega)$, when $\tau\omega$ is comparable to 1 or $\omega$ is comparable to $1/\tau$. These three regions are shown in Figure 6.6(a). The frequency where $\omega = 1/\tau$ is called the *corner frequency* $\omega_c$.

(a)    $$A(s) = (\tau s + 1)^n \tag{6.22}$$

When $\tau s \gg 1$,

$$A(s) = (\tau s)^n \tag{6.23}$$
$$M(\omega) = (\tau\omega)^n$$
dB $= 20n \log(\tau\omega)$ same as that in Case 1.

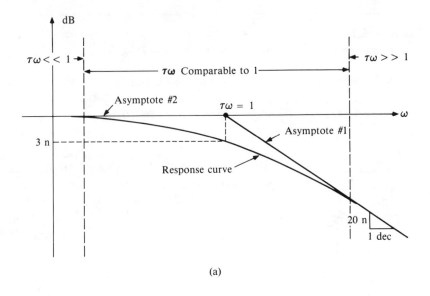

(a)

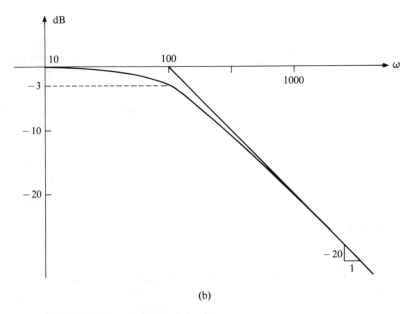

(b)

FIGURE 6.6. (a) Magnitude Bode plot for $(\tau s + 1)^n$. (b) Magnitude Bode plot for $(0.01s + 1)^{-1}$.

The magnitude Bode plot is a straight line with a slope of $20n$ dB/decade *starting* at $\omega_c = 1/\tau$. This line does not cross the $\omega$-axis since $\tau s \gg 1$ is not satisfied for values of $\omega$ less than $\omega_c$. This line is called an *asymptote*. An asymptote is a line to which a curve approaches eventually. This asymptote and the curve coincide only when $\omega \gg 1$. The actual curve deviates from the asymptote in the vicinity of the corner frequency $\omega_c$.

(b) $A(s) = (\tau s + 1)^n$, when $\tau s \ll 1$, $A(s) = 1$, and dB $= 0$

This is the $\omega$-axis. It is the asymptote for the condition where $\tau s \ll 1$. The actual curve approaches the $\omega$-axis when $\omega_c \ll 1$.

(c) When $\omega$ is comparable to $\omega_c$, the actual Bode plot deviates from the asymptotes. The maximum deviation occurs at the corner frequency $\omega_c = 1/\tau$.

$$A(j\omega) = (j\tau\omega + 1)^n \tag{6.24}$$

At the corner frequency $\omega = 1/\tau$

$$A(j\omega) = (1 + j)^n \tag{6.25}$$
$$M(\omega) = (1 + 1)^{0.5n} = 2^{0.5n} \tag{6.26}$$
$$dB = 10n \log 2 \simeq 3n \tag{6.27}$$

The magnitude Bode plot of a function of the form $(\tau s + 1)^n$ is asymptotic to two straight lines, one starting at $\omega_c = 1/\tau$ on $\omega$-axis with a slope of $20n$ dB/decade and the other on the $\omega$-axis ending at $\omega_c$. The maximum deviation between the asymptotes and the actual plot occurs at the corner frequency and is $3n$ dB, as indicated in Figure 6.6(a). The Bode plot is often left as the straight-line approximation. However, it must be understood that the actual curve rounds the corner with varying deviation, the maximum deviation occurring at the corner frequency. The magnitude Bode plot of $(0.01s + 1)^{-1}$ is given in Figure 6.6(b).

The corner frequency is $1/\tau = 1/0.01 = 100$ rad/s. The slope of the asymptote is $20n$ dB/decade $= -20$ dB/decade. One point is located on the $\omega$-axis at $100$ rad/s. Another point is located one decade from $\omega_c$ at $1000$ rad/s and $-20$ dB. The asymptote is drawn through these two points.

---

## Problems

**6.2** Draw the magnitude Bode plots for each of the following:

(a) $A(s) = 10/(s + 10)$        (b) $A(s) = 25/s^2$

(c) $A(s) = (s + 25)/25$        (d) $A(s) = 100/(s + 10)^2$

---

## 6.5  Graphical Addition of Bode Plots

Once the individual Bode plots are drawn, they are then graphically added for the resultant plot. This is done starting at the lowest frequency, then proceeding, taking into account any new asymptote started. The important point to keep in mind is that the resultant line replaces the component lines.

## Example 6.4

Draw the approximate Bode plot for the following transfer function:
$A(s) = (0.1s)(0.001s)/(0.01s + 1)^2$

*Solution.* $A(s) = (0.1s)^1(0.01s + 1)^{-2}(0.001s + 1)^1$

| $(0.1s)^1$ | crosses at $1/\tau = 10$ rad/s with $20n = 20$ dB/decade |
| $(0.01s + 1)^{-2}$ | starts at $1/\tau = 100$ rad/s with $20n = -40$ dB/decade |
| $(0.001s + 1)^1$ | starts at $1/\tau = 1000$ rad/s with $20n = 20$ dB/decade |

where $A(s)$ is broken into three functions, each of which is of the standard form. The Bode plots for the three individual functions and their resultant lines are given in Figure 6.7.

For very low frequencies, up to 100 rad/s, the only curve is due to $A_1(s) = (0.1s)^1$, and therefore this line represents the Bode plot in this interval. At 100 rad/s, a

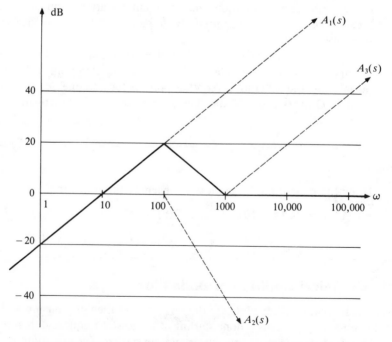

FIGURE 6.7. Magnitude Bode plot of $A(s)$ of Example 6.4

line with −40 dB/decade starts due to $A_2(s) = (0.01s + 1)^{-2}$. The resultant line of $A_1(s)$ and $A_2(s)$ has a slope of −20 dB/decade starting at (100 rad/s, +20 dB) point. This line replaces $A_1(s)$ and $A_2(s)$, and in further additions only this resultant line can be used instead of $A_1(s)$ and $A_2(s)$. An $A_1(s) + A_2(s)$ resultant line represents the Bode plot from 100 rad/s to 1000 rad/s, where another asymptote is started with +20 dB/decade due to $A_3(s) = (0.001s + 1)^1$. The resultant line has a 0 slope starting at (1000 rad/s, 0 dB) point.

## Example 6.5

Draw the magnitude Bode plot for

$$A(s) = \frac{100(s + 10)(s + 500)}{s(s + 100)(s + 1000)}$$

*Solution.*   The first step is to correct the given transfer function to the time-constant form.

$$A(s) = \frac{100 \times 10 \times 500}{100 \times 1000} \frac{(0.1s + 1)(0.002s + 1)}{s(0.01s + 1)(0.001s + 1)}$$

$$A(s) = (0.2s)^{-1}(0.1s + 1)^1(0.01s + 1)^{-1}(0.002s + 1)^1(0.001s + 1)^{-1}$$

| | |
|---|---|
| $(0.2s)$ | crosses at 5 with slope −20 |
| $(0.1s + 1)$ | starts at 10 with slope 20 |
| $(0.01s + 1)$ | starts at 100 with slope −20 |
| $(0.002s + 1)$ | starts at 500 with slope 20 |
| $(0.001s + 1)$ | starts at 1000 with slope 20 |

The straight-line approximation of the magnitude Bode plot is given in Figure 6.8.

## Problems

**6.3**  Draw the Bode plots for the following:

(a) $A(s) = \dfrac{0.4(0.2s + 1)}{(0.01s + 1)}$

(b) $A(s) = \dfrac{0.5(0.01s + 1)}{(0.2s + 1)}$

(c) $A(s) = \dfrac{10(s + 10)^2}{s(s + 800)}$

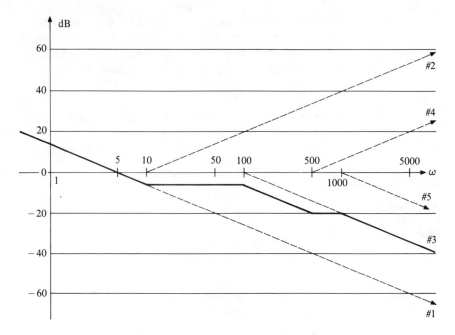

FIGURE 6.8. Magnitude Bode plot of Example 6.5

(d) $A(s) = \dfrac{s(s + 20)}{(s + 100)^2}$

(e) $A(s) = \dfrac{1,000,000}{(0.00001s + 1)^3}$

(f) $A(s) = \dfrac{100(0.1s + 1)(0.02s + 1)}{s(0.01s + 1)^2}$

(g) $A(s) = \dfrac{100(s + 2000)}{s(s + 500)(s + 200)}$

(h) $A(s) = \dfrac{200(s + 600)(s + 3000)}{s(s + 1000)(s + 100)}$

## 6.6  Bode Plot of Quadratic Functions

It is possible that one or more factors of the transfer function may be a quadratic of the form $(\tau s)^2 + 2z\tau s + 1$. This quadratic can be factored as $(\tau_1 s + 1)(\tau_2 s + 1)$ if $z > 1$. If $z = 1$, the quadratic is a perfect square of the form $(\tau s + 1)^2$. As a first approximation, $z$ is arbitrarily assumed to be 1 and the asymptote is drawn with $20n$ dB/decade. The actual middle term only changes the response in the vicinity of the corner frequency $1/\tau$. At the corner frequency the deviation is 6 dB when $z = 1$. For other values of damping factor $z$, the deviation at the corner frequency differs. The deviation at $\omega_c$ when

| | |
|---|---|
| $z > 1$ | is more than 6 dB |
| $z = 1$ | 6 dB |
| $z = 0.707$ | 3 dB (maximally flat response) |
| $z < 0.707$ | starts peaking in the pass band |

A magnitude Bode plot of the quadratic factor is presented for various values of $z$ in Figure 6.9. The actual response due to a quadratic term of the form $(\tau s)^2 + 2\tau z s + 1$ with a damping factor $z > 0.707$ is said to be flat. A flat response rounds the corner frequency without peaks or valleys. The graph will monotonically increase if the quadratic term is in the numerator of the transfer function, and decrease if the term is in the denominator. When $z = 0.707$, the response is said to be maximally flat, meaning that the response is the flattest. Any further reduction in $z$ will cause peaking of the response curve in the pass band.

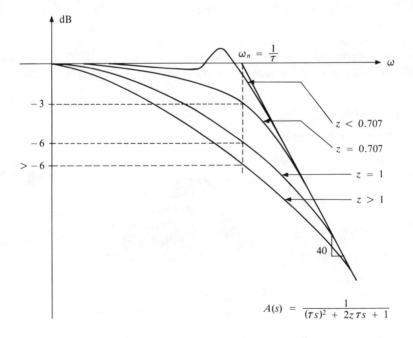

$$A(s) = \frac{1}{(\tau s)^2 + 2z\tau s + 1}$$

FIGURE 6.9. Magnitude Bode plot for $\dfrac{1}{(\tau s)^2 + 2z\tau s + 1}$

## Problems

**6.4** For the following transfer functions, find $z$ and draw the approximate magnitude response curve.

(a) $A(s) = \dfrac{1,000,000}{s^2 + 1000s + 1,000,000}$

(b) $A(s) = \dfrac{1000s}{s^2 + 1000s + 1,000,000}$

(c) $A(s) = \dfrac{s^2}{s^2 + 1000s + 1,000,000}$

(d) $A(s) = \dfrac{s^2 + 1,000,000}{s^2 + 1000s + 1,000,000}$

## 6.7 Summary

The magnitude and phase response constitute the steady-state characteristics of a network for sinusoidal inputs. The Bode plot is a relatively fast way of plotting the response. As such, the Bode plot is a very useful analytical tool. Very often the straight-line approximation of the Bode plot is left as the response curve. The rounding of the corners is understood. The Bode plot is also used for stability analysis of feedback systems.

## Key Terms

Define the following terms:

Bode plot
decade
stability
dB
$V_o(t)_{ss}$
magnitude response
corner frequency
damping factor
maximum deviation

polar form
$V_o(s)_{ss}$
phase response
maximally flat
graphical addition
resultant plot
peaking
asymptotes

# CHAPTER 7

# First-Order Networks

## 7.1 Introduction

First-order networks were introduced in section 4.7. In this chapter various first-order networks are classified based on their end use. Of all the circuits discussed in this chapter, filters and integrators are most often encountered in networks. For that reason, the sections dealing with these topics merit an expanded presentation. The general approach of study of each network will be as follows:

1. Find the transfer function $A(s)$.
2. Draw the approximate magnitude Bode plot.
3. Change the transfer function to P-Z form.
4. Draw the pole-zero map.
5. Establish the design equations.
6. Design networks for given specifications.

## 7.2 Filters

Filters are frequency-selective networks, where one or more bands of frequencies are allowed to pass through, while one or more bands of frequencies are rejected. An *active filter* is capable of providing a gain for pass-band frequencies. An operational amplifier can be used as the active device that provides the pass-band gain. Specially designed integrated circuits such as the Intersil FLT-U2 are available. However, any general-purpose operational amplifier can be used in the design of active filters, if the pass-band frequencies are well within the capabilities of the operational amplifier.

An *ideal filter* rejects 100 percent of the signals in its rejection band and allows 100 percent of the signals to pass through its pass band. The four basic types of filters are the low-pass filter, high-pass filter, band-pass filter, and band-elimination filter. The frequency response curves of all four types of filters are shown in Figure 7.1.

For the low-pass filter, the pass band is from 0 rad/s to $\omega_c$ rad/s and the rejection band is all frequencies above $\omega_c$ rad/s. $\omega_c$ is called the *cutoff frequency* of the low-pass filter.

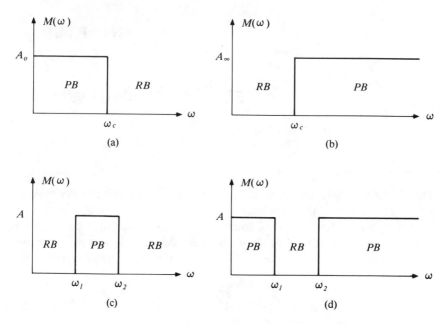

FIGURE 7.1. Frequency response curves for ideal filters: (a) Low-pass. (b) High-pass. (c) Band-pass. (d) Band-elimination.

The pass band for the high-pass filter contains all frequencies above its cutoff frequency $\omega_c$. The band of frequencies below $\omega_c$ is the rejection band of the high-pass filter.

The band-pass filter has two rejection bands, one band below $\omega_1$ and another above $\omega_2$. The band of frequencies between $\omega_1$ and $\omega_2$ is the pass band. The bandwidth of the band-pass filter is thus $(\omega_2 - \omega_1)$ rad/s.

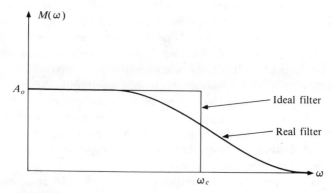

FIGURE 7.2. Frequency response of ideal and real low-pass filter

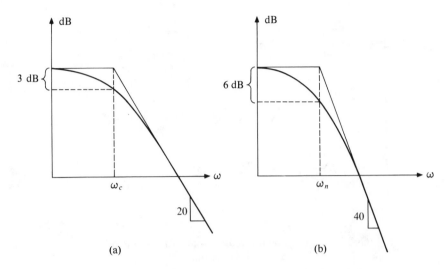

FIGURE 7.3. Magnitude Bode plot for: (a) Single pole low-pass filter. (b) Double pole low-pass filter.

The band-elimination filter is the opposite of the band-pass filter in that the rejection band of one is the pass band of the other.

Realizable filters (i.e., the filters that are physically attainable) will transmit the signals in the rejection band and attenuate signals in the pass band as indicated in the diagram for a low-pass filter in Figure 7.2.

In order to make the real filter response as close as possible to that of the ideal filter response, the attenuation of the signal in the pass band has to be minimized and the attenuation in the rejection band increased. For a single-pole filter, there is an attenuation of 3 dB at the corner frequency. The attenuation in the rejection band is 20 dB/decade as indicated in Figure 7.3(a). If the filter transfer function has two poles, the attenuation in the rejection band can be improved to 40 dB/decade. However, the attenuation in the pass band may also increase as shown in Figure 7.3(b).

Single-pole filters are called first-order filters. Filters with two poles are called second-order filters. The transfer function of an $n$th-order filter contains $n$ poles. From Figure 7.3(b) it can be seen that a higher order filter may not improve the filter characteristics. However, properly designed higher order filters can improve the filter response enough to closely approximate that of the ideal filters.

## 7.3  Low-Pass Filter

The transfer function of a single-pole low-pass filter is given in the time-constant form by equation (7.1), and in P-Z form by equation (7.2).

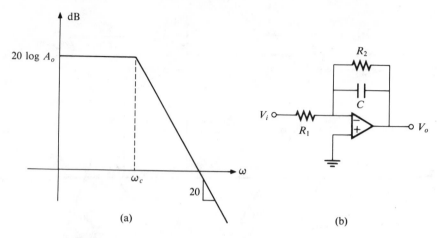

(a)

(b)

FIGURE 7.4. (a) Magnitude Bode plot for a single pole low-pass filter. (b) Inverting low-pass filter.

$$A(s) = \frac{A_0}{\tau s + 1} \qquad (7.1)$$

$$A(s) = \frac{A_0 \omega_c}{s + \omega_c}, \ \omega_c = 1/\tau \qquad (7.2)$$

where $A_0$ is the pass-band gain, $\omega_c$ is the cutoff frequency, and $\tau$ is the time constant and the reciprocal of $\omega_c$. A magnitude Bode plot is given in Figure 7.4(a).

Consider the network of Figure 7.4(b). The network shown represents an inverting amplifier. Its transfer function is given by equation (7.3) and is simplified to equation (7.4).

$$A(s) = -\frac{R_2 \| (1/sC)}{R_1} \qquad (7.3)$$

$$A(s) = \frac{-(R_2/R_1)}{R_2 C s + 1} \qquad (7.4)$$

The transfer function of the network is then changed to P-Z form in equation (7.5).

$$A(s) = \frac{-(R_2/R_1)(1/R_2C)}{s + (1/R_2C)} \qquad (7.5)$$

The magnitude Bode plot and pole-zero map are given in Figure 7.5(a) and (b), respectively.

Comparing equation (7.4) and the standard equation of a single-pole low-pass filter given by equation (7.2),

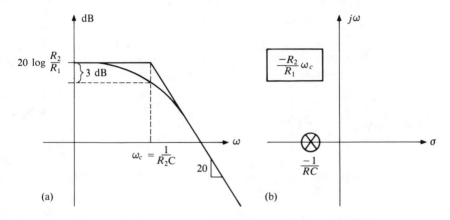

FIGURE 7.5. (a) Magnitude Bode plot of the inverting low-pass filter. (b) Pole-zero map of the inverting low-pass filter.

$$A_0 = -(R_2/R_1) \tag{7.6}$$

$$\omega_c = 1/\tau = 1/(R_2C) \tag{7.7}$$

Equations (7.6) and (7.7) are the two design equations of the inverting low-pass filter of Figure 7.4(b).

---

**Example 7.1**

Design an inverting low-pass filter for a pass-band gain of $-10$ and a cutoff frequency of 100 rad/s.

*Solution.*    There are three components, $R_1$, $R_2$, and $C$, to be designed and two design equations to satisfy. Therefore, one component can be assumed.

Let $C = 0.1\ \mu\text{F}$. From equation (7.7),

$$100 = \frac{1}{R_2 \times 10^{-7}} \text{ or } R_2 = 100\ \text{k}\Omega$$

From equation (7.6),

$$-10 = \frac{-100,000}{R_1} \text{ or } R_1 = 10\ \text{k}\Omega$$

The designed circuit and its magnitude Bode plot are given in Figure 7.6.

---

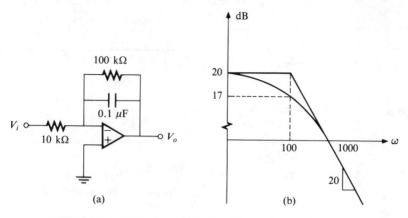

(a)

(b)

FIGURE 7.6. (a) Designed circuit of Example 7.1. (b) Magnitude Bode plot of (a).

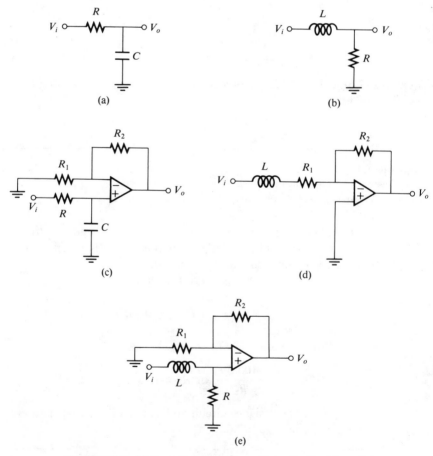

(a)

(b)

(c)

(d)

(e)

FIGURE 7.7. (a) through (e) Low-pass filters for Problems 7.1 and 7.2

## Problems

**7.1**  For the first-order low-pass filters of Figure 7.7 on page 176, find the transfer function and the required number of design equations.

**7.2**  Formulate a design procedure for each network of Figure 7.7.

## 7.4  High-Pass Filter

The transfer function of a single-pole high-pass filter is given by equation (7.8). The transfer function is changed to P-Z form in equation (7.9).

$$A(s) = \frac{(A_\infty/\omega_c)s}{(1/\omega_c)s + 1} \tag{7.8}$$

$$A(s) = \frac{A_\infty s}{s + \omega_c} \tag{7.9}$$

where $A_\infty$ is the pass-band gain and $\omega_c$ the cutoff frequency. The magnitude Bode plot and pole-zero map are given in Figure 7.8.

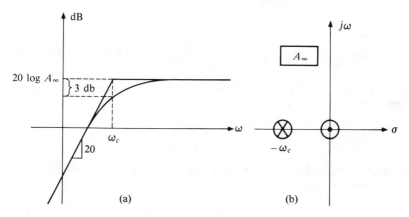

(a)                                         (b)

FIGURE 7.8. (a) Magnitude Bode plot for single pole high-pass filter. (b) Pole-zero map for single pole high-pass filter.

Figure 7.9(a) illustrates a noninverting high-pass filter. This amplifier has a gain of $(1 + R_f/R_i)$ for signals appearing at its positive terminal. However, the input signal experiences an attenuation by the passive network made up of $R$ and $C$. Hence, the transfer function is

$$A(s) = \frac{KR}{R + (1/sC)}$$

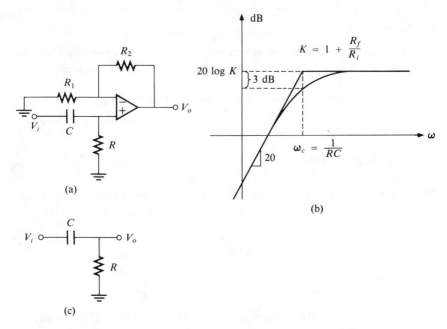

(a)

(b)

(c)

FIGURE 7.9. (a) Noninverting high-pass filter. (b) Magnitude Bode plot of (a). (c) Passive high-pass filter.

$$A(s) = \frac{KRCs}{RCs + 1} \qquad (7.10)$$

where $K = 1 + R_f/R_i$. The transfer function is changed to P-Z form in equation (7.11).

$$A(s) = \frac{Ks}{s + 1/(RC)} \qquad (7.11)$$

The magnitude Bode plot is given in Figure 7.9(b).

Comparing equation (7.11) and (7.9),

$$\omega_c = 1/(RC) \qquad (7.12)$$

$$A_\infty = K = 1 + R_f/R_i \qquad (7.13)$$

Equations (7.12) and (7.13) are the two design equations of the noninverting high-pass filter.

---

### Example 7.2

Design the passive high-pass filter of Figure 7.9(c) for a cutoff frequency of 1000 rad/s.

*Solution.*    $A(s) = \dfrac{R}{R + 1/(sC)} = \dfrac{RCs}{RCs + 1}$

$$= \frac{1s}{s + 1/(RC)}$$

$A_\infty = 1$ and $\omega_c = 1/(RC)$

There are two components and one equation to satisfy. One component can be assumed.

Let $C = 0.01 \ \mu\text{F}$

$$1000 = \frac{1}{RC} \quad \text{or} \quad R = \frac{1 \times 1,000,000}{1000 \times 0.01}$$

$$R = 100 \ \text{k}\Omega$$

## Problems

**7.3**  For each of the networks of Figure 7.10 complete the following: (a) find the transfer function, (b) obtain the design equations, and (c) list a design procedure.

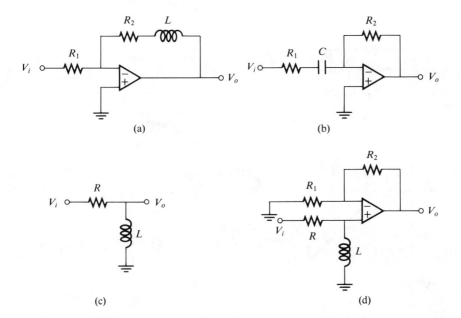

FIGURE 7.10. (a) through (d) Networks for Problem 7.3

## 7.5  All-Pass Filter

Both the magnitude and phase shift of the output for networks such as filters are frequency dependent. In many cases the magnitude response of the
network is of prime importance. In others, the phase response and the associated time shift are main considerations. For all-pass filters, the magnitude
is independent of frequency, whereas the phase angle is a function of frequency. The network of Figure 7.11(a) is a phase-lag all-pass filter.

$$V_o = -V_i + 2V_i \frac{1/(sC)}{R + 1/(sC)} \tag{7.14}$$

$$= V_i \left( \frac{2}{RCs + 1} - 1 \right)$$

$$A(s) = \frac{1 - \tau s}{1 + \tau s} \tag{7.15}$$

where $\tau = RC$

$$A(j\omega) = \frac{1 - j\omega\tau}{1 + j\omega\tau} = M(\omega) \underline{/\phi(\omega)} \tag{7.16}$$

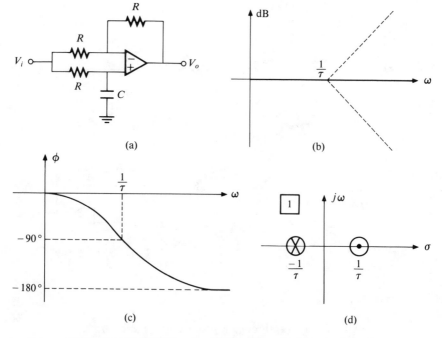

FIGURE 7.11. (a) Phase-lag all-pass filter. (b) Magnitude Bode
plot. (c) Phase Bode plot. (d) Pole-zero map.

$$M(\omega) = \left[ \frac{(1 + \omega^2\tau^2)}{(1 + \omega^2\tau^2)} \right]^{0.5} = 1 \qquad (7.17)$$

The magnitude Bode plot is given in Figure 7.11(b).

$$\phi(\omega) = -\arctan \tau\omega - \arctan \tau\omega = -2 \arctan \tau\omega \qquad (7.18)$$

when $\omega = 0$,      $\phi(\omega) = 0°$          at very low frequency
when $\omega = 1/\tau$, $\phi(\omega) = -90°$      at corner frequency
when $\omega = \infty$,  $\phi(\omega) = -180°$   at very high frequency

An approximate phase Bode plot is drawn in Figure 7.11(c). The pole-zero map is given in Figure 7.11(d).

## Problems

**7.4**   For each of the all-pass filters of Figure 7.12, find the transfer function and draw the magnitude and phase Bode plots and pole-zero map.

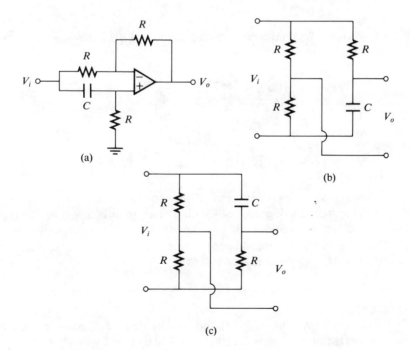

(a)

(b)

(c)

FIGURE 7.12. (a), (b), and (c) All-pass networks for Problem 7.4

## 7.6  Integrator

Integrators are very useful circuits in computing, signal processing, and signal-generating applications. Integrators remain the major building block of analog computers. Since integrators are the basic network component of state variable design of analog circuits, we will examine them in detail in this section.

### The Basic Integrator

The circuit of Figure 7.13(a) illustrates a basic integrator.

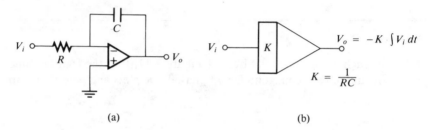

(a)                                              (b)

FIGURE 7.13. (a) Basic integrator circuit. (b) Block diagram of (a).

$$A(s) = \frac{V_o(s)}{V_i(s)} = \frac{-1}{RCs} \qquad (7.19)$$

$$V_o(s) = \frac{-1}{RC} \frac{V_i(s)}{s}$$

$$V_o(t) = \frac{-1}{RC} \mathcal{L}^{-1}\left[\frac{V_i(s)}{s}\right] = \frac{-1}{RC} \int V_i \, dt \qquad (7.20)$$

The output is essentially the integral of the input.

Recall that a function divided by $s$ indicates an integration in the time domain. The initial conditions will have an effect, but they will simply determine the value of the integration constant. A block diagram representation of an integrator is given in Figure 7.13(b).

### Example 7.3

Find the output voltage $V_o(t)$ and its time-domain response curve for the integrator of Figure 7.13(a). $R = 1$ M$\Omega$, $C = 1$ $\mu$F, $V_i = 10$ V dc, $V_{sat} = \pm 20$ V. The capacitor is initially de-energized.

Solution. $\qquad V_o = -1 \int 10 \, dt = -10t + A$

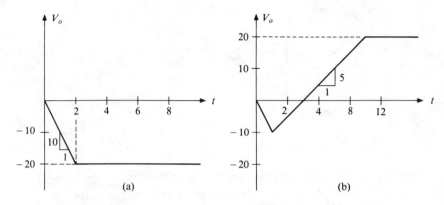

FIGURE 7.14. Response curves for: (a) Example 7.3. (b) Example 7.4.

where $A$ is the integration constant and is due to the initial condition of the capacitor. For the problem at hand, $A = 0$. The time-domain response curve is given in Figure 7.14(a).

---

**Example 7.4**

After 1 s, the input of Example 7.3 is suddenly changed to $-5$ V. Draw the time-domain response curve of $V_o$.

*Solution.* For 1 s the output is the same as that in Figure 7.14(a). At $t = 1$ s, the output is $-10$ V. This is the initial condition for the integration of the new input.

$$V_o = -1 \int -5 \, dt = 5t + A$$

where $A = -10$    $V_o = 5t - 10$

The time-domain response curve is shown in Figure 7.14(b).

---

**Error Ramp Voltages of an Integrator**

The output of an integrator will contain error voltages resulting from the offset voltage and biasing current of the op-amp. The effect of offset voltage is illustrated in Figure 7.15(a). The input voltage $V_i$ and bias current $I_b$ are assumed to be zero.

$$V_o = \frac{1}{RC} \int V_{os} \, dt + V_{os} + A \tag{7.21}$$

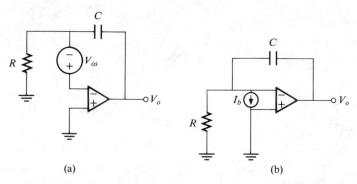

FIGURE 7.15. (a) Effect of offset voltage on an integrator. (b) Effect of bias current on integrator.

Assuming $V_c = 0$ at $t = 0$, $A = 0$

$$V_o = \frac{V_{os}}{RC} t + V_{os} \qquad (7.22)$$

This output voltage varies with time and eventually reaches saturation voltage. If the integration interval is small, the error due to the offset voltage can be ignored.

---

**Example 7.5**

For the integrator of Example 7.15(a), $V_i = 0$. The offset input voltage is $-50$ mV, $R = 1$ M$\Omega$, and $C = 1$ $\mu$F. How long will it take for the output voltage to reach (a) 1 V and (b) saturation voltage of 20 V?

*Solution.*

$$V_o = \frac{-1}{RC} \int -50 \times 10^{-3} \, dt - 50 \times 10^{-3}$$

$$V_o = 50 \times 10^{-3}t - 50 \times 10^{-3} = 50 \times 10^{-3}(t - 1)$$

(a)  $\qquad\qquad V_o = 1000$ mV

$$1000 \times 10^{-3} = 50 \times 10^{-3}(t - 1)$$

or $t - 1 = 20$ and $t = 21$ s

(b)  $\qquad 20,000 \times 10^{-3} = 50 \times 10^{-3}(t - 1)$

or $t - 1 = 400$ s and $t = 401$ s

The integrator will self-saturate after 401 s.

---

The effect of the bias current is indicated in Figure 7.15(b).

$$V_o = (1/C) \int I_b \, dt = (1/C) I_b t \qquad (7.23)$$

Both the bias current and offset polarities must be taken into account in determining the slope of the ramp voltage. The combined effect of the two error ramps determine the upper limit of integration time for the integrator.

---

**Example 7.6**

For the integrator of Figure 7.15(b), $R = 1$ M$\Omega$, $C = 1$ $\mu$F, and $I_b = 20 \times 10^{-9}$ A. How long will the op-amp remain in the analog region? $V_{sat} = 20$ V.

*Solution.*

$$V_o = \frac{1}{C} I_b t \quad \text{or} \quad t = \frac{V_o C}{I_b} = \frac{20 \times 10^{-6}}{20 \times 10^{-9}} = 2000 \text{ s}$$

It will take 2000 s before the amplifier goes into saturation.

---

Figure 7.16 is an integrator compensated to eliminate error voltages. $A_1$ and $A_2$ are two integrators using two of the four op-amps of a quad (i.e., four op-amps in a package). Both integrators create equal error ramps which are fed to a differential amplifier. The error ramps are the common mode inputs for the differential amplifier and are thus rejected.

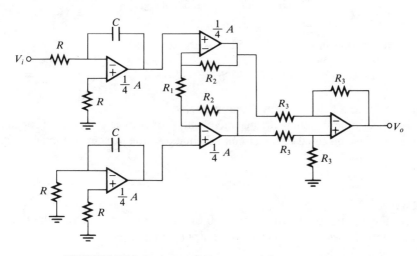

FIGURE 7.16. Integrator compensated for error ramps

The error ramps in integrators can be minimized by selecting amplifiers with very-low offset voltage and bias current. A larger capacitance reduces the ramp voltage due to bias current. The dielectric leakage current of the capacitor must be less than the bias current of the amplifier. Capacitors made of polystyrene and Teflon are the best choice. For short-term integrations, Mylar or silver-mica capacitors are satisfactory. For high-frequency signals at high amplitudes, slew-rate distortion will also occur.

### Three-Mode Integrator

A switching arrangement is used to start and terminate the integration function of the three-mode integrator shown in Figure 7.17. An initial condition mode, where a voltage is placed across the capacitor prior to the integration mode, is enacted by switch S2. The hold mode is placed on the integrator with both switches S1 and S2 kept open.

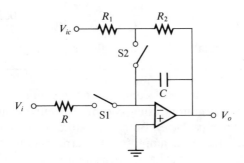

FIGURE 7.17. Three-mode integrator

Integration mode        S1 closed, S2 open
Initial condition mode    S1 open, S2 closed
Hold mode              S1 open, S2 open

Both S1 and S2 closed is an illegal mode.
Electronic switching arrangement with proper logic can be used for the two switches indicated in the circuit schematic of the three-mode integrator.

---

### Example 7.7

For the basic integrator, $RC = 0.01$ s and $V_i = 9e^{-3t}$. Draw the time-domain response curve of the output voltage.

$$V_{sat} = \pm 30 \text{ V}$$

*Solution.*

$$V_o = \frac{-1}{RC} \; 9 \int e^{-3t} \, dt = \frac{-900}{-3} \, e^{-3t} + \text{initial condition}$$

The initial condition is assumed to be zero.

$$V_o = 300e^{-3t} \quad \text{or} \quad V_{sat} \text{ (whichever is smaller)}$$
$$300e^{-3T_1} = 30 \quad \text{or} \quad e^{-3T_1} = 0.1$$
$$-3T_1 = \log_e 0.1 \quad \text{or} \quad T_1 = \tfrac{1}{3} \log_e 10$$

The time-domain response curve is given in Figure 7.18.

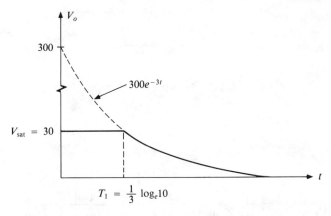

FIGURE 7.18. Response curve of Example 7.7

## Problems

**7.5**  Find the transfer function of the networks of Figure 7.19.

**7.6**  For the basic integrator of Figure 7.13(a), $R = 10 \text{ k}\Omega$ and $C = 0.001 \; \mu\text{F}$. Draw the time-domain response curves for the inputs listed. $V_{sat} = 20$ V.

(a) 5 V dc

(b) 3 V for 0 to 20 $\mu$s, then switched to zero

(c) $3e^{-3t}$

(d) 4 sin 8$t$

**7.7**  Do Problem 7.6 for the inputs given in Figure 7.20.

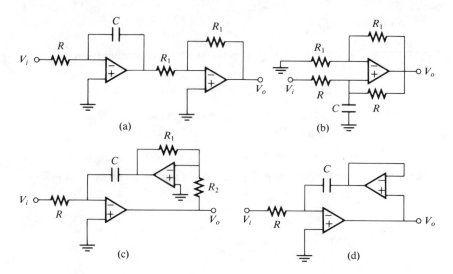

FIGURE 7.19. Networks for Problem 7.5

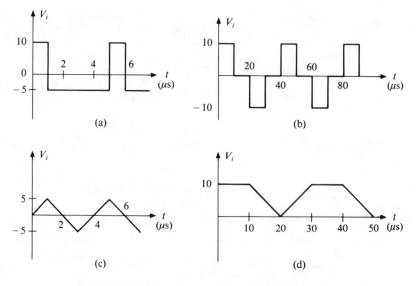

FIGURE 7.20. Input waveforms for Problem 7.7

**7.8** For the integrator of Figure 7.13(a), $R = 10 \, \text{k}\Omega$, $C = 0.0001 \, \mu\text{F}$, $V_{os} = 20 \, \text{mV}$, $I_b = 10 \, \text{nA}$, and $V_{sat} = 10 \, \text{V}$. How long will it take for the integrator to self-saturate?

## 7.7  Differentiator

By interchanging the resistor and capacitor of the basic integrator circuit, the basic differentiator circuit is realized, as indicated in Figure 7.21(a).

$$I_c = -V_o/R \tag{7.24}$$

$I_c$ is the charging current and is given by

$$I_c = C \frac{dV_i}{dt} \tag{7.25}$$

$$C \frac{dV_i}{dt} = \frac{-V_o}{R} \tag{7.26}$$

$$V_o = -RC \frac{dV_i}{dt} \tag{7.27}$$

The output depends on the differentiation of the input.

From the magnitude Bode plot of Figure 7.21(b), it can be seen that the gain of the differentiator increases as the frequency increases. This is a major problem of a differentiator. It should be noted that the high-frequency component of the noise can be amplified to such an extent that the amplifier may go into saturation.

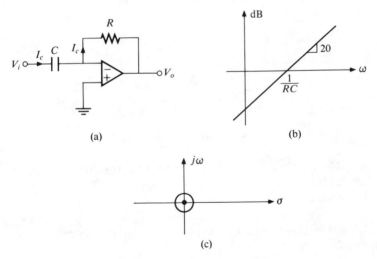

(a)                              (b)

(c)

FIGURE 7.21. (a) Basic differentiator circuit. (b) Magnitude Bode plot of (a). (c) Pole-zero map of (a).

---

**Example 7.8**

For the differentiator of Figure 7.21(a), $R = 100$ k$\Omega$ and $C = 0.1$ $\mu$F. $V_{sat} = 20$ V.

(a) Find $V_o$ if $V_i = 2 \sin 40t$

(b) Find $V_o$ if $V_i = 2 \sin 4000t$

(c) Draw the time-domain response curve for $V_o$ of (b)

*Solution.*

(a) $V_o = -10^5 \times 10^{-7} \dfrac{d(2 \sin 40t)}{dt}$

   $= -0.8 \cos 4t$

(b) $V_o = -80 \cos 4000t$ or $V_{sat}$

(c) The time-domain response curve is given in Figure 7.22.

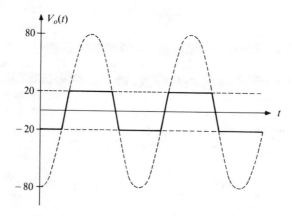

FIGURE 7.22. Response curve of $V_o(t)$ of Example 7.8

**Problems**

**7.9** $R = 10 \text{ k}\Omega$, $C = 0.1 \text{ }\mu\text{F}$, and $V_{sat} = 10$ V for the differentiator of Figure 7.21(a). Calculate the output voltage for all input voltages listed for Problem 7.6.

**7.10** Draw the time-domain response curves of the output voltages of Problem 7.9.

## 7.8 Lead and Lag Networks

Lead and lag networks are used primarily for their phase shift characteristics. The all-pass filters of section 7.5 are lead and lag networks as well. The effect of frequency on the phase shift can be observed in the phase Bode plot of the gain functions of the networks. In general, these circuits also affect the magnitude. Consider the phase lag network of Figure 7.23(a). Note that the network configuration is identical to the all-pass filter.

$$V_o = V_i \left( -\frac{R_2}{R_1} + \frac{R_1 + R_2}{R_1} \frac{(1/sC)}{R + (1/sC)} \right) \tag{7.28}$$

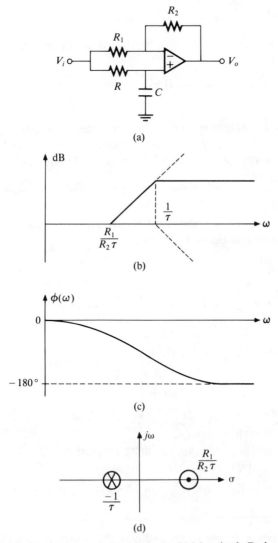

FIGURE 7.23. (a) Phase-lag network. (b) Magnitude Bode plot for (a). (c) Phase Bode plot for (a). (d) Pole-zero map for (a).

$$A(s) = -\frac{R_2}{R_1} + \frac{(R_1 + R_2)}{R_1(RCs + 1)}$$

$$A(s) = \frac{-R_2(\tau s + 1) + R_1 + R_2}{R_1(\tau s + 1)}$$

where $\tau = RC$

$$A(s) = \frac{-R_2\tau s - R_2 + R_1 + R_2}{R_1(\tau s + 1)} = \frac{R_1(-(R_2/R_1)\tau s + 1)}{R_1(\tau s + 1)}$$

$$A(s) = \frac{-((R_2/R_1)\tau s + 1)}{\tau s + 1} \tag{7.29}$$

The magnitude Bode plot is drawn in Figure 7.23(b), assuming $(R_2/R_1) > 1$.

$$\phi(\omega) = -\arctan((R_2/R_1)\tau\omega) - \arctan \tau\omega \tag{7.30}$$

$$\phi(0) = 0 \quad \text{and} \quad \phi(\infty) = -180°$$

The phase response curve between these two extreme frequencies depends on the ratio $R_2/R_1$. The phase Bode plot is given in Figure 7.23(c). The pole-zero map of the network is shown in Figure 7.23(d).

---

### Example 7.9

For the phase-lag network of Figure 7.24(a), draw the approximate magnitude and phase Bode plots.

*Solution.*

$$V_o = V_i\left(-2 + 3\,\frac{R}{R + (1/sC)}\right)$$

$$A(s) = -2 + \frac{3RCs}{RCs + 1}$$

$$= \frac{-2RCs - 2 + 3RCs}{RCs + 1} = \frac{2(0.5\tau s - 1)}{\tau s + 1}$$

where $\tau = RC$.

The approximate magnitude Bode plot is given in Figure 7.24(b).

$$\phi(\omega) = 180° - \arctan(0.5\tau\omega) - \arctan(\tau\omega)$$

$$\boxed{-a + bj = r\,\underline{/\theta} \quad \text{where} \quad \phi = 180 - \arctan(b/a)}$$

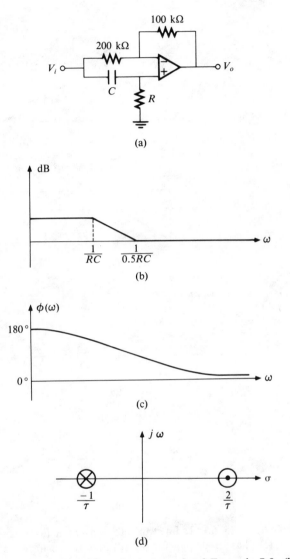

FIGURE 7.24. (a) Phase-lead network of Example 7.9. (b) Magnitude Bode plot for (a). (c) Phase Bode plot for (a). (d) Pole-zero map for (a).

Note that the angle $\phi(\omega)$ lies in the second quadrant.

The phase Bode plot is shown in Figure 7.24(c) and the pole-zero map in Figure 7.24(d).

Consider the phase-lead network of Figure 7.25(a). This is a passive network and its transfer function is given by equation (7.32).

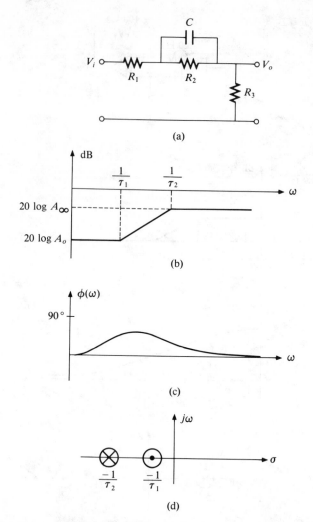

FIGURE 7.25. (a) Lead network. (b) Magnitude Bode plot for (a). (c) Phase Bode plot for (a). (d) Pole-zero map for (a).

$$A(s) = \frac{R_3}{R_1 + R_2 \| (1/sC) + R_3} \tag{7.31}$$

$$= \frac{R_3}{R_1 + (R_2/(R_2 Cs + 1)) + R_3}$$

$$= \frac{R_3(R_2 Cs + 1)}{(R_1 + R_3)R_2 Cs + R_1 + R_3 + R_3}$$

$$A(s) = \frac{\dfrac{R_3}{R_1 + R_2 + R_3}(R_2 Cs + 1)}{\dfrac{(R_1 + R_3)}{R_1 + R_2 + R_3}R_2 Cs + 1} = \frac{A_0(\tau_1 s + 1)}{\tau_2 s + 1} \qquad (7.32)$$

where

$$A_0 = \frac{R_3}{R_1 + R_2 + R_3} \qquad (7.33)$$

$$\tau_1 = R_2 C \qquad (7.34)$$

$$\tau_2 = \frac{R_1 + R_3}{R_1 + R_2 + R_3}R_2 C \qquad (7.35)$$

$$A_\infty = \frac{R_3}{R_1 + R_3} \qquad (7.36)$$

The magnitude Bode plot, the phase Bode plot, and the pole-zero map are given in Figure 7.25(b), (c), and (d), respectively.

Note the following relationships:

1. $A_0$ is a fraction and hence $20 \log A_0 < 0$ dB.
2. $\tau_2 < \tau_1$ and therefore $1/\tau_2 > 1/\tau_1$
3. At very high frequencies the gain is given by

$$A_\infty = \lim_{s \to \infty} A(s) = A_0 \tau_1/\tau_2 = R_3/(R_1 + R_3)$$

4. Also, $A_\infty < 1$ and hence $20 \log A_\infty < 0$.

We can qualitatively examine the network and see the significance of the gains, $A_0$ at low frequencies and $A_\infty$ at high frequencies. At low frequencies the capacitance acts as an open circuit and the gain is $R_3/(R_1 + R_2 + R_3)$. At high frequencies the capacitor acts as a short circuit, and the gain is $R_3/(R_1 + R_3)$.

The lead and lag circuits are very useful networks. One application is magnitude and phase compensation in feedback systems. The external or internal compensation of the op-amp is one familiar example. Lead networks can be used to improve the response of a system. Problem 7.11 is such a case where a lead network is used to improve the response of an otherwise slow-responding thermoelectric device.

## Problems

**7.11**  A thermocouple used as a feedback sensing device is found to behave as a first-order system with a time constant of 6 s. Its response is to be speeded up by a factor of 5. A lead network of Figure 7.24(a) is to be used. This network works from a source with an impedance of 20 kΩ and into an amplifier of input impedance of 100 kΩ. The amplifier is capable of addition gain, meaning that the attenuation of the lead network is not a concern. Design the network.

**7.12**  For the lead and lag networks of Figure 7.26, draw the magnitude and phase Bode plots.

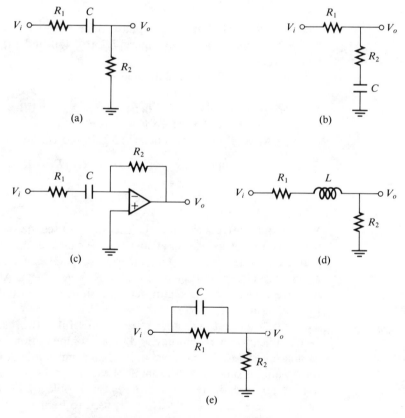

FIGURE 7.26. Networks for Problem 7.12

## 7.9  Frequency-Independent Networks

If the transfer function of a network contains a pole, the effect of this pole on frequency response can be cancelled by introducing a zero at the same location. The capacitive probe used with oscilloscopes to measure voltage is an example.

---

**Example 7.10**

Prove that the network of Figure 7.27 is frequency independent if $R_1 C_1 = R_2 C_2$, even if $R_1$ is not equal to $R_2$.

*Solution.*   If a network is frequency independent, its transfer function will not be a function of $s$.

$$A(s) = Z_2/(Z_1 + Z_2)$$

where

$$Z_1 = R_1 + 1/(sC_1)$$
$$= (R_1 C_1 s + 1)/sC_1$$

and

$$Z_2 = R_2 + 1/sC_2 = (R_2 C_2 s + 1)/sC_2$$

Let $R_1 C_1 = R_2 C_2 = \tau$

$$A(s) = \cfrac{\cfrac{\tau s + 1}{sC_2}}{\cfrac{\tau s + 1}{sC_1} + \cfrac{\tau s + 1}{sC_2}} = \cfrac{\cfrac{1}{C_2}}{\cfrac{1}{C_1} + \cfrac{1}{C_2}}$$

$$= \frac{C_1}{C_1 + C_2} \quad \text{is not a function of } s.$$

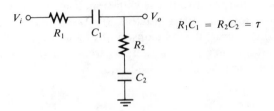

$$R_1 C_1 = R_2 C_2 = \tau$$

FIGURE 7.27. Network for Example 7.10

**Problems**

**7.13** $R_2 C_2 = R_1 C_1$ for all the networks of Figure 7.28. Check if these networks are frequency independent.

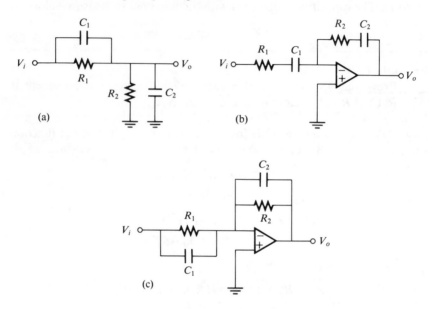

FIGURE 7.28. Networks for Problem 7.13

## 7.10 Summary

Filters, integrators, differentiators, and lead and lag networks may have the same circuit configurations. The particular name simply depends on the application. In low-pass and high-pass filters, the *magnitude* response with respect to frequency is the main consideration. For all-pass filters and lead and lag networks, the *phase* response with respect to frequency is of importance. For integrators and differentiators, the time-domain response is the major concern. However, it can be observed that a low-pass filter has both a phase lag and an integration aspect, whereas a high-pass filter can be looked at as a differentiator or phase-lead network.

**Key Terms**

Define the following terms:

active filter                          bandwidth
ideal filter                           first-order filter

$A_0$

real filter

pass band

$A$

rejection band

low-pass filter

integrator

high-pass filter

all-pass filter

error ramp

band-pass filter

cutoff frequency

second-order filter

three-mode integrator

integration mode

time shift

phase-lag network

hold mode

differentiator

lead network

filter

frequency-independent network

initial condition mode

See Appendix A, Lab 1 *Magnitude Bode Plot* for further applications of the concepts discussed in this chapter.

# CHAPTER 8

# Second-Order Filters

## 8.1  Introduction

A second-order filter can be recognized by the quadratic function of $s$ in the denominator of its transfer function. The response of a second-order filter is attenuated at 40 dB/decade in its rejection band. The pass-band response depends on the middle term of the quadratic. The utility of second-order filters is evidenced by their appearance in component designs for higher order systems. For example, a fifth-order filter can be implemented by two second-order filters and one first-order filter. There are several second-order filter configurations that have been developed. Of these configurations, the *multiple feedback* and the *voltage-controlled voltage source* (VCVS) filters are widely used.

## 8.2  Transfer Functions of Second-Order Filters

The denominator of the transfer function of a second-order filter is expressed as

$$D(s) = s^2 + 2z\omega_n s + \omega_n^2 \qquad (8.1)$$

where $D(s)$ is the denominator of $A(s)$ of a second-order filter, $\omega_n$ is the *natural frequency*, and $z$ is the *damping factor*. Regardless of the kind of second-order filter, the denominator of its transfer function is always expressed as given by equation (8.1). The numerator of the transfer function determines the kind of filter being used. For example, $2Az\omega_n s$ is the numerator of the transfer function of the band-pass filter. The standard transfer functions of second-order low-pass, high-pass, band-pass, and band-rejection filters are given by the following equations—(8.2), (8.3), (8.4), and (8.5), respectively.

$$A(s) = \frac{A_0 \omega_n^2}{s^2 + 2z\omega_n s + \omega_n^2} \qquad LP \qquad (8.2)$$

$$A(s) = \frac{A_\infty s^2}{s^2 + 2z\omega_n s + \omega_n^2} \qquad HP \qquad (8.3)$$

$$A(s) = \frac{2Az\omega_n s}{s^2 + 2z\omega_n s + \omega_n^2} \qquad \text{BP} \qquad (8.4)$$

$$A(s) = \frac{A(s^2 + \omega_n^2)}{s^2 + 2z\omega_n s + \omega_n^2} \qquad \text{BR} \qquad (8.5)$$

where $A_0$, $A_\infty$, and $A$ are pass-band gains. For a band-pass filter, the bandwidth $B$ is usually given, rather than the damping factor $z$. The quality factor $Q$ and the damping factor $z$ are related by equation (8.6).

$$Q = 1/2z \qquad (8.6)$$

$$B = \omega_n/Q = 2z\omega_n \qquad (8.7)$$

The transfer function for a band-pass filter can be modified as

$$A(s) = \frac{ABs}{s^2 + Bs + \omega_n^2} \qquad (8.8)$$

where $B$ is the bandwidth of the band-pass filter. Note that with the exception of the gain term $A$ the numerators of all types of filters contain one or more denominator terms.

## 8.3   Effect of Damping on Filter Response

For the following discussion, assume a second-order low-pass filter. Its transfer function is given by equation (8.2).

### Critically Damped Filter

Let $z = 1$. The denominator quadratic becomes a perfect square $(s + \omega_n)^2$. In this case, the filter is said to be critically damped. The transfer function is

$$A(s) = \frac{A_0\omega_n^2}{(s + \omega_n)^2} \qquad (8.9)$$

$$= \frac{A_0}{\left(\dfrac{1}{\omega_n} s + 1\right)^2}$$

The magnitude Bode plot for this filter is shown in Figure 8.1(a). Compared to a first-order low-pass filter response, this second-order filter has a higher rejection percentage in its rejection band, that is, it is a closer approximation of the *ideal* filter than the first-order filter. However, the pass-band response of this second-order filter is worse than that of the first-order low-pass filter, that is, the first-order filter is a closer approximation of the *ideal* filter than this second-order filter in the pass-band.

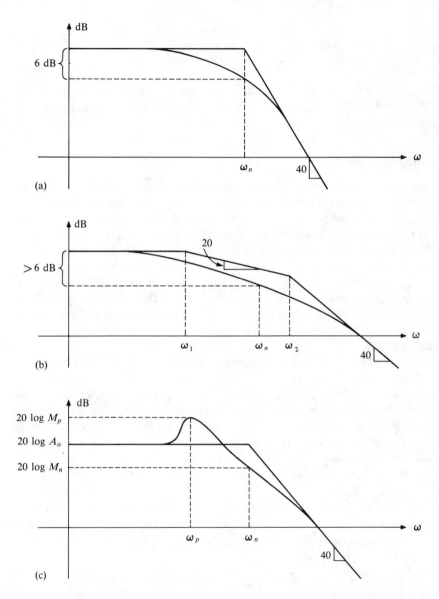

FIGURE 8.1. Magnitude response curves for second-order low-pass filters: (a) $z = 1$. (b) $z > 1$. (c) $0 < z < 1$.

## Overdamped Filter

Let $z > 1$. This filter is said to be overdamped. The denominator quadratic can be split into two linear factors $(s + \omega_1)$ and $(s + \omega_2)$.

$$A(s) = \frac{A_0 \omega_1 \omega_2}{(s + \omega_1)(s + \omega_2)} \tag{8.10}$$

$$\omega_n = (\omega_1 \omega_2)^{0.5} \tag{8.11}$$

The magnitude Bode plot for $A(s)$ when $z > 1$ is given in Figure 8.1(b). The pass-band attenuation of the overdamped filter is larger than the critically damped filter.

### Underdamped Filter

Let $z < 1$. This filter is underdamped. The roots of the denominator quadratic of the transfer function are a pair of complex conjugates. For this reason, the underdamped filters are sometimes called complex conjugate filters. In order to draw the magnitude Bode plot, first it is assumed that $z = 1$. Based on this assumption the asymptotes are drawn. The value of $z$ controls the actual response in the vicinity of $\omega_n$. Depending on the value of $z$, the pass-band response of the filter can be improved. When $z = 0.707$ the attenuation at the natural frequency matches that of a first-order low-pass filter. If $z < 0.707$, peaking will occur in the pass band as indicated in Figure 8.1(c). The *peaking frequency* $\omega_p$ is the frequency at which the frequency response curve peaks.

Normally, the cutoff frequency of a filter is defined as the frequency where the gain has dropped to 70.7% of the pass-band gain (which corresponds to a 3-dB drop in Bode plots). This frequency is the *half-power frequency* $\omega_h$. Note that $\omega_n = \omega_h$ only when $z = 0.707$. For band-pass filters and band-rejection filters, $\omega_n$ is the *center frequency*. The upper and lower half-power frequencies are approximately a half-bandwidth above and a half-bandwidth below the center frequency.

---

**Example 8.1**

The transfer function of a band-rejection filter is

$$A(s) = \frac{2(s^2 + 10{,}000)}{s^2 + 10s + 10{,}000}$$

Find the center frequency, the pass-band gain bandwidth, and the upper and lower half-power frequencies.

*Solution.* Comparing the transfer function of the band-rejection filter given by equation (8.5), we find the following:

> Center frequency = 100 rad/s
> Damping factor = 0.05; $Q = 1/0.1 = 10$
> Bandwidth = $\omega_n/Q = 10$ rad/s
> Pass-band gain = 2

Lower half-power frequency, $\omega_1 = 95$ rad/s
Upper half-power frequency, $\omega_2 = 105$ rad/s
Gain at $\omega_1$ and $\omega_2 = 0.707 \times 2 = 1.414$

---

## Problems

**8.1** Find $\omega_n$, $z$, and $A_0$ for the low-pass filters.

(a) $A(s) = \dfrac{20{,}000}{s^2 + 200s + 10{,}000}$    (b) $A(s) = \dfrac{10{,}000}{s^2 + 100s + 10{,}000}$

(c) $A(s) = \dfrac{20{,}000}{s^2 + 500s + 10{,}000}$

---

## 8.4 Magnitude Response of Second-Order Low-Pass Filter

In order to obtain an expression for the magnitude response of a second-order low-pass filter, $s$ is replaced by $j\omega$ in equation (8.2).

$$A(j\omega) = \frac{A_0\omega_n^2}{-\omega^2 + j2z\omega\omega_n + \omega_n^2} \tag{8.12}$$

$$= \frac{A_0\omega_n^2}{(\omega_n^2 - \omega^2) + j2z\omega_n\omega}$$

$$M(\omega) = \frac{A_0\omega_n^2}{\sqrt{(\omega_n^2 - \omega^2)^2 + 4z^2\omega_n^2\omega^2}} \tag{8.13}$$

$$\phi(\omega) = -\arctan\left[\frac{2z\omega_n\omega}{\omega_n^2 - \omega^2}\right] \tag{8.14}$$

where $M(\omega)$ is the magnitude of $A(j\omega)$ and $\phi(\omega)$ the phase angle of $A(j\omega)$.

### Peaking Frequency

The *peaking* of the magnitude occurs, if at all, at a frequency $\omega_p$, where the first derivative of $M(\omega)$ with respect to $\omega$ is zero since the *maxima* condition is valid in this case. A rather difficult process of differentiating a quotient (V/U) can be simplified somewhat by taking $\log_e$ on both sides of the equation. The $\log_e$ operator will change division to subtraction.

$$\log_e M(\omega) = \log_e(A_0\omega_n^2) - 0.5\,[\log_e(\omega_n^2 - \omega^2)^2 + 4z^2\omega_n^2\omega^2] \tag{8.15}$$

By differentiating both sides of equation (8.15) with respect to $\omega$, we obtain

$$\frac{1}{M}\frac{dM}{d\omega} = 0 - \frac{0.5[2(\omega_n^2 - \omega^2)(-2\omega) + 8z^2\omega_n^2\omega]}{(\omega_n^2 - \omega^2)^2 + 4z^2\omega_n^2\omega^2} \tag{8.16}$$

$$d(\log_e x)/dx = 1/x \tag{8.17}$$

when $dM/d\omega = 0$, $\omega = \omega_p$

$$0 = \frac{2(\omega_n^2 - \omega_p^2)\omega_p - 4z^2\omega_n^2\omega_p}{(\omega_n^2 - \omega_p^2)^2 + 4z^2\omega_n^2\omega_p^2} \tag{8.18}$$

For equation (8.18) to be true, the numerator must be zero:

$$2(\omega_n^2 - \omega_p^2)\omega_p - 4z^2\omega_n^2\omega_p = 0$$
$$2(\omega_n^2 - \omega_p^2) = 4z^2\omega_n^2$$
$$\omega_n^2 - \omega_p^2 = 2z^2\omega_n^2 \quad \text{or} \quad \omega_p^2 = \omega_n^2 - 2z^2\omega_n^2$$
$$\omega_p = \omega_n\sqrt{1 - 2z^2} \tag{8.19}$$

The peaking frequency exists only when $1 - 2z^2 > 0$ or $z < 0.707$. When $z = 0.707$, the filter has what is called a maximally flat response, or a *Butterworth response*.

## Magnitude at the Peaking Frequency

The magnitude of a filter is given by equation (8.13) and the peaking frequency by (8.19). The magnitude $M_p$ at the peaking frequency is the magnitude when $\omega = \omega_p$.

$$M_p = \frac{A_0\omega_n^2}{\sqrt{(\omega_n^2 - \omega_n^2(1 - 2z^2))^2 + 4z^2\omega_n^4(1 - 2z^2)}} \tag{8.20}$$

$$= \frac{A_0\omega_n^2}{\omega_n^2\sqrt{4z^4 + 4z^2(1 - 2z^2)}} = \frac{A_0}{\sqrt{(4z^2 - 4z^4)}}$$

$$M_p = \frac{A_0}{2z\sqrt{1 - z^2}} \quad \text{for } 0 < z < 0.707 \tag{8.21}$$

## Magnitude at the Natural Frequency

The magnitude at the natural frequency is found by substituting $\omega = \omega_n$ in equation (8.13).

$$M_n = \frac{A_0\omega_n^2}{\sqrt{(\omega_n^2 - \omega_n^2)^2 + 4z^2\omega_n^4}} = \frac{A_0}{2z} \tag{8.22}$$

when $M_n$ is the magnitude at the natural frequency.

**Example 8.2**

For a maximally flat low-pass filter, show that the half-power frequency $\omega_h = \omega_n$.

*Solution.*  The half-power frequency is the frequency at which the magnitude has dropped to 0.707 of the pass-band gain. For a maximally flat filter $z = 0.707$,

$$M_n = \frac{A_0}{2(0.707)} = 0.707 A_0.$$

The frequency at which the magnitude is $0.707 A_0$ is the half-power frequency. Hence $\omega_n = \omega_h$ when $z = 0.707$.

**Half-Power Frequency**

When the gain is $0.707 A_0$, the frequency is $\omega_h$.

$$0.707 A_0 = \frac{A_0 \omega_n^2}{\sqrt{(\omega_n^2 - \omega_h^2)^2 + 4z^2 \omega_n^2 \omega_h^2}}$$

Squaring both sides of the equation, we have

$$0.5 = \frac{\omega_n^4}{\omega_n^4 - 2\omega_n^2 \omega_h^2 + \omega_h^4 + 4z^2 \omega_n^2 \omega_h^2}$$

$$0.5\omega_n^4 - \omega_n^2 \omega_h^2 + 0.5\omega_h^4 + 2z^2 \omega_n^2 \omega_h^2 = \omega_n^4$$

$$\omega_n^4 - 2\omega_n^2 \omega_h^2 + \omega_h^4 + 4z^2 \omega_n^2 \omega_h^2 - 2\omega_n^4 = 0$$

$$\omega_h^4 + \omega_h^2(4z^2 \omega_n^2 - 2\omega_n^2) - \omega_n^4 = 0$$

Let $\omega_h^2 = x$, such that $\omega_h = \sqrt{x}$

$$x^2 + 2\omega_n^2(2z^2 - 1)x - \omega_n^4 = 0$$

$$x_1 = \frac{-2\omega_n^2(2z^2 - 1) + \sqrt{[4\omega_n^4(2z^2 - 1)^2 - 4(-\omega_n^4)]}}{2}$$

$$x_1 = \omega_n^2[(1 - 2z^2) + \sqrt{[(2z^2 - 1)^2 + 1]}]$$

$$x_1 = \omega_n^2[(1 - 2z^2) + \sqrt{4z^4 - 4z^2 + 2}]$$

therefore,

$$\omega_h = \omega_n \sqrt{1 - 2z^2 + \sqrt{4z^4 - 4z^2 + 2}} \qquad (8.23)$$

**Example 8.3**

The transfer function of a low-pass filter is

$$A(s) = \frac{2,000,000}{s^2 + 1000s + 1,000,000}$$

Find:    (a) The natural frequency $\omega_n$

(b) The damping factor $z$

(c) The pass-band gain $A_0$

(d) The peaking frequency $\omega_p$

(e) The half-power frequency $\omega_h$

(f) The magnitude of gain $M_n$

(g) The magnitude of gain $M_p$ at $\omega_p$

(h) The magnitude of gain at half-power frequency.

Draw an approximate frequency-domain response curve.

*Solution.*    Comparing the given transfer function and the standard low-pass transfer function of equation (8.2),

(a) $\omega_n^2 = 1,000,000$    or    $\omega_n = 1000$ rad/s

(b) $2z\omega_n = 1000$    or    $z = 0.5$

(c) $A_0\omega_n^2 = 2,000,000$    or    $A_0 = 2$

Since $z < 0.707$ the response will peak in the pass band.

(d) $\omega_p = \omega_n \sqrt{1 - 2z^2} = 707$ rad/s

(e) $\omega_h = \omega_n[1 - 2z^2 + \sqrt{4z^4 - 4z^2 + 2}]^{0.5} = 1270$ rad/s

(f) $M_n = \dfrac{A_0}{2z} = 2$

(g) $M_p = \dfrac{A_0}{2z\sqrt{1 - z^2}} = 2.3$

(h) $M_h = 0.707A_0 = 1.414$

The approximate frequency-domain response curve is shown in Figure 8.2.

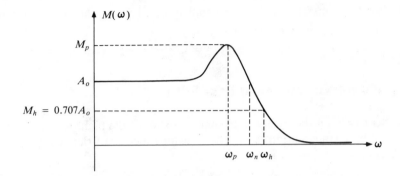

FIGURE 8.2. Approximate frequency-domain response curve of Example 8.3

The transfer function of the low-pass filter is often normalized for a natural frequency of 1 rad/s. The network components designed for such a filter can be scaled to any desired frequency. The transfer function of the low-pass filter with a unity pass-band gain is often considered the standard transfer function of a second-order system. The low-pass parameters are often provided for higher order transfer functions for Butterworth, Chebyshave, Bessell, and other filters. We have already mentioned that the Butterworth filter is a maximally flat filter. The Chebyshave filter, on the other hand, has peaks in its pass band. The Bessell filter is primarily intended to provide a relatively constant phase shift in its pass band. All these special characteristics are obtained by adjusting the damping factors of the second-order filters that are components of higher order filters. The high-pass, band-pass, and band-reject parameters are then transcribed from the listed low-pass parameters. Further coverage of these filters can be found in many excellent sources, some of which are referenced at the end of this book. The time-domain response curve of a second-order low-pass filter is covered in section 4.9.

---

### Problems

**8.2**  Find the transfer function of a low-pass filter with a cutoff (half-power) frequency of 1000 rad/s, a pass-band gain of 10, and the magnitude at the peak frequency of 12. Also find the peak frequency and the magnitude at the natural frequency.

**8.3**  The transfer function of a low-pass filter is

$$A(s) = \frac{10}{0.0000001s^2 + 0.0001s + 1}$$

Find $\omega_n$, $A_0$, and $z$. Also find $\omega_p$, $M_p$, $M_n$, and $\omega_h$.

**8.4** For the transfer functions of Problem 8.1, find $\omega_h$ and $\omega_n$. Also find $\omega_p$ and $M_p$ where applicable.

## 8.5 High-Pass and Band-Pass Filters

In order to obtain the steady-state characteristics of the high-pass filter, $s$ is replaced by $j\omega$ in equation (8.3). The transfer function of the high-pass filter becomes:

$$A(j\omega) = \frac{A_\infty (j\omega)^2}{-\omega^2 + j2z\omega_n\omega + \omega_n^2} \tag{8.24}$$

$$= \frac{A_\infty \omega^2 \big/ 180° - \arctan\,[2z\omega_n\omega/(\omega_n^2 - \omega^2)]}{\sqrt{(\omega_n^2 - \omega^2)^2 + 4z^2\omega_n^2\omega^2}}$$

$$M(\omega) = \frac{A_\infty\omega^2}{\sqrt{(\omega_n^2 - \omega^2)^2 + 4z^2\omega_n^2\omega^2}} \tag{8.25}$$

$$\phi(\omega) = 180° - \arctan\,[(2z\omega_n\omega)/(\omega_n^2 - \omega^2)] \tag{8.26}$$

By replacing $s$ with $j\omega$ for the transfer function of the band-pass filter,

$$A(j\omega) = \frac{jAB\omega}{\omega_n^2 - \omega^2 + jB\omega} \tag{8.27}$$

where $B = 2z\omega_n$ is the bandwidth.

$$M(\omega) = \frac{AB\omega}{\sqrt{(\omega_n^2 - \omega^2)^2 + B^2\omega^2}} \tag{8.28}$$

$$\phi(\omega) = 90° - \arctan\,[B\omega/(\omega_n^2 - \omega^2)] \tag{8.29}$$

---

**Example 8.4**

The transfer function of a band-pass filter is

$$A(s) = \frac{200s}{s^2 + 20s + 10,000}$$

Find the following: (a) the center frequency, (b) the bandwidth, (c) the pass-band gain, (d) the upper and lower cutoff frequencies.

*Solution.*

(a) $\omega_n^2 = 10,000 \qquad \omega_n = 100$ rad/s
  The center frequency $= 100$ rad/s

(b) $B = 20$ rad/s
  The bandwidth is 20 rad/s.

(c) $AB = 200$    $A = 200/20$
The pass-band gain is 10.

(d) The upper half-power frequency $\omega_2 = \omega_n + 0.5B = 110$ rad/s.
The lower half-power frequency $\omega_1 = \omega_n - 0.5B = 90$ rad/s.

## 8.6  Multiple Feedback Filter

The multiple feedback filter configuration is illustrated in Figure 8.3(a). $Y_1$, $Y_2$, $Y_3$, $Y_4$, and $Y_5$ are admittances. These elements are either capacitors or resistors. Depending on which ones are capacitors or resistors, the low-pass, high-pass, or band-pass filters can be realized. There are two feedback loops, one through $Y_5$ and another through $Y_4$. By a series of circuit reduction techniques, the network is simplified into an inverting amplifier as illustrated in Figure 8.3(b), (c), and (d).

The Thevenin equivalent circuit is obtained across the admittance $Y_2$.

$$V_{th} = V_i \frac{Y_1}{Y_1 + Y_2} \tag{8.30}$$

$$Y_{th} = Y_1 + Y_2 \tag{8.31}$$

Recall that the admittances in parallel are added, and the voltage divider equation involving admittances is similar to the current divider equation involving impedances. The resulting delta network is shown in Figure 8.3(b). A delta network is formed by $Y_3$, $Y_4$, and $Y_5$. The delta network is then converted to a wye network. The wye network admittances are $Y_{3CY}$, $Y_{4BY}$, and $Y_{5AY}$ as indicated in Figure 8.3(b). These are given by:

$$Y_{3CY} = \frac{NR}{Y_3} \tag{8.32}$$

$$Y_{4BY} = \frac{NR}{Y_4} \tag{8.33}$$

$$Y_{5AY} = \frac{NR}{Y_5} \tag{8.34}$$

where

$$NR = Y_3Y_4 + Y_3Y_5 + Y_4Y_5 \tag{8.35}$$

The simplified network is shown in Figure 8.3(c). The wye admittance $Y_{4BY}$ is simply in series with the very-high input impedance of the operational amplifier. Hence, this admittance can be ignored. The admittances $Y_{th}$ and $Y_{5AY}$ can be combined to form the input admittance $Y_i$. Recall that the admittances in series are combined according to the product divided by the sum rule, similar to impedances in parallel.

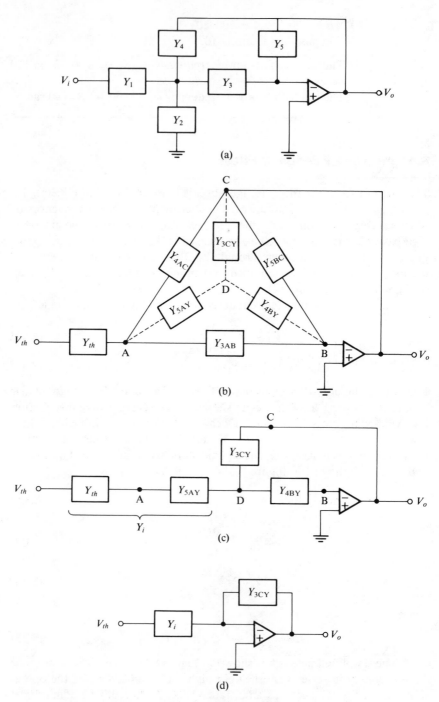

FIGURE 8.3. (a) Multiple feedback filter. (b), (c), and (d)
Series of simplification of multiple feedback filter of (a).

$$Y_i = \frac{Y_{th} Y_{5AY}}{Y_{th} + Y_{5AY}} \tag{8.36}$$

The simplified final circuit is given in Figure 8.3(d).

The gain of the amplifier is $-Y_i/Y_f$, and hence the output is given by:

$$V_o = -V_{th} \frac{Y_i}{Y_{3CY}} \tag{8.37}$$

$$= -V_i \frac{Y_1}{(Y_1 + Y_2)} \frac{Y_{th} Y_{5AY}}{(Y_{th} + Y_{5AY}) Y_{3CY}} \tag{8.38}$$

$$A(s) = V_o/V_i = \frac{-Y_1 (Y_1 + Y_2) Y_{5AY}}{(Y_1 + Y_2)(Y_1 + Y_2 + Y_{5AY}) Y_{3CY}} \tag{8.39}$$

$$= \frac{-Y_1 Y_3 NR}{Y_5(Y_1 + Y_2 + Y_{5AY}) NR}$$

$$A(s) = \frac{-Y_1 Y_3}{Y_5(Y_1 + Y_2 + NR/Y_5)}$$

$$= \frac{-Y_1 Y_3}{Y_5 Y_1 + Y_5 Y_2 + NR}$$

$$= \frac{-Y_1 Y_3}{Y_5 Y_1 + Y_5 Y_2 + Y_5 Y_3 + Y_5 Y_4 + Y_3 Y_4}$$

$$A(s) = \frac{-Y_1 Y_3}{Y_5(Y_1 + Y_2 + Y_3 + Y_4) + Y_3 Y_4} \tag{8.40}$$

By judiciously selecting $Y_1$, $Y_2$, $Y_3$, $Y_4$, and $Y_5$ as either resistors or capacitors, the low-pass, high-pass, and band-pass filters can be implemented.

## Problems

**8.5**  Derive the transfer function of the multiple feedback filter by considering the amplifier to be a two-input amplifier, with $V_i$ and $V_o$ as the two inputs (see Figure 8.4).

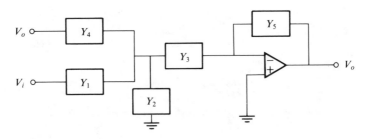

FIGURE 8.4. Multiple feedback redrawn for Problem 8.4

## 8.7  Low-Pass, High-Pass, and Band-Pass Configurations

The admittances may be either of the form $1/R$ which is not a function of $s$, or $sC$ which is a function of $s$.

### Low-Pass Filter

The transfer function of a second-order low-pass filter (equation (8.2)) has a numerator which is not a function of $s$. The numerator of the transfer function of the multiple feedback filter (equation (8.40)) is $-Y_1 Y_3$. Therefore, $Y_1$ and $Y_3$ must be resistors such that $Y_1 = 1/R_1$ and $Y_3 = 1/R_3$. The denominator of the network transfer function must contain an $s^2$ term, an $s$ term, and a term independent of $s$. At best, $Y_3 Y_4$ can contain an $s$ term because we have already established that $Y_3$ is not a function of $s$. In order to have an $s^2$ term, $Y_5$ must be a capacitor such that $Y_5 = sC_5$. The constant term must be $Y_3 Y_4$, and therefore $Y_4 = 1/R_4$. For the $s^2$ term, $Y_2 = sC_2$. The required multiple feedback low-pass filter circuit is shown in Figure 8.5. For this figure the components are $Y_1 = 1/R_1$, $Y_2 = sC_2$, $Y_3 = 1/R_3$, $Y_4 = 1/R_4$, and $Y_5 = sC_5$.

$$A(s) = \frac{-\dfrac{1}{R_1 R_3}}{sC_5\left(\dfrac{1}{R_1} + sC_2 + \dfrac{1}{R_3} + \dfrac{1}{R_4}\right) + \dfrac{1}{R_4 R_3}} \tag{8.41}$$

$$= \frac{-\dfrac{1}{R_1 R_3}}{s^2 C_5 C_2 + sC_5\left(\dfrac{1}{R_1} + \dfrac{1}{R_3} + \dfrac{1}{R_4}\right) + \dfrac{1}{R_3 R_4}}$$

$$= \frac{-\dfrac{1}{R_1 R_3 C_2 C_5}}{s^2 + s\dfrac{1}{C_2}\left(\dfrac{1}{R_1} + \dfrac{1}{R_3} + \dfrac{1}{R_4}\right) + \dfrac{1}{R_3 R_4 C_2 C_5}} \tag{8.42}$$

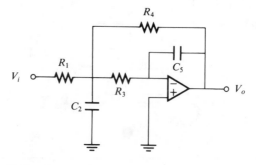

FIGURE 8.5. Multiple feedback low-pass filter

Comparing equation (8.42) and the transfer function of a second-order low-pass filter of equation (8.2),

$$\omega_n^2 = \frac{1}{R_3 R_4 C_2 C_5} \tag{8.43}$$

$$2z\omega_n = \frac{1}{C_2} \left( \frac{1}{R_1} + \frac{1}{R_3} + \frac{1}{R_4} \right) \tag{8.44}$$

$$A_0 \omega_n^2 = \frac{-1}{R_1 R_3 C_2 C_5} \quad \text{or} \quad A_0 = -\frac{R_4}{R_1} \tag{8.45}$$

The equations (8.43), (8.44), and (8.45) are the three design equations of the multiple feedback low-pass filter. $\omega_n$, $z$, and $A_0$ are known, given, or specified. There are five components to be designed and three equations to be satisfied. The three components must be solved using the three design equations, leaving two components to be assumed.

**Design procedure:** Two components are arbitrarily selected and the remaining three components are calculated using the three design equations. $A_0$, $z$, and $\omega_n$ are given or known.

1. Assume a value for $R_4$. From equation (8.45), solve for $R_1$.

$$R_1 = \frac{R_4}{A_0}$$

2. Assume a value for $R_3$. From equation (8.44), solve for $C_2$.

$$C_2 = \frac{1}{2z\omega_n} \left( \frac{1}{R_1} + \frac{1}{R_3} + \frac{1}{R_4} \right)$$

3. Calculate $C_5$ from equation (8.43).

$$C_5 = \frac{1}{R_4 R_3 C_2 \omega_n^2}$$

---

**Example 8.5**

Design a second-order low-pass filter with a pass-band gain of $A_0 = -10$, $z = 0.5$, and $\omega_n = 1000$ rad/s.

*Solution.*

1. Assume    $R_1 = 10 \text{ k}\Omega$
             $R_4 = 100 \text{ k}\Omega$

2. Assume    $R_3 = 10 \text{ k}\Omega$
             $C_2 = 210 \text{ nF}$

3. Calculate $C_5 = 1/21 \ \mu\text{F}$

---

The designed values of components are practical values. As a rule of thumb, all resistors are kept in the range of 1 kΩ to 1 MΩ and the capacitors from 0.1 μF to 100 pF, when used with op-amps. The selection of an op-amp depends on its frequency response capabilities, and the frequency response required of the network. For an audio range of frequencies, a 741 op-amp may suffice. If any of the designed components are too small or too large, the network will have to be redesigned.

### High-Pass Filter

By reasoning similar to that used for a low-pass filter, it can be shown that the components of the high-pass filter circuit are $Y_1 = sC_1$, $Y_2 = 1/R_2$, $Y_3 = sC_3$, $Y_4 = sC_4$, and $Y_5 = 1/R_5$. The network is shown in Figure 8.6.

$$A(s) = \frac{-\dfrac{C_1}{C_4} s^2}{s^2 + \dfrac{1}{R_5 C_3 C_4}(C_1 + C_3 + C_4) + \dfrac{1}{R_5 R_2 C_3 C_4}} \tag{8.46}$$

Comparing equation (8.46) and the transfer function of the high-pass filter of equation (8.3),

$$|A_\infty| = C_1/C_4 \tag{8.47}$$

$$2z\omega_n = \frac{1}{R_5 C_3 C_4}(C_1 + C_3 + C_4) \tag{8.48}$$

$$\omega_n^2 = \frac{1}{R_2 R_5 C_3 C_4} \tag{8.49}$$

Equations (8.47), (8.48), and (8.49) are the three design equations for the multiple feedback high-pass filter.

**Design procedure:** $A_\infty$, $z$, and $\omega_n$ are known. Three equations are to be satisfied and five components are to be designed. Two components are assumed.

1. Assume $C_1$ and calculate $C_4$.

$$C_4 = C_1/|A_\infty|$$

2. Assume $C_3$ and calculate $R_5$.

$$R_5 = \frac{1}{2z\omega_n C_3 C_4}(C_1 + C_3 + C_4)$$

3. Calculate $R_2$.

$$R_2 = \frac{1}{\omega_n^2 R_5 C_3 C_4}$$

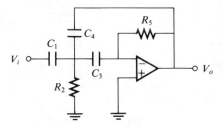

FIGURE 8.6. Multiple feedback high-pass filter

## Example 8.6

Design a second-order high-pass filter.

$$|A_\infty| = 10, \; z = 0.5, \text{ and } \omega_n = 1000 \text{ rad/s}.$$

*Solution.*

1. Assume   $C_1 = 10$ nF
   $C_4 = 1$ nF

2. Assume   $C_3 = 10$ nF
   $R_5 = 2.1$ MΩ

3. Calculate $R_2 = 49$ kΩ.

   The value of $R_5$ is too high. If we redesign the network assuming $C_1$ and $C_3$ as 100 nF, $R_5$ will be 210 kΩ. The new set of values are: $C_1 = 100$ nF, $C_3 = 100$ nF, $C_2 = 10$ nF, $R_2 = 4.9$ kΩ, and $R_5 = 210$ kΩ.

## Band-Pass Filter

For a multiple feedback band-pass filter, the components are $Y_1 = 1/R_1$, $Y_2 = 1/R_2$, $Y_3 = sC_3$, $Y_4 = sC_4$, and $Y_5 = 1/R_5$.

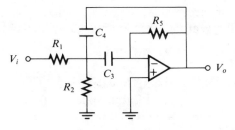

FIGURE 8.7. Multiple feedback band-pass filter

$$A(s) = \frac{-\frac{1}{R_1 C_4} s}{s^2 + s \frac{1}{R_5 C_3 C_4}(C_3 + C_4) + \frac{1}{R_5 C_3 C_4}\left(\frac{1}{R_1} + \frac{1}{R_2}\right)} \tag{8.50}$$

The three design equations are obtained.

$$AB = \frac{-1}{R_1 C_4} \tag{8.51}$$

$$B = \frac{C_3 + C_4}{R_5 C_3 C_4} \tag{8.52}$$

$$\omega_n^2 = \frac{(R_1 + R_2)}{R_1 R_2 R_5 C_3 C_4} \tag{8.53}$$

### Problems

**8.6**  Make a design procedure for a second-order band-pass filter.

**8.7**  Design a band-pass filter with a pass-band gain of −2, a bandwidth of 5 k rad/s, and a center frequency of 50 k rad/s.

**8.8**  Find the damping factor $z$ and quality factor $Q$ of Problem 8.7.

**8.9**  Draw an approximate frequency response curve for Problem 8.7.

**8.10**  Draw approximate frequency response curves for the designed networks of Examples 8.5 and 8.6.

## 8.8  Network Scaling

In Example 8.6, our initial design produced a set of component values that were not practical. Our redesign, however, resulted in a new set of component values that were acceptable. A close examination of both sets of component values will reveal that they are related by a constant.

$$\begin{aligned}
C_1 &= 10 \text{ nF} &&\longrightarrow 100 \text{ nF (divided by 0.1)} \\
C_4 &= 1 \text{ nF} &&\longrightarrow 10 \text{ nF (divided by 0.1)} \\
C_3 &= 10 \text{ nF} &&\longrightarrow 100 \text{ nF (divided by 0.1)} \\
R_5 &= 2.1 \text{ M}\Omega &&\longrightarrow 210 \text{ k}\Omega \text{ (multiplied by 0.1)} \\
R_2 &= 49 \text{ k}\Omega &&\longrightarrow 4.9 \text{ k}\Omega \text{ (multiplied by 0.1)}
\end{aligned}$$

It seems that all capacitors are divided by the same number (0.1) that all the resistors are multiplied by to obtain the new set of values. This technique of changing component values of designed circuit elements is called *impedance scaling*, and the constant used is called the *impedance scale factor* $K_z$.

The transfer function of a filter is the ratio of output voltage and input voltage, and therefore it is dimensionless (i.e., no unit). It is always a ratio of impedances. If all impedances are multiplied by a factor $K_z$, the impedance ratio, and hence the transfer function, will remain unchanged. Thus it is possible to scale all impedances by a factor $K_z$ without altering the transfer function. Note that impedance scaling does affect impedances and currents within the network. What is not changed is the transfer function. Impedance scaling can only be used for transfer functions that are dimensionless.

Scaled impedance of inductor

$$K_z Z_1 = s(K_z L)$$

Scaled impedance of capacitor

$$K_z Z_c = \frac{K_z}{sC} = \frac{1}{s\left(\dfrac{C}{K_z}\right)}$$

Scaled impedance of resistor

$$K_z Z_r = K_z R$$

Thus, inductors and resistors are *multiplied* by the impedance scale factor and capacitors are *divided* by the impedance scale factor.

---

**Example 8.7**

Design a second-order high-pass filter. $A_\infty = 10$, $z = 0.5$, and $\omega_n = 1000$ rad/s.

*Solution.* Example 8.7 is identical to Example 8.6. As in Example 8.6, we can start by assuming a practical value such as 10 nF for $C_1$. However, we almost always need to scale impedances. Hence, there is no reason to assume practical values. It is better to assume convenient values instead. A 1-F capacitor is certainly not practical, but it is an easy value to work with.

1. Assume   $C_1 = 1$ F
$C_4 = 0.1$ F

2. Assume   $C_3 = 1$ F
$R_5 = 0.021$ Ω

3. Calculate $R_2 = 0.00049$ Ω

From the above set of values, $R_2$ is the worst resistor. In order to make it to the nearest kΩ, a $K_z$ of $10^7$ is used. Now the set of components becomes:

$C_1 = 0.1 \ \mu F$
$C_4 = 0.01 \ \mu F$
$C_3 = 0.1 \ \mu F$
$R_5 = 210 \ k\Omega$
$R_2 = 4.9 \ k\Omega$

If these values are not acceptable, we can use another impedance scale factor.

---

The transfer function of the required filter is often arbitrarily provided for the natural frequency or cutoff frequency as 1 rad/s. The frequency in this case is said to be *normalized*. The network components designed for $\omega_n = 1$ rad/s can be scaled to any other natural frequency $\omega_n$ using *frequency scaling*. The frequency scale factor $K_f$ is the required natural frequency. Frequency scaling is performed by multiplying the frequency terms of all the impedances by the frequency scale factor $K_f$. $Z_r = R$ and is not a function of frequency. Hence the frequency scaling does not affect the resistors.

$Z_1 = L(K_f s)$      As frequency increases, the impedance increases. In order to keep the impedance the same as that for $\omega_n = 1$ rad/s, the inductance $L$ is divided by $K_f$.

$Z_c = 1/C(K_f s)$      As frequency increases, the impedance decreases. In order to keep the impedance the same as that for $\omega_n = 1$ rad/s, the capacitance $C$ is divided by $K_f$.

In order to scale frequencies, the following conditions must be met:

1. All resistors are left as they are.
2. All inductors are divided by $K_f$.
3. All capacitors are divided by $K_f$.

---

**Example 8.8**

Design five band-pass filters with central frequencies of (a) 1000 rad/s, (b) 2000 rad/s, (c) 3000 rad/s, (d) 4000 rad/s, and (e) 5000 rad/s. For all filters $Q = 10$ and $A = -10$.

*Solution.*    The natural frequency is assumed to be 1 rad/s.

$\omega_n = 1$ rad/s, $A = -10$, and $B = 0.1$ rad/s ($B = \omega_n/Q$)

1. Let $C_3 = 1$ F. From equation (8.51),

$$-1 = -1/R_1 \quad \text{or} \quad R_1 = 1 \ \Omega$$

2. Let $C_3 = 1$ F. From equation (8.52),

$$0.1 = 2/R_5 \quad \text{or} \quad R_5 = 20 \ \Omega$$

3. From equation (8.53),

$$1 = (1 + R_2)/20R_2 \quad \text{or} \quad R_2 = 1/19 = 0.056 \ \Omega$$

The solution for part (a) of this example is as follows:

| Unscaled components | Frequency scale $K_f = 1000$ | Impedance scale $K_z = 40,000$ |
|---|---|---|
| $R_1 = 1$ | 1 | 40 k$\Omega$ |
| $R_2 = 0.056$ | 0.056 | 2.24 k$\Omega$ |
| $C_3 = 1$ | 0.001 | 25 nF |
| $C_4 = 1$ | 0.001 | 25 nF |
| $R_5 = 20$ | 20 | 800 k$\Omega$ |

In this example, (b), (c), and (d) parts can be similarly designed.

## Problems

**8.11**  Do parts (b), (c), and (d) of Example 8.8.

**8.12**  Design high-pass filters with $z = 0.707$ and pass-band gains of $-2$. The half-power frequencies are 200 Hz, 500 Hz, 800 Hz, and 1000 Hz.

[**Hint:** Note that frequencies are given in Hz. Also cutoff frequencies are given. Recall $\omega_h = \omega_n$ when $z = 0.707$.]

**8.13**  Design low-pass filters with $z = 0.5$ and the magnitude of pass-band gain of 5. The cutoff frequencies are 60 Hz, 120 Hz, 800 Hz, and 1000 Hz.

[**Hint:** First find $\omega_n$ using equation (8.22).]

## 8.9  VCVS Filters

Voltage-controlled voltage source (VCVS) filters use a noninverting amplifier with a dc gain of $K = (1 + R_f/R_i)$. The amplifier is represented by Figure 8.8(b). Figure 8.8(a) is the schematic of the noninverting amplifier. The VCVS filter configuration is shown in Figure 8.8(c). $Y_1$, $Y_2$, $Y_3$, and $Y_4$ are admittances. These admittances can be either capacitive or resistive. The same configuration can yield low-pass, high-pass, and band-pass filters. Because the amplifier is noninverting, the input impedance of the amplifier is very high. Furthermore, unlike multiple feedback filters, the input and the output of VCVS filters do not have the additional 180° phase shift. Referring to the VCVS configuration of Figure 8.8(c):

$$i_1 = I_2 + I_3 \tag{8.54}$$

$$(V_i - V_2)Y_i = (V_2 - V_o)Y_4 + (V_2 - V_o/K)Y_2 \tag{8.55}$$

$$\frac{V_o}{K} = V_2 \frac{Y_2}{Y_2 + Y_3} \tag{8.56}$$

$$V_2 = V_o \frac{(Y_2 + Y_3)}{KY_2} \tag{8.57}$$

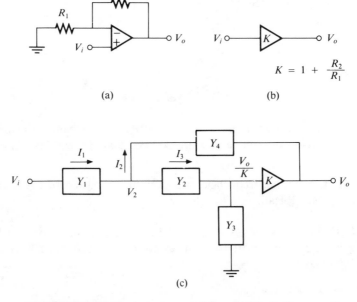

FIGURE 8.8. (a) Noninverting amplifier. (b) Block diagram of noninverting amplifier of (a). (c) VCVS filter.

From equation (8.55),

$$Y_1\left(V_i - V_o \frac{Y_2 + Y_3}{KY_2}\right) = Y_4\left(V_o \frac{Y_2 + Y_3}{KY_2} - V_o\right) + Y_2\left(V_o \frac{Y_2 + Y_3}{KY_2} - \frac{V_o}{K}\right)$$

$$Y_1 V_i = V_o \frac{Y_2 + Y_3}{KY_2}(Y_1 + Y_4 + Y_2) - V_o Y_4 - V_o \frac{Y_2}{K}$$

$$KY_1 Y_2 V_i = V_o(Y_2 + Y_3)(Y_1 + Y_2 + Y_4) - V_o KY_2 Y_4 - V_o Y_2 Y_2$$

$$\frac{V_o}{V_i} = A(s)$$

$$= \frac{KY_1 Y_2}{(Y_1 Y_2 + Y_2 Y_2 + Y_2 Y_4 + Y_1 Y_3 + Y_3 Y_2 + Y_3 Y_4 - Y_2 Y_2 - KY_2 Y_4}$$

$$A(s) = \frac{KY_1 Y_2}{Y_1 Y_2 + Y_2 Y_4 + Y_1 Y_3 + Y_2 Y_3 + Y_3 Y_4 - KY_2 Y_4}$$

$$A(s) = \frac{KY_1 Y_2}{Y_2(Y_1 + Y_3 + Y_4 - KY_4) + Y_1 Y_3 + Y_3 Y_4} \qquad (8.58)$$

## Low-Pass Filter

For a low-pass filter, $Y_1 = 1/R_1, Y_2 = 1/R_2, Y_3 = sC_3$, and $Y_4 = sC_4$. The circuit is given in Figure 8.9(a).

$$A(s) = \frac{K\dfrac{1}{R_1 R_2}}{\dfrac{1}{R_2}\left(\dfrac{1}{R_1} + sC_3 + sC_4 - sKC_4\right) + sC_3 \dfrac{1}{R_1} + s^2 C_3 C_4}$$

$$= \frac{\dfrac{K}{R_1 R_2}}{s^2 C_3 C_4 + s\left(\dfrac{C_3}{R_2} + \dfrac{C_4}{R_2} + \dfrac{C_3}{R_1} - \dfrac{KC_4}{R_2}\right) + \dfrac{1}{R_1 R_2}}$$

$$A(s) = \frac{\dfrac{K}{R_1 R_2 C_3 C_4}}{s^2 + s\left(\dfrac{1}{R_2 C_4} + \dfrac{1}{R_2 C_3} + \dfrac{1}{R_1 C_4} - \dfrac{K}{R_2 C_3}\right) + \dfrac{1}{R_1 R_2 C_3 C_4}}$$

The three design equations are now derived as

$$\omega_n^2 = \frac{1}{R_1 R_2 C_3 C_4} \qquad (8.59)$$

$$2z\omega_n = \frac{1}{R_2 C_4} + \frac{1}{R_2 C_3} + \frac{1}{R_1 C_4} - \frac{K}{R_2 C_3} \qquad (8.60)$$

$$A_o = K = 1 + \frac{R_f}{R_i} \tag{8.61}$$

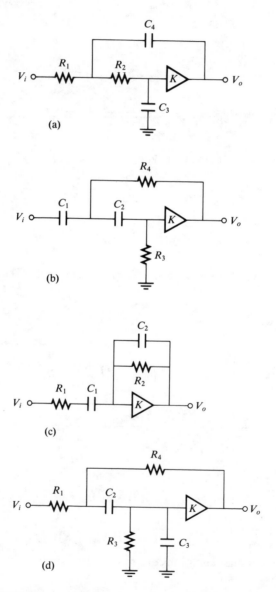

(a)

(b)

(c)

(d)

FIGURE 8.9. (a) VCVS low-pass filter. (b) VCVS high-pass filter. (c) VCVS band-pass filter. (d) Another band-pass configuration.

**Design procedure:** There are six components to be designed and three equations to satisfy. Hence, three components can be assumed, one of which must be either $R_f$ or $R_i$, but not both.

1. Choose $R_f$ and find $R_i$ from equation (8.61).
2. Choose $C_3 = C$
3. Choose $C_4 = C$
4. Find $R_2$ from:

$$R_2 = \frac{z}{\omega_n C}\left(1 + \sqrt{1 + \frac{K-2}{z^2}}\right) \tag{8.62}$$

where $K$ must be larger than 2.
5. Find $R_1$ from:

$$R_1 = \frac{1}{R_2 \omega_n^2 C^2} \tag{8.63}$$

---

### Example 8.9

Derive equation (8.62).

*Solution.* When $C_3 = C_4 = C$, from equations (8.59) and (8.60),

$$\omega_n^2 C^2 = \frac{1}{R_1 R_2} \tag{8.64}$$

$$2z\omega_n C = \frac{2-K}{R_2} + \frac{1}{R_1} \tag{8.65}$$

From equation (8.64),

$$\frac{1}{R_1} = R_2 \omega_n^2 C^2$$

$$2z\omega_n C = \frac{2-K}{R_2} + R_2 \omega_n^2 C^2$$

$$(R_2\omega_n C)^2 - 2z(R_2\omega_n C) + (2-K) = 0 \tag{8.66}$$

The equation (8.66) is a quadratic in $R_2\omega_n C$.

$$R_2\omega_n C = z + \sqrt{z^2 + K - 2}$$

$$= z + z\sqrt{1 + \frac{K-2}{z^2}} = z\left(1 + \sqrt{1 + \frac{K-2}{z^2}}\right)$$

$$R_2 = \frac{z}{\omega_n C}\left(1 + \sqrt{1 + \frac{K-2}{z^2}}\right)$$

**Example 8.10**

Design a low-pass filter with $A_0 = 10$, $z = 1$, and $\omega_n = 1000$ rad/s.

*Solution.*   Following the design procedure given on page 225,

1. Let $R_f = 1$ $\Omega$ and $R_i = 0.11$ $\Omega$
2. Let $C_3 = 1$ F
3. Let $C_4 = 1$ F. Assume a normalized natural frequency of 1 rad/s.
4. $R_2 = 1 + 3 = 4$ $\Omega$
5. $R_1 = 0.24$ $\Omega$

| Unscaled components | Frequency scale $K_f = 1000$ | Impedance scale $K_z = 100{,}000$ |
|---|---|---|
| $R_f = 1$ | 1 | 100 k$\Omega$ |
| $R_i = 0.11$ | 0.11 | 11 k$\Omega$ |
| $R_2 = 4$ | 4 | 400 k$\Omega$ |
| $R_1 = 0.25$ | 0.25 | 25 k$\Omega$ |
| $C_3 = 1$ | 0.001 | 10 nF |
| $C_4 = 1$ | 0.001 | 10 nF |

## High-Pass Filter

For a high-pass filter $Y_1 = sC_1$, $Y_2 = sC_2$, $Y_3 = 1/R_3$, and $Y_4 = 1/R_4$. The network is given in Figure 8.9(b).

$$A(s) = \frac{Ks^2}{s^2 + s\left(\dfrac{1}{R_3 C_1} + \dfrac{1}{R_3 C_2} + \dfrac{1}{R_4 C_1} - \dfrac{K}{R_4 C_1}\right) + \dfrac{1}{C_1 C_2 R_3 R_4}} \tag{8.67}$$

$$A = K = 1 + \frac{R_f}{R_i} \tag{8.68}$$

$$2z\omega_n = \frac{1}{R_3 C_1} + \frac{1}{R_3 C_2} + \frac{1}{R_4 C_1} - \frac{K}{R_4 C_1} \tag{8.69}$$

$$\omega_n^2 = \frac{1}{C_1 C_2 R_3 R_4} \tag{8.70}$$

**Design procedure:**

1. Choose $R_f$ and find $R_i$ from equation (8.68).
2. Choose $C_1 = C$
3. Choose $C_2 = C$

4. $R_4 = \dfrac{1}{2\omega_n C} [z + \sqrt{z^2 + 2K - 2}]$

Calculate $R_3$ from equation (8.70).

## Band-Pass Filter

A VCVS band-pass realization is given in Figure 8.9(c). $Y_1$ is made up of a resistor $R_1$ connected in series with a capacitor $C_1$.

$$Y_1 = \frac{sC_1/R_1}{(1/R_1) + sC_1} = \frac{sC_1}{R_1 C_1 s + 1} \tag{8.71}$$

where  $Y_2$ is a short and hence its admittance is infinity
$Y_3$ is open and its admittance is zero
$Y_4$ is a parallel combination of resistor $R_2$ and capacitor $C_2$.

$$Y_4 = \frac{1}{R_2} + sC_2 = \frac{R_2 C_2 s + 1}{R_2} \tag{8.72}$$

$$A(s) = \frac{KY_1 Y_2}{Y_2(Y_1 + Y_3 + Y_4 - KY_4) + Y_1 Y_3 + Y_3 Y_4}$$

Dividing numerator and denominator by $Y_2$, we obtain

$$A(s) = \frac{KY_1}{Y_1 + Y_3 + Y_4 + -KY_4 + \dfrac{Y_1 Y_3}{Y_2} + \dfrac{Y_3 Y_4}{Y_2}}$$

When $Y_2 = \infty$,

$$A(s) = \frac{KY_1}{Y_1 + Y_3 + Y_4 - KY_4}$$

and when $Y_3 = 0$,

$$A(s) = \frac{KY_1}{Y_1 + Y_4(1 - K)} \tag{8.73}$$

Substituting for $Y_1$ and $Y_4$,

$$A(s) = \frac{K \dfrac{sC_1}{R_1 C_1 s + 1}}{\dfrac{sC_1}{R_1 C_1 s + 1} + \dfrac{R_2 C_2 s + 1}{R_2}(1 - K)}$$

$$A(s) = \frac{K(R_2 C_1 s)}{R_2 C_1 s + (R_1 C_1 s + 1)(R_2 C_2 s + 1)(1 - K)}$$

$$= \frac{KR_2 C_1 s}{R_1 R_2 C_1 C_2(1 - K)s^2 + (R_2 C_2 + (1 - K)(R_1 C_1 + R_2 C_2))s + (1 - K)}$$

$$A(s) = \cfrac{Ks \cfrac{1}{(1-K)R_1 C_2}}{s^2 + s\left(\cfrac{1}{R_2 C_2} + \cfrac{1}{R_1 C_1} + \cfrac{1}{R_1 C_2(1-K)}\right) + \cfrac{1}{R_1 R_2 C_1 C_2}} \tag{8.74}$$

$$\omega_n^2 = \frac{1}{R_1 R_2 C_1 C_2} \tag{8.75}$$

$$B = \frac{1}{R_2 C_2} + \frac{1}{R_1 C_1} + \frac{1}{R_1 C_2(1-K)} \tag{8.76}$$

$$AB = \frac{K}{(1-K)R_1 C_2} \tag{8.77}$$

$$K = 1 + \frac{R_f}{R_i} \tag{8.78}$$

Equations (8.85), (8.76), (8.77), and (8.78) are the design equations for this band-pass filter. The three design parameters are the center frequency $\omega_n$, the bandwidth $B$, and the pass-band gain $A$. The design procedure can be greatly simplified if the pass-band gain $A$ is left as a free parameter, thereby removing one constriction.

**Design procedure:** The center frequency and bandwidth are given. The band-pass gain is left as a free parameter.

1. Let $R_1 = R_2 = R$ and $C_1 = C_2 = C$

$$\omega_n^2 = \left(\frac{1}{RC}\right)^2 \quad \text{or} \quad \omega_n = \frac{1}{RC} \tag{8.79}$$

$$B = \frac{3 - 2K}{RC(1-K)} = \frac{\omega_n(3-2K)}{1-K}$$

$$\frac{\omega_n}{B} = Q = \frac{1-K}{3-2K} \tag{8.80}$$

$$AB = \frac{\omega_n K}{1-K} \quad \text{or} \quad A = \frac{K}{3-2K} \tag{8.81}$$

2. Choose $C$. Calculate $R$ from equation (8.79). Calculate $K$ from equation (8.80). Calculate $R_f$ and $R_i$ from equation (8.78).
3. The pass-band gain is calculated from equation (8.81).

---

## Problems

**8.14** Derive the design equations for the band-pass filter of Figure 8.9(d).

**8.15** Do Problem 8.12 using the VCVS configuration.

**8.16**   Do Problem 8.13 using the VCVS configuration.

**8.17**   Design a band-pass filter with center frequency of 5 k rad/s and a bandwidth of 500 rad/s. Use the network of Figure 8.9(c). Calculate the pass-band gain of the designed circuit.

---

## 8.10   Computer-Aided Design

The design process can be simplified by using a computer. A number of very good software packages are commercially available. The programs for multiple feedback and VCVS filter designs are presented in Appendix B. These programs are written in Applesoft BASIC with minimum sophistication.

## 8.11   State Variable Filters

Filter circuits can be synthesized using analog computer simulation techniques. A detailed presentation of this approach of designing circuits is given in Chapter 9. In this section, a three-in-one filter that can provide low-pass, high-pass, or band-pass responses is analyzed. In Figure 8.10(a), $A_2$ and $A_3$ are integrators and $A_1$ is a three-input amplifier. The three inputs of the amplifier $A_1$ are $V_i$, $V_o$, and $V_3$. The output $V_2$ is given by:

$$V_2 = -K_1V_o + K_3V_3 + K_2V_i \tag{8.82}$$

where

$$K_1 = \frac{R_2}{R_1}, \ K_2 = \left(1 + \frac{R_2}{R_1}\right)\left(\frac{R_4}{R_3 + R_4}\right)$$

and

$$K_3 = \left(1 + \frac{R_2}{R_1}\right)\left(\frac{R_3}{R_3 + R_4}\right)$$

A block diagram for equation (8.82) is given in Figure 8.10(b). The block diagram contains a *summing block*. To review, a summing block is where two or more signals are algebraically added. The signals $-K_1V_o$, $K_3V_3$, and $K_2V_i$ are added to obtain the signal $V_2$. The output and input of integrator $A_2$ are related by equation (8.83). The output and input of integrator $A_3$ are related by equation (8.84).

$$\frac{V_3}{V_2} = \frac{-1}{R_5C_5s} \tag{8.83}$$

$$\frac{V_o}{V_3} = \frac{-1}{R_6C_6s} \tag{8.84}$$

The block diagrams of equations (8.83) and (8.84) are given in Figure 8.10(c) and (d), respectively. The three block diagrams are combined in Figure

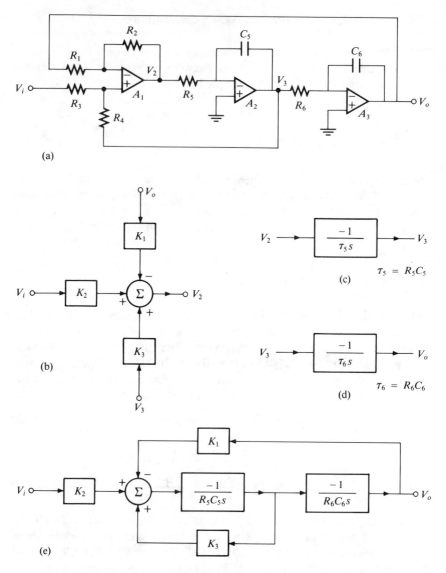

FIGURE 8.10. (a) State variable filter. (b) Block diagram of $A_1$. (c) Block diagram of $A_2$. (d) Block diagram of $A_3$. (e) Block diagram of state variable filter.

8.10(e). $V_o$ is the output and $V_i$ is the input. The objective is to find $V_o/V_i$. The summing point is split into two as indicated in Figure 8.11(a). Equation (8.81) is restated in equation (8.85) to indicate the splitting of a summing block.

$$V_2 = (-K_1 V_o + K_2 V_i) + K_3 V_3 \tag{8.85}$$

$-K_1 V_o$ and $K_2 V_i$ are the inputs of the first summing block. The output of the first summing block and $K_3 V_3$ form the inputs of the second summing block.

The circled portion of the block diagram of Figure 8.11(a) represents the block diagram of a feedback amplifier. A block diagram of a typical feedback amplifier is presented in Figure 8.11(b). The closed-loop gain is given by equation (8.86).

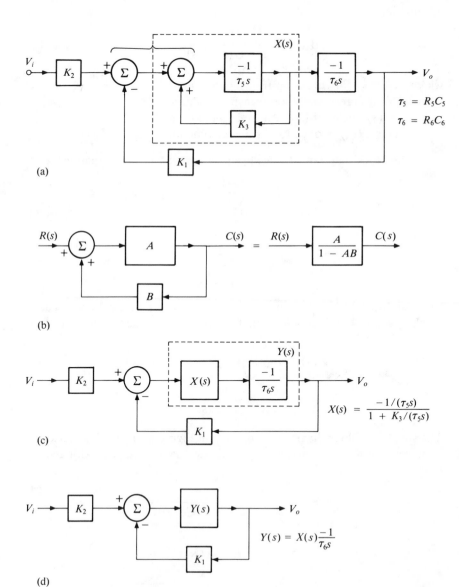

FIGURE 8.11. Block diagram reduction of state variable filter

$$W = \frac{A}{1 - AB} \tag{8.86}$$

where   $W$ is the gain with feedback
       $A$ is the gain if there were no feedback, and
       $B$ the feedback factor

The equation (8.86) can be generalized for any transfer function, as given by equation (8.87).

$$W(s) = \frac{G(s)}{1 - G(s)H(s)} \tag{8.87}$$

where   $G(s)$ = forword-loop transfer function
       $H(s)$ = feedback-loop transfer function
       $W(s)$ = closed-loop transfer function, and
       $G(s)H(s)$ = open-loop transfer function

The block diagram of a feedback system can now be replaced by

$$X(s) = \frac{\dfrac{-1}{R_5 C_5 s}}{1 - \dfrac{-K_3}{R_5 C_5 s}} \tag{8.88}$$

$$= \frac{-1}{R_5 C_5 s + K_3}$$

The simplified block diagram is shown in Figure 8.11(c). Two cascaded blocks are circled in Figure 8.11(c). They can be combined as their product.

$$Y(s) = X(s)\, \frac{-1}{R_6 C_6 s} \tag{8.89}$$

$$= \frac{1}{R_6 C_6 s (R_5 C_5 s + 1)}$$

The simplified block diagram is provided in Figure 8.11(c). This block diagram contains a block diagram of a feedback system in cascade with another block.

$$A(s) = \frac{V_o}{V_i} = K_2 \frac{\dfrac{1}{R_6 C_6 s (R_5 C_5 s + 1)}}{1 - \dfrac{-K_1}{R_6 C_6 s (R_5 C_5 s + 1)}} \tag{8.90}$$

$$= \frac{K_2}{R_6 R_5 C_6 C_5 s^2 + K_3 R_6 C_6 s + K_1}$$

$$A(s) = \cfrac{\cfrac{K_2}{R_5 R_6 C_5 C_6}}{s^2 + \cfrac{K_3}{R_5 C_5} s + \cfrac{K_1}{R_5 R_6 C_5 C_6}} \tag{8.91}$$

The transfer function of the network is of the same form as the standard transfer function of a low-pass filter.

$$\omega_n^2 = \frac{K_1}{R_5 R_6 C_5 C_6} \tag{8.92}$$

$$A_0 = \frac{K_2}{K_1} \tag{8.93}$$

$$2z\omega_n = \frac{K_3}{R_5 C_5} \tag{8.94}$$

Now consider $V_3$ as the output and $V_i$ as the input.

$$A_1(s) = \frac{V_3}{V_i} = \frac{V_o}{V_i} \frac{V_3}{V_o} = A(s) \frac{V_3}{V_o}$$

$$\frac{V_o}{V_3} = \frac{-1}{R_6 C_6 s} \quad \text{or} \quad \frac{V_3}{V_o} = -R_6 C_6 s$$

$$A_1(s) = \frac{V_3}{V_i} = \cfrac{-K_2 \cfrac{s}{R_5 C_5}}{s^2 + \cfrac{K_3}{R_5 C_5} s + \cfrac{K_1}{R_5 R_6 C_5 C_6}} \tag{8.95}$$

The equation (8.95) shows that the transfer function relating the output $V_3$ and the input $V_i$ is that for a band-pass filter. Now consider $V_2$ as the output and $V_i$ as the input.

$$A_2(s) = \frac{V_2}{V_i} = \cfrac{K_2 s^2}{s^2 + \cfrac{K_3}{R_5 C_5} s + \cfrac{K_1}{R_5 R_6 C_5 C_6}} \tag{8.96}$$

When $V_2$ is considered the output, a high-pass response is obtained. This network is suited for a high-$Q$ (narrow bandwidth) band-pass filter.

---

## Problems

8.18   Derive equation (8.96).

8.19   Derive the three design equations for both band-pass and high-pass realizations.

---

## 8.12 Undamped Filter: An Oscillator

Consider the transfer function of a second-order filter with the damping factor $z = 0$. The transfer function is given by equation (8.97).

$$A(s) = \frac{A_0\omega_n^2}{s^2 + \omega_n^2} \qquad (8.97)$$

The *impulse response* is the output of a system for a unit impulse. This response is simply the inverse Laplace transform of the transfer function of equation (8.97).

$$h(t) = \mathcal{L}^{-1}[A(s)] \qquad (8.98)$$

where $h(t)$ is the unit impulse response.

$$h(t) = A_0\omega_n \sin \omega_n t u(t) \qquad (8.99)$$

The output is a sinusoidal signal. The network is an oscillator. In order to obtain a sinusoidal output, the input terminal is grounded so that no steady-state input is applied. A small impulse signal automatically appears at the input terminal at $t = 0$ when the power is initially applied to the filter circuit. The amplitude of this impulse function is much smaller than the unit impulse signal which has an amplitude of infinity. Thus we expect a much smaller amplitude for the output than $A_0\omega_n$ as given in equation (8.99).

Consider a VCVS circuit configuration for a low-pass filter with $R_1 = R_2 = R$, $C_3 = C_4 = C$, and the input grounded as shown in Figure 8.12.

$$A(s) = \frac{\dfrac{K}{R^2C^2}}{s^2 + s\left(\dfrac{3}{RC} - \dfrac{K}{RC}\right) + \dfrac{1}{(RC)^2}} \qquad (8.100)$$

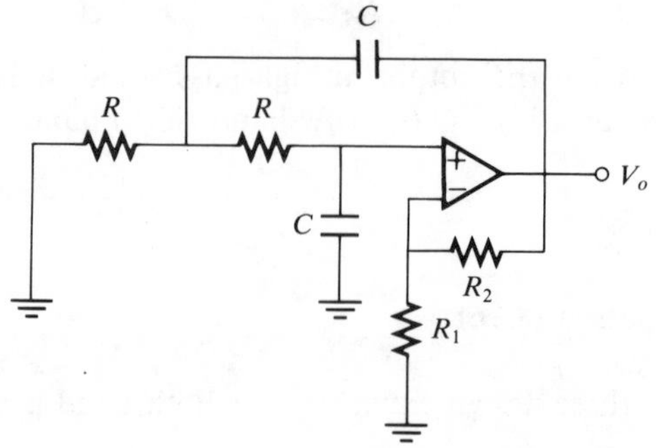

damping
factor

FIGURE 8.12. VCVS filter configured as an oscillator

In order to make this low-pass filter an oscillator, the damping factor $z$ is set to zero.

$$\frac{3}{RC} - \frac{K}{RC} = 0 \quad \text{or} \quad K = 3 \tag{8.101}$$

The network will oscillate if the gain $(1 + R_f/R_i)$ is set to 3. If $K < 3$, the circuit will not oscillate. If $K > 3$, the output will be distorted.

## 8.13. Summary

In this chapter the transfer functions of second-order filters and their frequency responses are investigated. The damping factor determines the response in the vicinity of the natural frequency. When $z < 0.707$, the magnitude response will peak within the pass band. The VCVS and multiple feedback configurations were examined as typical examples. The VCVS band-pass filter was first introduced by R. P. Sallen and E. L. Key in 1955. In recognition of their work, the VCVS filter is also known as the Sallen-Key circuit. The discovery of the multiple feedback configuration is attributed to T. Delyannis and J. J. Friend (1970). Hence, this configuration is also known as the Delyannis-Friend circuit. The state variable filter of the type given in section 8.11 is also known as the Biquad filter, a name first coined by J. Tow in 1968. The VCVS filter can also be configured as an oscillator.

### Key Terms

Define the following terms:

| | |
|---|---|
| multiple feedback | half-power frequency |
| VCVS | lower half-power frequency |
| bandwidth | upper half-power frequency |
| damping factor | complex conjugate |
| underdamped | maximally flat |
| natural frequency | Butterworth response |
| overdamped | normalized |
| center frequency | Chebyshave |
| critically damped | impedance scaling |
| peaking frequency | frequency scaling |
| cutoff frequency | |

See Appendix A, Labs 2, 3, 4, and 5 for further applications of *second-order low-pass filters*, *second-order band-pass filters*, *second-order high-pass filters*, and *oscillators*, respectively.

# CHAPTER 9

# State Variable Networks

## 9.1  Introduction

Historically, operational amplifiers are associated with analog computers, which are used to simulate system responses. These same simulation techniques can be utilized to design electrical networks for desired responses. The basic building blocks of network simulators are as follows:

1. Inverting amplifiers
2. Summing amplifiers
3. Integrators, and
4. Summing integrators

Although they are not standardized, special symbols and terminologies are used within the analog computation field. It will greatly simplify the effort in the design of state variable networks if we follow the same techniques and terminologies.

State variable refers to the output variable of the system at various states (e.g., magnitude and phase) that is reapplied to various points within the system as inputs. In this sense, it is a multiple feedback system.

## 9.2  Building Blocks of State Variable Networks

To begin designing networks, let us examine two of the building blocks mentioned above: inverting amplifiers and integrators. For an inverting configuration, the gain is proportional to the feedback impedance $Z_f$. If $Z_f$ is doubled, the gain is also doubled. This does not hold true with a noninverting amplifier. The only reason we restrict the networks to the inverting configuration, however, is that it is easier to design this type. The schematic of an inverting amplifier and its block diagram representation are shown in Figure 9.1(a) and (b), respectively. Note that the absolute value of $A$ is indicated on the input line of the amplifier symbol of Figure 9.1(b). It is understood that the signal is phase shifted at the output, as is always the case with inverting amplifiers. Figure 9.1(c) is the schematic of an inverter which is simply an inverting amplifier with a unity gain. A summing amplifier and its block diagram are shown in Figure 9.1(d) and (e), respectively. For the summing amplifier, the output $V_o$ is expressed as

$$V_o = -(A_1 V_1 + A_2 V_2 + \ldots + A_n V_n) \tag{9.1}$$

where $A_n = R_f/R_n$

An integrator is illustrated in Figure 9.2(a) and its block diagram is shown in Figure 9.2(b). The output $V_o(s)$ is given by:

$$V_o(s) = -\frac{K}{s} V_i(s) \tag{9.2}$$

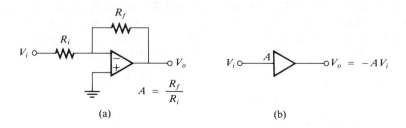

(a)  (b)

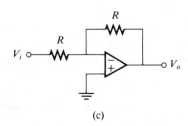

(c)

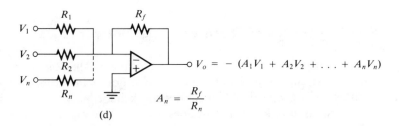

(d)

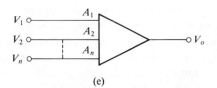

(e)

FIGURE 9.1. (a) Inverting amplifier. (b) Block diagram of (a). (c) Inverter. (d) Summing amplifier. (e) Block diagram of (d).

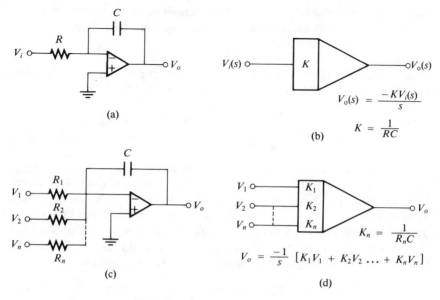

FIGURE 9.2. (a) Integrator. (b) Block diagram of (a). (c) Summing integrator. (d) Block diagram of (c).

where $V_i(s)$ is the input and $K$ the *integration factor*.

$$K = \frac{1}{RC} \tag{9.3}$$

A *summing integrator* and its symbolic representation are shown in Figure 9.2(c) and (d), respectively. The output of the summing integrator is expressed as

$$V_o(s) = -\frac{1}{s}\,(K_1 V_1 + K_2 V_2 + \ldots + K_n V_n) \tag{9.4}$$

where

$$K_n = \frac{1}{R_n C}$$

## 9.3  Simulation of First-Order Transfer Functions

We begin our simulation technique with a first-order transfer function because of its simplicity. A first-order transfer function is given by equation (9.5).

$$A(s) = \frac{V_o(s)}{V_i(s)} = \frac{As}{s + \omega_c} \tag{9.5}$$

The denominator and numerator are polynomials of the first degree in $s$. The transfer function can be recognized as that of a high-pass filter.

$$V_o(s + \omega_c) = V_i As \qquad (9.6)$$

Note that the function of $s$ notation is omitted for $V_i$ and $V_o$ in equation (9.6) for the sake of clarity.

$$sV_o + V_o\omega_c = sAV_i$$

$$sV_o = sAV_i - V_o\omega_c \qquad (9.7)$$

Recall that a signal in the frequency domain when multiplied by $s$ indicates a time-domain differentiation of the signal. The equation (9.6), therefore, indicates that *the differentiated output of the network is equal to the difference between $d(AV_i)/dt$ and $V_o\omega_c$*. The equation as given in (9.6) can be implemented using a differentiator circuit and a summing amplifier circuit. However, it is preferred that integrators are used rather than differentiators in network designs. The equation (9.7) is rearranged as

$$V_o = AV_i - \omega_c \frac{V_o}{s} \qquad (9.8)$$

Recall that a signal in the frequency domain when divided by $s$ indicates a time-domain integration of the signal. The output is the algebraic sum of two signals, $AV_i$ and $\omega_c V_o/s$. The sum of these two signals can be obtained as the output of a summing amplifier. The summing amplifier output is always negative with respect to its inputs.

$$V_o = -\left(\omega_c \frac{V_o}{s} - AV_i\right) \qquad (9.9)$$

The two inputs and the respective gains of the summing amplifier are

$$\omega_c \frac{V_o}{s} \quad \text{with a gain of 1}$$

$$-V_i \quad \text{with a gain of } A$$

The block diagram of the summing amplifier is shown in Figure 9.3(a).

The input $\omega_c V_o/s$ is the output of an integrator with an integration factor of $\omega_c$ and an input of $-V_o$. This can be seen in equation (9.10).

$$\omega_c \frac{V_o}{s} = -\frac{1}{s}\,\omega_c(-V_o) \qquad (9.10)$$

The input $-V_i$ is the output of an inverting amplifier with an input $V_i$ and a gain of 1. The complete block diagram is shown in Figure 9.3(b), and the schematic in Figure 9.3(c). The component values can be scaled for practical values by applying the impedance scale factor.

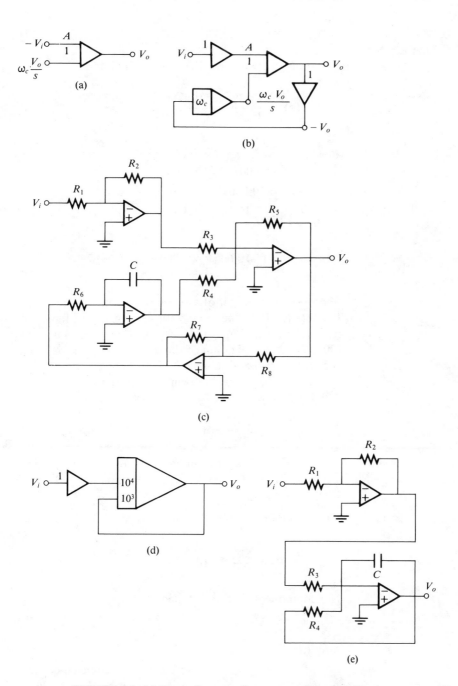

FIGURE 9.3. (a) Block diagram of output amplifier. (b) Block diagram of network. (c) Schematic of network. (d) Block diagram of network of Example 9.1. (e) Schematic of (d).

**Example 9.1**

Design a state variable network for the transfer function

$$A(s) = \frac{V_o(s)}{V_i(s)} = \frac{10{,}000}{s + 1000}$$

*Solution.*

$$sV_o + 1000V_o = 10{,}000V_i$$

$$sV_o = 10{,}000V_i - 1000V_o$$

$$V_o = 10{,}000\ \frac{V_i}{s} - 1000\ \frac{V_o}{s}$$

$$= \frac{-1}{s}\ (-10{,}000V_i + 1000V_o)$$

where $V_o$ is the output of a two-input summing integrator. The input $-V_i$ is one input with an integration factor of 10,000. The other input is $V_o$ with an integration factor of 1000. The block diagram of the required network is given in Figure 9.3(d) and its schematic in Figure 9.3(e).

Amplifier 1 is a single-input amplifier with a gain of $A = 1$. Assume $R_2 = 1\ \Omega$.

$$R = \frac{R_2}{A} = 1\ \Omega$$

Amplifier 2 is a two-input integrator with integration factors of $K_1 = 10^4$ and $K_2 = 10^3$. Assume $C = 1$ F.

$$R_3 = \frac{1}{CK_1} = 10^{-4}\ \Omega$$

$$R_4 = \frac{1}{CK_2} = 10^{-3}\ \Omega$$

The components are now scaled for impedance.

**Amplifier 1**

|  |  | Impedance scale $K_z = 10{,}000$ |
|---|---|---|
| 1. Assume | $R_1 = 1\ \Omega$ | 10 k$\Omega$ |
| 2. Calculate | $R_1 = 1\ \Omega$ | 10 k$\Omega$ |

**Amplifier 2**

|  |  |  | Impedance scale $K_z = 100,000,000$ |
|---|---|---|---|
| 1 | Assume | $C_2 = 1$ F | 10 nF |
| 2. | Calculate | $R_3 = 10^{-4}$ Ω | 10 kΩ |
| 3. | Calculate | $R_4 = 10^{-3}$ Ω | 100 kΩ |

For amplifiers, $R_F$ is assumed (1 Ω is a good choice) and $R_1$, $R_2$, etc., is calculated using the equation $A_n = R_F/R_n$. For integrators, the capacitance is assumed (1 F is a good choice) and $R_1$, $R_2$, etc., is calculated using $K_n = 1/CR_n$.

## Problems

**9.1** The transfer function $A(s)$ relates the output voltage and input voltage of a first-order system. For each transfer function given, draw a block diagram for the state variable implementation of the network.

(a) $A(s) = \dfrac{10s}{s + 1000}$

(b) $A(s) = \dfrac{20}{s + 1000}$

(c) $A(s) = \dfrac{20(s + 1000)}{(s + 10,000)}$

(d) $A(s) = \dfrac{s - 10,000}{s + 10,000}$

**9.2** Design the networks and draw the schematics for the block diagrams of Problem 9.1.

**9.3** Identify the first-order networks of Problem 9.1 according to which filter it represents (low-pass, high-pass, etc.) for the transfer functions of Problem 9.1.

## 9.4 Simulation of Higher Order Transfer Functions

Consider the second-order transfer function given by equation (9.11).

$$A(s) = \frac{V_o(s)}{V_i(s)} = \frac{10,000,000}{s^2 + 1200s + 1,000,000} \qquad (9.11)$$

The transfer function can be identified as that of a second-order low-pass filter with $\omega_n = 1000$ rad/s, $z = 0.6$, and $A_0 = 10$.

$$V_o(s^2 + 1200s + 1,000,000) = 10,000,000 V_i \qquad (9.12)$$

$$s^2 V_o = 10,000,000 V_i - 1200 s V_o - 1,000,000 V_o$$

$$V_o = 10,000,000 \, \frac{V_i}{s^2} - 1200 \, \frac{V_o}{s} - 1,000,000 \, \frac{V_o}{s^2}$$

$$V_o = \frac{-1}{s} \left( -10,000,000 \, \frac{V_i}{s} + 1,000,000 \, \frac{V_o}{s} + 1200 V_o \right)$$

The output $V_o$ is realized as the output of a summing integrator with three inputs. Two of the inputs are to be further integrated. These two inputs can be combined as a single input, making the integrator a two-input summing integrator.

Input 1: $\left( -10,000 \, \dfrac{V_i}{s} + 1000 \, \dfrac{V_o}{s} \right)$ with an integration factor of 1000

Input 2: $V_o$ with an integration factor of 1200

Note how like terms are grouped in order to reduce the number of required integrators. The input and the output of the integrator are indicated in Figure 9.4(a). The input 1 is the output of another two-input summing integrator as indicated by equation (9.13):

$$-10,000 \, \frac{V_i}{s} + 1000 \, \frac{V_o}{s} = \frac{-1}{s} \, (10,000 V_i - 1000 V_o) \tag{9.13}$$

Two inputs of this summing integrator are:

$V_i$ with an integration factor of 10,000, and

$-V_o$ with an integration factor of 1000.

The complete block diagram of the required network is shown in Figure 9.4(b) and the schematic in 9.4(c). Practical values are obtained by scaling for impedance.

**Amplifier 1**

|  | Impedance scale $K_z = 100,000,000$ |
|---|---|
| $C_1 = 1$ F | 10 nF |
| $R_1 = 10^{-4} \, \Omega$ | 10 k$\Omega$ |
| $R_2 = 10^{-3} \, \Omega$ | 1000 k$\Omega$ |

**Amplifier 2**

|  | Impedance scale $K_z = 10,000$ |
|---|---|
| $R_5 = 1 \, \Omega$ | 10 k$\Omega$ |
| $R_6 = 1 \, \Omega$ | 10 k$\Omega$ |

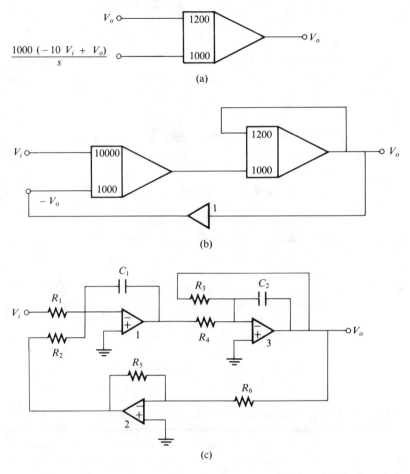

FIGURE 9.4. (a) Block diagram of output amplifier. (b) Block diagram of network. (c) Schematic of network.

**Amplifier 3**

|  | Impedance scale<br>$K_z = 100,000,000$ |
| --- | --- |
| $C_2 = 1$ F | 10 nF |
| $R_3 = 8.33 \times 10^{-4}$ Ω | 83.3 kΩ |
| $R_4 = 10^{-3}$ Ω | 100 kΩ |

**Example 9.2**

Design a third-order low-pass filter with a natural frequency of 1000 rad/s and a low frequency gain of 10. The normalized transfer function of a third-order low-pass filter is given by:

$$A(s) = \frac{15A_0}{s^3 + 6s^2 + 15s + 15}$$

where $A_0$ is the pass-band gain.

*Solution.* A step-by-step design procedure was developed with this solution.

**Step 1.** Rewrite the transfer function in the form: $V_0 D(s) = V_i N(s)$, where $D(s)$ is the denominator and $N(s)$ the numerator of the transfer function.

$$s^3 V_o + 6s^2 V_o + 15s + 15 = 150 V_i$$

**Step 2.** Isolate the most differentiated $V_o$. In our case $s^3 V_o$ is the most differentiated output voltage.

$$s^3 V_o = 150 V_i - 6s^2 V_o - 15s V_o - 15 V_o$$

**Step 3.** Divide both sides of the equation by $s^n$ where $n$ is the highest power of $s$. In our case, divide both sides by $s^3$.

$$V_o = 150 \frac{V_i}{s^3} - 15 \frac{V_o}{s^3} - 15 \frac{V_o}{s^2} - 6 \frac{V_o}{s}$$

Note that the items are arranged to keep like terms (i.e., terms to be integrated by the same number) side by side.

**Step 4.** Rearrange the left-hand side of the equation as the output of a summing integrator or a summing amplifier. If each term is divided by $s$, the signal is the output of a summing integrator, otherwise it is the output of a summing amplifier. Take $(-1)$ outside the bracket for the amplifier and $(-1/s)$ outside the bracket for the integrator. What remains inside the bracket are the inputs. Whole or part of the input can be incorporated as the gain or the integration factor for the input. All the input terms that are to be further integrated are bunched as a single input.

$$V_o = \frac{-1}{s} \left[ \underbrace{\left( \frac{-150 V_i + 15 V_o}{s^2} + \frac{15 V_o}{s} \right)}_{\text{input 1}} + \underbrace{6 V_o}_{\text{input 2}} \right]$$

**Step 5.** Draw the block diagram of the integrator (or amplifier). The block diagram is shown in Figure 9.5(a). An integration factor of 15 is allowed for input 1 and 6 for input 2.

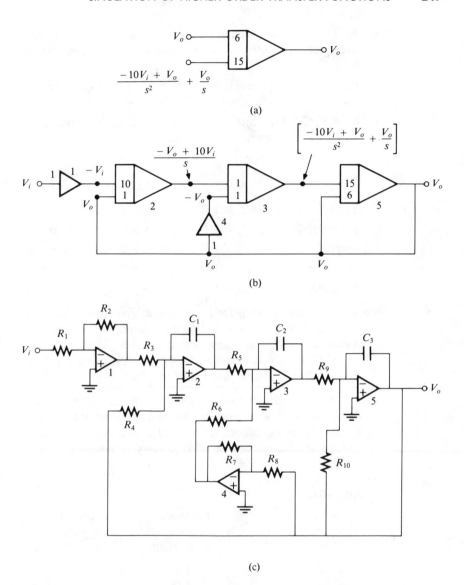

FIGURE 9.5. (a) and (b) Block diagrams for designed circuit for Example 8.2. (c) Unscaled electric network for (b).

**Step 6.** Each input to the integrator (or amplifier) is in turn generated as the output of the integrator or amplifier. The block diagram is given in Figure 9.5(b).

**Step 7.** An electric network is drawn for the block diagram developed (Figure 9.5(c)).

**Step 8.** The feedback element ($R_f$ for amplifiers and $C$ for integrators) is assumed. The other components are calculated from:

$R_n = R_f/A_n$   for amplifiers, where $A_n$ is the gain for the input, and

$R_n = K_n C$   for integrators, where $K_n$ is the integration factor for the input.

|  | **Assume** | **Calculate** | **Calculate** |
|---|---|---|---|
| Amplifier 1 | $R_2 = 1 \ \Omega$ | $R_1 = 1 \ \Omega$ | |
| Amplifier 2 | $C_1 = 1$ F | $R_3 = 0.1 \ \Omega$ | $R_4 = 1 \ \Omega$ |
| Amplifier 3 | $C_2 = 1$ F | $R_5 = 1 \ \Omega$ | $R_6 = 1 \ \Omega$ |
| Amplifier 4 | $R_7 = 1 \ \Omega$ | $R_8 = 1 \ \Omega$ | |
| Amplifier 5 | $C_3 = 1$ F | $R_9 = \frac{1}{15} \ \Omega$ | $R_{10} = \frac{1}{6} \ \Omega$ |

**Step 9.** A normalized transfer function was given, meaning that the transfer function is based on a frequency of 1 rad/s. The component values are now scaled for the given frequency ($K_f = 1000$ rad/s). Recall that all capacitors are divided by $K_f$ and all the resistors are left alone.

**Step 10.** Scale the circuit components for practical values. Recall that all resistors are multiplied by the impedance scale factor $K_z$ and all the capacitors are divided by $K_z$. Different impedance scale factors can be selected for different amplifiers.

**Amplifier 1**

|  | **Frequency scale** $K_f = 1000$ | **Impedance scale** $K_z = 10{,}000$ |
|---|---|---|
| $R_2 = 1 \ \Omega$ | $1 \ \Omega$ | 10 k$\Omega$ |
| $R_1 = 1 \ \Omega$ | $1 \ \Omega$ | 10 k$\Omega$ |

**Amplifier 2**

|  | | **Impedance scale** $K_z = 100{,}000$ |
|---|---|---|
| $C_1 = 1$ F | 0.001 F | 10 nF |
| $R_3 = 0.1 \ \Omega$ | $0.1 \ \Omega$ | 10 k$\Omega$ |
| $R_4 = 1 \ \Omega$ | $1 \ \Omega$ | 100 k$\Omega$ |

**Amplifier 3**

| | Frequency scale $K_f = 1000$ | Impedance scale $K_z = 100,000$ |
|---|---|---|
| $C_2 = 1$ F | 0.001 F | 10 nF |
| $R_5 = 1$ $\Omega$ | 1 $\Omega$ | 100 k$\Omega$ |
| $R_6 = 1$ $\Omega$ | 1 $\Omega$ | 100 k$\Omega$ |

**Amplifier 4**

| | | |
|---|---|---|
| $R_7 = 1$ $\Omega$ | 1 $\Omega$ | 100 k$\Omega$ |
| $R_8 = 1$ $\Omega$ | 1 $\Omega$ | 100 k$\Omega$ |

**Amplifier 5**

| | | |
|---|---|---|
| $C_3 = 1$ F | 0.001 F | 10 nF |
| $R_9 = 0.0667$ $\Omega$ | 0.0667 $\Omega$ | 6.67 k$\Omega$ |
| $R_{10} = 0.1667$ $\Omega$ | 0.1667 $\Omega$ | 16.67 k$\Omega$ |

---

If several filters with different natural frequencies are required, the nominal component values can be scaled for as many frequencies as needed.

---

**Problems**

**9.4**  Design the normalized second-order networks. Do not scale for impedance.

(a) $A(s) = \dfrac{A}{s^2 + 2zs + 1}$

(b) $A(s) = \dfrac{2Azs}{s^2 + 2zs + 1}$

(c) $A(s) = \dfrac{As^2}{s^2 + 2zs + 1}$

(d) $A(s) = \dfrac{A(s^2 + 1)}{s^2 + 2zs + 1}$

(e) $A(s) = \dfrac{A(s^2 - 2zs + 1)}{s^2 + 2zs + 1}$

(f) $A(s) = \dfrac{A(s + 1)}{s^2 + 2zs + 1}$

**9.5**  Design the networks for $A(s)$ of Problem 9.4, if

(a) $\omega_n = 5000$ rad/s, $A = 2$, and $z = 0.5$

(b) $\omega_n = 10,000$ rad/s, $A = 10$, and $z = 0.707$

(c) $\omega_n = 2000$ rad/s, $A = 5$, and $z = 0.2$

**9.6**  Find the transfer function of the network of Figure 9.6, and show that it is a noninverting integrator.

---

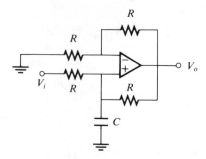

FIGURE 9.6. Noninverting integrator

## 9.5  Summary

There are two ways to design networks. One method can be described as an analytic technique where the network configuration is previously established and analyzed. Based on the analysis, the design equations are established and are used to design networks. The design of a multiple feedback filter is an example of this method.

The other method is a synthesis technique where the network configuration is unknown until designed. This method of designing networks is powerful in that any transfer function can be thus synthesized. The extra number of operational amplifiers needed may not become an excessive burden if *quad* amplifiers are used. The major drawback of state variable design is the upper limit on the frequency response. The restriction is caused by the limitation of the operational amplifiers. Yet another consideration is the stability of the network. Stability of a higher order system with feedback is very much dependent on loop gain.

### Key Terms

Define the following terms:

inverting amplifier                      integration factor
summing amplifier                        state variable
summing integrator

In Appendix A, you will find a further review of the frequency and time-domain responses of second-order networks (see Labs 6 and 7, respectively).

# CHAPTER 10

# Gyrators

## 10.1 Introduction

A *gyrator* is a two-port network that simulates an impedance $Z$. When used with a high-quality (or high-$Q$) capacitor, it can simulate the characteristics of a high-quality coil. Gyrators are often used as inductance simulators. They can also be used as capacitance simulators or even resistance simulators. However, there is limited practical importance for a capacitance or resistance simulation. The general problems associated with coils, such as their large size, low $Q$, winding capacitance, nonlinearity, and magnetic susceptibility are significant reasons to employ inductance simulations. Another important reason is that the inductance cannot be fabricated as an integrated circuit.

## 10.2 Impedance Simulations

The impedances of a coil, an inductor, a capacitor, and a resistor are given by equations (10.1) through (10.4).

$$Z_{\text{coil}} = R + sL \tag{10.1}$$

$$Z_L = sL \tag{10.2}$$

$$Z_C = \frac{1}{sC} \tag{10.3}$$

$$Z_R = R \tag{10.4}$$

Any network that exhibits an impedance between two terminals of the form given by equation (10.1) can be considered a coil of resistance $R$ and inductance $L$. If $R = 0$, the coil then becomes a pure inductor.

## 10.3 Coil Simulator with Frequency-Dependent Resistance and Inductance

The impedance between the terminal A and the ground of the circuit of Figure 10.1(a) is that of a coil with resistance $R$ and inductance $L$. Both the inductance and the resistance of the simulated coil are frequency dependent.

The maximum $Q$ of the coil occurs only at a particular frequency. For all other frequencies, the quality factor $Q$ remains lower than the maximum. Figure 10.1(b) is the equivalent impedance seen between the terminal A and the ground.

For the circuit of Figure 10.1(a), the impedance between the terminal A and the ground (A′) is given by equation (10.5).

$$Z_{AA'} = \frac{V_A}{I_A} \tag{10.5}$$

where $V_A$ is the voltage at the terminal A (with respect to ground) and $I_A$, $I_1$, and $I_2$ are currents, as indicated in Figure 10.1(a).

$$I_A = I_1 + I_2 \tag{10.6}$$

By Ohm's law, current is the voltage across the impedance divided by the impedance.

The voltage across the capacitance is expressed as

$$V_C = V_A - V_B$$

Since the amplifier has a unity gain, its output voltage is the same as $V_B$, as shown in Figure 10.1(a).

The voltage across the resistor $R_2$ is expressed as

$$V_R = V_A - V_B$$

Therefore,

$$I_A = (V_A - V_B)sC + \frac{(V_A - V_B)}{R_2}$$

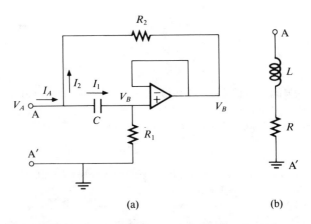

(a)                                    (b)

FIGURE 10.1. (a) Coil simulator. (b) Simulated coil between terminal A and ground.

$$I_A = (V_A - V_B)\left[sC + \frac{1}{R_2}\right] \qquad (10.7)$$

$$= (V_A - V_B)\frac{R_2Cs + 1}{R_2}$$

$$V_B = V_A \frac{R_1}{R_1 + 1/sC} \qquad (10.8)$$

$$= V_A \frac{R_1Cs}{R_1Cs + 1}$$

Substituting $V_B$ in equation (10.7),

$$I_A = V_A\left(1 - \frac{R_1Cs}{R_1Cs + 1}\right)\frac{R_2Cs + 1}{R_2}$$

$$= V_A\left(\frac{R_1Cs + 1 - R_1Cs}{R_1Cs + 1}\right)\frac{R_2Cs + 1}{R_2}$$

$$I_A = V_A \frac{R_2Cs + 1}{R_2(R_1Cs + 1)} \qquad (10.9)$$

$$Z_{AA'} = \frac{R_2(R_1Cs + 1)}{R_2Cs + 1} \qquad (10.10)$$

$s$ is now replaced by $j\omega$ to obtain equation (10.11):

$$Z_{AA'} = \frac{R_2(1 + jR_1C\omega)}{(1 + jR_2C\omega)} \qquad (10.11)$$

In order to remove the complex number from the denominator of equation (10.11), both the numerator and denominator of this equation are multiplied by the *complex conjugate* of the denominator.

$$Z_{AA'} = \frac{R_2(1 + jR_1C\omega)(1 - jR_2C\omega)}{(1 + jR_2C\omega)(1 - jR_2C\omega)} \qquad (10.12)$$

$$= \frac{R_2(1 + R_1R_2C^2\omega^2 + jR_1C\omega - jR_2C\omega)}{1 + R_2^2C^2\omega^2}$$

$$Z_{AA'} = \frac{R_2(1 + R_1R_2C^2\omega^2)}{1 + R_2^2C^2\omega^2} + j\omega\frac{CR_2(R_1 - R_2)}{1 + R_2^2C^2\omega^2} \qquad (10.13)$$

The impedance $Z_{AA'}$ expressed by equation (10.13) is of the form of the impedance expressed by equation (10.1). Between terminal A and the ground, the network behaves as a coil with a resistance $R$ and inductance $L$ as given in equations (10.14) and (10.15), respectively.

$$R = \frac{R_2(1 + R_1R_2C^2\omega^2)}{1 + R_2^2C^2\omega^2} \qquad (10.14)$$

$$L = \frac{CR_2(R_1 - R_2)}{1 + R_2^2 C^2 \omega^2} \qquad (10.15)$$

Very often $R_2$ is made much much smaller than $R_1$ such that $(R_1 - R_2)$ approaches $R_1$. $(R_1 - R_2) \simeq R_1$ because $R_1 \gg R_2$. Under this condition, the inductance is given by equation (10.16).

$$L \simeq \frac{CR_1 R_2}{1 + R_2^2 C^2 \omega^2} \qquad (10.16)$$

when $R_1 \gg R_2$. Note that the impedance becomes resistive if $R_1 = R_2$, and it becomes capacitive if $R_1 < R_2$.

The quality factor $Q$ of a coil is defined by equation (10.17).

$$Q \simeq \frac{\omega L}{R} \qquad (10.17)$$

$$Q \simeq \frac{\omega R_1 C}{1 + R_1 R_2 C^2 \omega^2} \qquad (10.18)$$

Note that the simulated inductance, resistance, and the $Q$ of the simulated coil are all frequency dependent. The maximum value of $Q$ occurs at a frequency where $dQ/d\omega = 0$ (maximum condition).

Taking $\log_e$ for both sides of equation (10.18), we obtain

$$\log_e Q = \log_e \omega R_1 C - \log_e (1 + R_1 R_2 C^2 \omega^2) \qquad (10.19)$$

Differentiating both sides of equation (10.19) with respect to $\omega$, we obtain

$$\frac{1}{Q} \frac{dQ}{d\omega} = \frac{R_1 C}{R_1 C \omega} - \frac{2R_1 R_2 C^2 \omega}{1 + R_1 R_2 C^2 \omega^2} \qquad (10.20)$$

$$\boxed{\frac{d(\log_e y)}{dx} = \frac{1}{y} \frac{dy}{dx}}$$

When the $Q$ is maximum, $dQ/d\omega = 0$

$$0 = \frac{1}{\omega} - \frac{2R_1 R_2 C^2 \omega}{1 + R_1 R_2 C^2 \omega^2} \qquad (10.21)$$

$$0 = 1 - \frac{2R_1 R_2 C^2 \omega^2}{1 + R_1 R_2 C^2 \omega^2} \; ; \; 1 + R_1 R_2 C^2 \omega^2 - 2R_1 R_2 C^2 \omega^2 = 0$$

$$R_1 R_2 C^2 \omega^2 = 1$$

$$\omega^2 = \frac{1}{R_1 C R_2 C} \qquad (10.22)$$

$$\omega_m = \frac{1}{C(R_1 R_2)^{0.5}} \qquad (10.23)$$

where $\omega_m$ is the frequency at which the $Q$ of the simulated coil is the maximum. Substituting this frequency in equation (10.18), an equation for maximum $Q$ can be derived:

$$Q_{max} = \frac{R_1}{2(R_1 R_2)^{0.5}} = \frac{1}{2}\left(\frac{R_1 R_1}{R_1 R_2}\right)^{0.5}$$

$$Q_{max} = 0.5\sqrt{\frac{R_1}{R_2}} \tag{10.24}$$

Substituting $\omega_m$ for $\omega$ in equations of inductance and resistance, equations for their values at the frequency where the quality factor $Q$ is maximum can be derived. Furthermore, since $R_1 + R_2 \approx R_1$ when $R_1 \gg R_2$, then

$$L_m = \frac{CR_1^2 R_2}{R_1 + R_2} \approx CR_1 R_2 \tag{10.25}$$

$$R_m = \frac{2R_1 R_2}{R_1 + R_2} \approx 2R_2 \tag{10.26}$$

---

**Example 10.1**

For the coil simulator of Figure 10.1(a):

$$R_1 = 100 \text{ k}\Omega, \ R_2 = 100 \ \Omega, \text{ and } C = 0.1 \ \mu\text{F}.$$

Find the following:

(a) the frequency at which the quality factor $Q$ is at maximum
(b) the maximum $Q$
(c) the effective inductance and resistance of the coil when the quality factor $Q$ is at maximum
(d) values of $Q$, $R$, and $L$ at 1000 rad/s

*Solution.* $R_2$ is much much smaller than $R_1$.

(a) $\omega_m = \dfrac{1}{C(R_1 R_2)^{0.5}} = 3150 \text{ rad/s}$

(b) $Q_{max} = 0.5\left(\dfrac{R_1}{R_2}\right)^{0.5} = 15.8$

(c) $L_m = CR_1 R_2 = 1 \text{ H}; \ R_m = 2R_2 = 200 \ \Omega$

(d) At 1000 rad/s,

$$L = \frac{R_2 R_1 C}{1 + R_2^2 C^2 \omega^2} \approx 1 \text{ H}$$

$$R = \frac{R_2(R_1 R_2 C^2 \omega^2 + 1)}{1 + R_2^2 C^2 \omega^2} \approx 110 \ \Omega$$

$$Q = \frac{\omega R_1 C}{1 + R_1 R_2 C^2 \omega^2} = 9.1$$

## Problems

**10.1**  Design a coil simulator to be used in a band-pass network with a center frequency of 10,000 rad/s. The $Q$ of the coil is to be maximum at this frequency. The bandwidth is to be 1000 rad/s. [**Hint:** Bandwidth $= \omega_n/Q$.]

## 10.4  Coil Simulator with Frequency-Independent Resistance and Inductance

Between terminals A and ground (A') the circuit of Figure 10.2(a) behaves like a coil of resistance $R$ and inductance $L$. An ac equivalent circuit for Figure 10.2(a) is given in Figure 10.2(b). When the voltage $V_o$ is the output voltage of a unity gain op-amp, it can be considered nearly ideal.

$$V_i = (R_1 + R_2)I - R_2 I_2 \tag{10.27}$$

$$-V_i = -R_2 I + \left(R_2 + \frac{1}{sC}\right) I_2 \tag{10.28}$$

where $I$ and $I_2$ are currents, as shown on Figure 10.2(a) and (b).

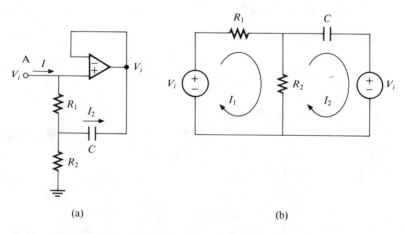

(a)                                    (b)

FIGURE 10.2. (a) Coil simulator. (b) ac equivalent circuit of (a).

$$\Delta = \begin{vmatrix} (R_1 + R_2) & -R_2 \\ -R_2 & \dfrac{R_2 Cs + 1}{sC} \end{vmatrix} \tag{10.29}$$

$$= R_2^2 - \frac{(R_1 + R_2)(R_2 Cs + 1)}{sC}$$

$$= \frac{R_2^2 sC - R_1 R_2 Cs - R_2^2 Cs - R_1 - R_2}{sC}$$

$$= \frac{-(R_1 R_2 Cs + R_1 + R_2)}{sC}$$

$$\Delta^I = \begin{vmatrix} V_i & -R_2 \\ -V_i & \dfrac{R_2 Cs + 1}{sC} \end{vmatrix} \tag{10.30}$$

$$= R_2 V_i - V_i \frac{R_2 Cs + 1}{sC} = V_i \frac{R_2 Cs - R_2 Cs - 1}{sC}$$

$$I = \frac{\Delta^I}{\Delta} = \frac{V_i}{Z_{AA'}} = V_i \frac{1}{R_1 R_2 Cs + R_1 + R_2} \tag{10.31}$$

$$Z_{AA'} = \frac{V_i}{I} = R_1 R_2 Cs + R_1 + R_2 \tag{10.32}$$

$$= (R_1 + R_2) + j\omega R_1 R_2 C$$

where $Z_{AA'}$ is the impedance seen between the terminals A and A'. It is the impedance of a coil with a resistance $R$ and inductance $L$ as given by equation (10.33) and (10.34), respectively.

$$R = R_1 + R_2 \tag{10.33}$$

$$L = R_1 R_2 C \tag{10.34}$$

As can be seen from equations (10.33) and (10.34), the effective resistance and inductance are independent of frequency.

## 10.5  Notch Filter

A *notch filter* is a special type of band-elimination (band-rejection) filter. A band-rejection filter is supposed to reject a band of frequencies, whereas a notch filter is intended to reject a single frequency. A notch filter is simply a narrow band-rejection filter. A frequency response of a notch filter is given in Figure 10.3. At the notch frequency $\omega_n$, the gain must be zero. Consider the network of Figure 10.4(a). It is a differential amplifier with a common

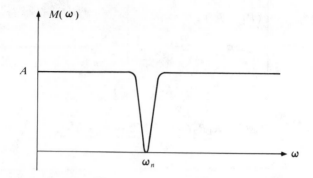

FIGURE 10.3. Frequency response curve of a notch filter

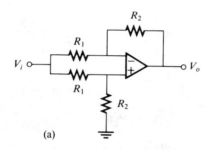

(a)

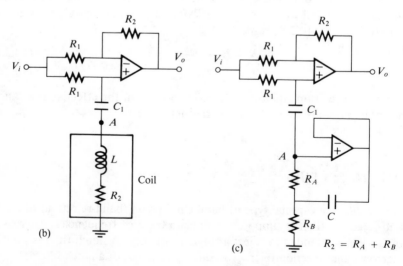

(b)

(c)

$R_2 = R_A + R_B$

FIGURE 10.4. (a) Differential amplifier with common-mode input. (b) Notch filter. (c) Notch filter with simulated coil.

mode gain of zero. Note that two sets of matched resistors $R_1$ and $R_2$ are required for the common mode gain to be zero. For a common mode input of $V_i$, the output stays at zero volts.

Now suppose a capacitor and an inductor are added to the circuit as shown in Figure 10.4(b). Except at the resonance frequency, where the net impedance remains, the circuit is no longer a differential amplifier. Therefore, the output is no longer zero.

$$V_o = 0$$

only when

$$\omega_n L = \frac{1}{\omega_n C_1}$$

or

$$\omega_n = 1/(LC_1)^{0.5} \tag{10.35}$$

The sharpness of the notch filter depends on the $Q$ of the series resonant circuit.

---

**Example 10.2**

Design a notch filter to eliminate a frequency of 1000 rad/s. The simulated inductance must be 1000 H.

*Solution.*   For the gyrator, assume

$$L = R_A R_B C = 1000 \text{ H}$$
$$R_2 = R_A + R_B$$
$$\text{Let} \quad R_A = R_B = 100 \text{ k}\Omega$$
$$R_2 = 200 \text{ k}\Omega$$
$$C = \frac{L}{R_A R_B} = 10^{-7} \text{ F}$$
$$\text{Let} \quad R_1 = 100 \text{ k}\Omega$$

$C_1$ is calculated from $\omega_n = \dfrac{1}{\sqrt{LC_1}}$

$$C_1 = 1 \text{ nF}$$
$$Q = \frac{\omega_n L}{R_2} = 5$$

Bandwidth $B = \dfrac{\omega_n}{Q} = 200 \text{ rad/s}$

$$\omega_1 = \omega_n - \frac{B}{2} = 900 \, \text{rad/s}$$

$$\omega_2 = \omega_n + \frac{B}{2} = 1100 \, \text{rad/s}$$

The designed circuit and an approximate frequency-domain response curve are given in Figure 10.5(a) and (b), respectively.

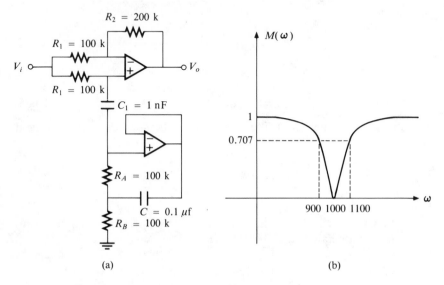

(a)                                    (b)

FIGURE 10.5. (a) Designed circuit of Example 10.2. (b) Frequency response curve of (a).

## 10.6   Inductance Simulator

A two-op-amp inductance simulator is shown in Figure 10.6. This simulator is a four-quadrant gyrator, which means that this circuit can simulate impedance in all four quadrants.

In Figure 10.6, $Y_1$, $Y_2$, $Y_3$, $Y_4$, and $Y_5$ are admittances. Our objective is to find the impedance between terminals A and A' ($Z_{AA'}$). Based on the fact that no current passes through the input terminals of the operational amplifier and that the voltage at the positive and negative terminals remains the same, equations (10.36), (10.37), and (10.38) are written as

$$(V_i - V_a) Y_1 = I \tag{10.36}$$

$$(V_a - V_i) Y_2 = (V_i - V_b) Y_3 \tag{10.37}$$

$$(V_b - V_i) Y_4 = V_i Y_5 \tag{10.38}$$

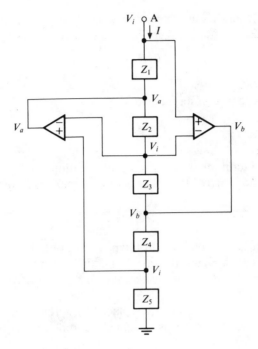

FIGURE 10.6. Four-quadrant gyrator

From equation (10.38),

$$(V_b - V_i) = \frac{Y_5}{Y_4} V_i$$

$$V_i - V_b = \frac{-Y_5}{Y_4} V_i \tag{10.39}$$

Substituting (10.39) in (10.37),

$$(V_a - V_i) Y_2 = \frac{-Y_5 Y_3}{Y_4} V_i$$

or

$$V_a - V_i = \frac{-Y_5 Y_3}{Y_2 Y_4} V_i \tag{10.40}$$

From equation (10.36),

$$I = \frac{Y_1 Y_3 Y_5}{Y_2 Y_4} V_i \tag{10.41}$$

$$Z_{AA'} = \frac{V_i}{I} = \frac{Z_1 Z_3 Z_5}{Z_2 Z_4} \tag{10.42}$$

$Z_1$, $Z_2$, $Z_3$, $Z_4$, and $Z_5$ are impedances. If $Z_1 = R_1$, $Z_2 = R_2$, $Z_3 = R_3$, $Z_5 = R_5$, and $Z_4 = 1/(sC_4)$, then $Z_{AA'}$ becomes:

$$Z_{AA'} = \frac{R_1 R_3 R_5 C_4}{R_2} s \qquad (10.43)$$

$Z_{AA'}$ is the impedance of an inductance $L$.

$$L = \frac{R_1 R_3 R_5 C_4}{R_2} \qquad (10.44)$$

There is no real term for the impedance of equation (10.43). Therefore, the network simulates a pure inductance between terminals A and ground (A′).

---

**Example 10.3**

The frequency-normalized prototype circuit of a third-order high-pass filter is given in Figure 10.7(a). Design the filter for a cutoff frequency of 100 rad/s and without using inductors.

*Solution.*    The inductors are replaced by gyrators in Figure 10.7(b). The gyrator is designed to replace 0.5 H inductance.

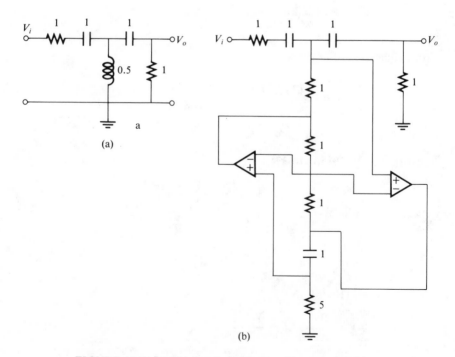

FIGURE 10.7. (a) Third-order high-pass filter. (b) Circuit of (a) without using inductors.

Assume $Z_1 = Z_2 = Z_3 = 1 \, \Omega$, $Z_4 = 1/s \, \Omega$ or $C_4 = 1 \, F$, and $Z_5 = 0.5 \, \Omega$, so that $L = 0.5 \, H$.

The components are now scaled for frequencies at 1000 rad/s. All resistors are unchanged and both capacitors are scaled to 1 mF. The components are scaled for practical values. An impedance scale factor of 10,000 is selected such that: $R_1 = R_2 = R_3 = R_6 = R_7 = 10 \, k\Omega$, $R_5 = 5 \, k\Omega$, and $C_4 = C_6 = C_7 = 0.1 \, \mu F$.

## Example 10.4

Prove that the network of Figure 10.8 is an inductance simulator when $Z$ is a capacitor element.

*Solution.*    The impedance between terminals A and A' is given by:

$$Z_{AA'} = \frac{V_a}{I_a} \tag{10.45A}$$

$$I_A = I_1 + I_2$$

$$I_1 = \frac{V_a - 2V_a}{R_1} \tag{10.45B}$$

$$I_2 = \frac{1}{R_1} \left( V_a + 2V_a \frac{Z}{R_2} \right) \tag{10.45C}$$

$$I_A = \frac{V_a}{R_1} \left( -1 + 1 + \frac{2Z}{R_2} \right) \tag{10.45D}$$

$$Z_{AA'} = \frac{V_a}{I_A} = \frac{R_1 R_2}{2Z}$$

When

$$Z = \frac{1}{sC}, \qquad Z_{AA'} = R_1 R_2 Cs$$

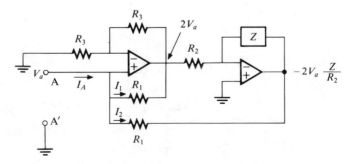

FIGURE 10.8. Circuit for Example 10.4

when

$$Z = \frac{1}{sC}, \qquad Z_{AA'} = 0.5R_1R_2Cs$$

This is an inductive impedance where the inductance is given by:

$$L = 0.5R_1R_2C$$

## 10.7   Frequency-Dependent Negative Resistance

The four-quadrant gyrator of Figure 10.6 can simulate a *negative resistance*. Let $Z_1 = R_1$, $Z_2 = 1/sC_2$, $Z_3 = R_3$, $Z_4 = 1/sC_4$, and $Z_5 = 1/sC_5$.

$$Z_{AA'} = -R_1R_3R_5C_2C_4\omega^2 \tag{10.46}$$

since $s^2 = -\omega^2$.

The impedance is a frequency-dependent negative resistance (FDNR). Consider the circuit of Figure 10.9.

$$I_1 = I_2 = (V_1 - V_2)/R_1 \tag{10.47}$$

$$I_3 = I_4 \quad \text{or} \quad (V_2 - V_1)/R_2 = V_1/Z \tag{10.48}$$

From equation (10.48),

$$V_2 = V_1(1 + R_2/Z) \tag{10.49}$$

Substituting (10.49) in (10.47),

$$I_1 = \left[ V_1 - V_1\left(1 + \frac{R_2}{Z}\right) \right] \Big/ R_1 = -V_1 \frac{R_2}{R_1 Z} \tag{10.50}$$

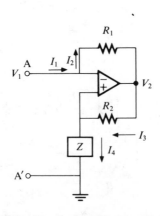

FIGURE 10.9. Negative impedance converter (NIC)

$$Z_{AA'} = \frac{V_1}{I_1} = -\frac{R_1}{R_2} Z \qquad (10.51)$$

$Z_{AA'}$ is negative of $Z$. If $Z$ is a resistance, $Z_{AA'}$ will be a negative resistance. This network is a negative impedance converter (NIC).

## 10.8  Switched Capacitor Networks

In section 10.1 it is stated that simulation of a resistance is almost never a practical necessity. It is true especially if the simulation itself requires resistances. However, there is one practical reason to simulate a resistance; i.e., when circuits are to be fabricated using MOS technology. In this technology, it is relatively easy to fabricate capacitors, switches, and operational amplifiers, but rather difficult to construct resistors. It is possible to simulate a resistance using MOS switches and capacitors. This technique provides *switched capacitor networks*. An MOS switch is shown in Figure 10.10(a) and is symbolically represented in Figure 10.10(b).

When the gate voltage is low, less than 2 V, the drain to source resistance is on the order of several hundred MΩ. On the other hand, the drain to source resistance is relatively low, on the order of few kΩ when the gate voltage is high (more than 2 V). The ratio of $R_{off}$ and $R_{on}$ is on the order of 100,000. When the gate voltage is low, the switch is considered opened. When the gate voltage is high, it is considered closed.

The voltage waveform that is used to operate the switch is called the system clock $\phi$. The clock frequency $f_c$ must be at least five times larger than the frequency of the input signal. Often, a two-phase clock, $\phi_1$ and $\phi_2$, is used with switched capacitance networks. The requirement is that when $\phi_1$ is high $\phi_2$ must be low and vice versa.

The clock signals are used in digital systems, usually for timing. A two-phase clock can be generated by a plan such as that indicated in Figure 10.11. The first block is a crystal oscillator, the output of which is fed to a "divide by $n$" network. The frequency of the output of this network can be

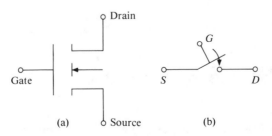

FIGURE 10.10. (a) MOS switch. (b) Symbol of (a).

FIGURE 10.11. Two-phase clock

varied and is a $\phi_1$ signal. This signal is applied to a two-phase generator to give the two outputs $\phi_1$ and $\phi_2$.

Consider the switched capacitor circuit of Figure 10.12(a). The network is redrawn in Figure 10.12(b) replacing FETs with switches.

At a given instant, $\phi_1$ is high and $\phi_2$ is low. If the clock frequency is large compared to the frequency of $V_i$, the input voltage can be considered to be constant for this short duration. The capacitor is charged as shown in Figure 10.12(c). The time constant is $R_{on}C$, and in about five time constants the capacitor will be fully charged. When the clock voltage changes, the capacitor discharges. The charge/discharge cycle happens in one clock period $T_c$. The net charge on the capacitor during $T_c$ is $\Delta q$.

$$\Delta q = C(V_i - V_o) \tag{10.52}$$

$$I = \frac{\Delta q}{\Delta t} = \frac{C(V_i - V_o)}{T_c} = Cf_c(V_i - V_o) \tag{10.53}$$

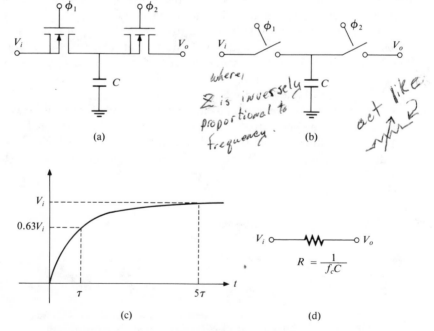

FIGURE 10.12. (a) Switched capacitor circuit. (b) Equivalent circuit. (c) Changing curve of $C$. (d) Simulated resistances.

$$\frac{V_i - V_o}{I} = R = \frac{1}{Cf_c} \tag{10.54}$$

where $f_c$ is the frequency of the clock signal, and $(V_i - V_o)/I$ is a resistor connected between a $V_i$-terminal and a $V_o$-terminal. The switched capacitor, therefore, simulates a resistance. The simulated resistance is indicated in Figure 10.12(d).

---

**Example 10.5**
   Draw a switched capacitance network for the integrator of Figure 10.13(a).

   *Solution.*   The resistance $R$ is to be designed using a switched capacitance. The network is given in Figure 10.13(b).

$$R = \frac{1}{f_c C_1}$$

$$A(s) = \frac{V_o(s)}{V_i(s)} = \frac{-f_c C_1}{Cs}$$

   where $K = f_c C_1 / C$.
   The integration factor $K$ depends on clock frequency and the ratio of the capacitors. The block diagram of the integrator is given in Figure 10.13(c).

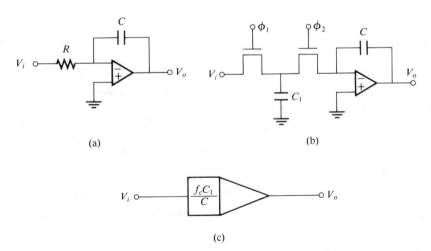

(a)                                   (b)

(c)

FIGURE 10.13. (a) Integrator of Example 10.6. (b) Switched capacitor network for (a). (c) Block diagram of (a).

### Example 10.6

Design the summing integrator indicated in Figure 10.14(a). The clock frequency is 100,000 Hz.

*Solution.* The two resistors are replaced by switched capacitors, and the circuit drawn in Figure 10.14(b).

Assume $C = 10$ pF, $C_1 = K_1 C/f_c = 0.1$ pF, and $C_2 = K_2 C/f_c = 0.01$ pF

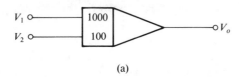

(a)

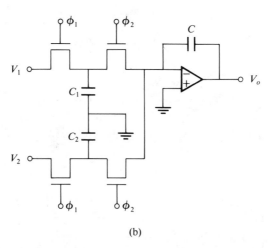

(b)

FIGURE 10.14. (a) Integrator of Example 10.7. (b) Switched capacitor design of (a).

### Problems

**10.2** Draw a multiple feedback high-pass filter using switched capacitors.

## 10.9 Summary

Gyrators are impedance converters. In fact, the gyrator of Figure 10.6 is known as a generalized impedance converter (GIC). With real elements, impedance can occur only in two quadrants (first and fourth). Gyrators can simulate negative resistances and thereby create impedances in all of the four quadrants. The frequency restriction on operational amplifiers is the major drawback of gyrators. Because op-amps are well suited for low frequencies, inductance simulation is a very practical solution to problems posed by large coils (several Henry). The switched capacitor network, which simulates a resistor, was developed in response to a specific need of the technology, where it was easier to fabricate capacitors and switches than it was to fabricate resistors.

## Key Terms

Define the following terms:

| | |
|---|---|
| coil | lower half-power frequency |
| coil simulator | clock frequency |
| $Q$ of the coil | upper half-power frequency |
| maximum $Q$ | oscillator |
| bandwidth | divide by $n$ network |
| common mode input | NIC |
| differential mode | GIC |
| notch filter | four-quadrant impedance |
| notch frequency | FDNR |

In Appendix A, you will find further review of gyrators (see Lab 9).

# CHAPTER 11

# Network Synthesis

## 11.1 Introduction

In Chapter 9, networks were designed using simulation techniques. In this chapter circuits are designed using impedance synthesis. This method of network design is well suited for both lead and lag compensation networks in control systems and for noise elimination and compensation networks in communication systems. The basic objective is to design networks in order to obtain the required transfer functions. This technique splits the transfer function into two impedances, so that their ratio is the required transfer function, and then synthesizes these two impedances to obtain the circuit components. Thus the problem of synthesizing a transfer function is reduced to synthesizing two impedances.

The objectives of network synthesis, as described above, can be achieved using operational amplifiers. The use of operational amplifiers eliminates one major problem of cascaded passive networks; i.e., loading.

## 11.2 Specification of Transfer Functions

A transfer function can be specified by an equation, a Bode plot, or a pole-zero map. If a Bode plot is given, the transfer function can be obtained in the time-constant form. The form of the transfer function can now be changed to the P-Z form to draw the pole-zero map.

---

**Example 11.1**
Find the transfer function in the P-Z form and draw the pole-zero map of the system, the Bode plot of which is shown in Figure 11.1(a).

*Solution.*

$$A(s) = \frac{K\left(\frac{1}{10}s + 1\right)\left(\frac{1}{50{,}000}s + 1\right)}{\left(\frac{1}{1000}s + 1\right)\left(\frac{1}{5000}s + 1\right)}$$

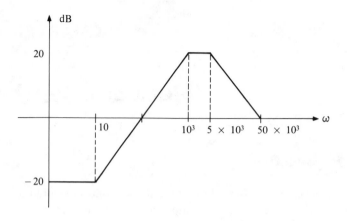

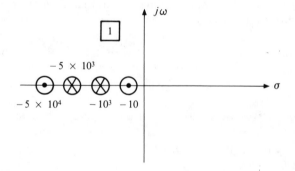

FIGURE 11.1. (a) Bode plot for Example 11.1. (b) Pole-zero map for Example 1.1.

where $K$ is such that $-20 = 20 \log K$ or $K = 0.1$.

$$A(s) = \frac{0.1 \times 1000 \times 5000}{10 \times 50,000} \frac{(s + 10)(s + 50,000)}{(s + 1000)(s + 5000)}$$

$$= \frac{(s + 10)(s + 50,000)}{(s + 1000)(s + 5000)}$$

There are two poles, one at $-1000$ and another at $-5000$. There are two zeros as well, one at $-10$ and the other at $-50,000$. The pole-zero map is shown in Figure 11.1(b).

## Problems

**11.1**   Draw the pole-zero maps for the systems with the Bode plots as given in Figure 11.2.

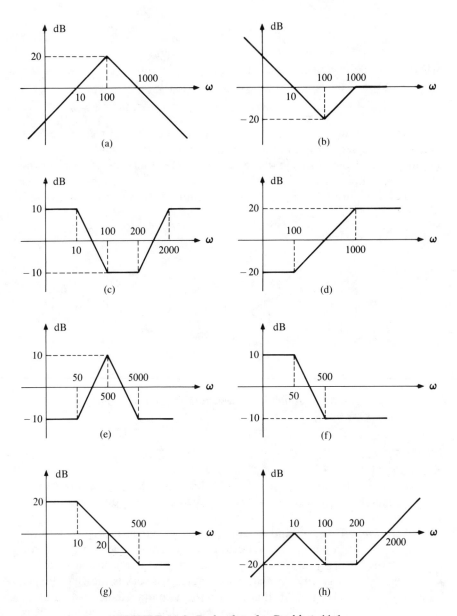

FIGURE 11.2. Bode plots for Problem 11.1

## 11.3  Transfer Function Synthesis

The transfer function $V_o(s)/V_i(s)$ of the network of Figure 11.3 is given by equation (11.1).

$$A(s) = \frac{V_o(s)}{V_i(s)} = \frac{KZ_f}{Z_i} = KZ_f Y_i \qquad (11.1)$$

where $Z_f$ is the feedback impedance and $Y_i$ is the input admittance of the first amplifier. The gain of the second amplifier is $-K$.

$$A(s) = KZ_f Y_i$$

The given transfer function contains poles and zeros. If some poles and zeros are grouped as $Z_f$, and the remaining poles and zeros as $Y_i$, the product of $Z_f$ and $Y_i$ will provide the required transfer function. If we can synthesize the impedance $Z_f$ and the admittance $Y_i$, and connect them as indicated in Figure 11.3, a circuit for the required transfer function will be realized.

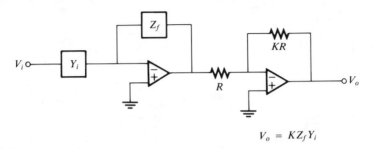

$$V_o = KZ_f Y_i$$

FIGURE 11.3. Amplifier to generate the transfer function $A(s) = KZ_f Y_i$

---

**Example 11.2**

For the pole-zero map of Figure 11.4(a), show how a network can be designed for the transfer function indicated by the pole-zero map.

*Solution.*   First, $Z_f$ and $Y_i$ are selected as shown in Figure 11.4(a). For now, the selection can be considered arbitrary. For practical reasons, however, such selections are restricted to a specific format. The required network is shown in Figure 11.4(b). At this point, the two impedances $Z_f$ and $Z_i$ should be synthesized. Note that $Z_i$ is known when $Y_i$ is known. In this case, $Z_i$ is $1/Y_i$.

---

## 11.4   Properties of *RC* Impedance Functions

For our purposes, we will restrict the transfer function synthesis to ladder networks only. A *ladder network* is a network that contains a simple series-

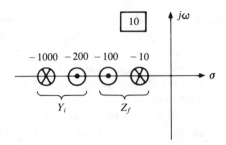

$$Y_i = \frac{s + 200}{s + 1000} \quad \text{or} \quad Z_i = \frac{s + 1000}{s + 200}$$

$$Z_f = \frac{s + 100}{s + 10} \qquad K = 10 = \frac{R_2}{R_1}$$

(a)

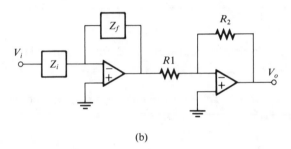

(b)

FIGURE 11.4. (a) Pole-zero map for Example 11.2. (b) Network to satisfy the pole-zero map of (a).

parallel connection of components. There are also *nonladder* networks, which include ladder networks connected in parallel and delta- and wye-connected components.

Three properties of the impedance function $Z(s)$ of an *RC* ladder network are listed below.

1. The highest power of $s$ in the denominator polynomial of $Z(s)$ must be equal to, or one degree more than, the highest power of $s$ in the numerator of $Z(s)$. This means that the number of poles of $Z(s)$ must be equal to or one more than the zeros of $Z(s)$.
2. All poles and zeros must be negative real numbers. A pole can be at the origin.
3. The poles and zeros must alternate, with a pole being the one nearest to the origin or at the origin.

Since $Y(s) = 1/Z(s)$, where poles of $Z(s)$ become the zeros of $Y(s)$ and the zeros of $Z(s)$ become the poles of $Y(s)$, the properties 1 and 3 listed above must be changed accordingly for the admittance function $Y(s)$.

Some of the restrictions result from the fact that negative resistors and negative capacitors are physically unavailable (although possible to simulate). Another reason is that inductors are not used. It is possible to obtain complex poles and complex zeros using nonladder networks.

The impedances and admittances are *driving-point* values, in that they are the impedances or admittances between two terminals. Impedances and admittances are two ways of describing the same physical element. A 10-$\Omega$ resistance or a 0.1 $\mho$ admittance describe the same resistor.

The impedance can be synthesized in some *basic* or *canonic forms*. A canonic form contains the minimum number of elements needed to realize the impedance. One such form uses partial fraction expansion and is known as the *Foster form*. Another method uses a repeated division technique and is often called the *Cauer form*.

---

**Problems**

**11.2** From the pole-zero maps obtained for Problem 11.1, select $Z_f(s)$ and $Y_i(s)$.

**11.3** Select $Z_f(s)$ and $Y_i(s)$ for the pole-zero maps of the systems given in Figure 11.5.

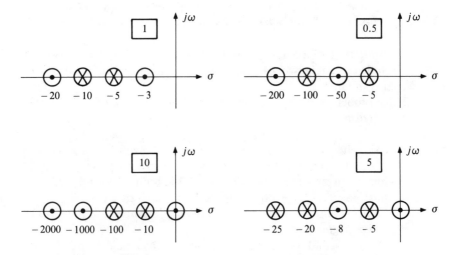

FIGURE 11.5. Pole-zero maps for Problem 9.4

## 11.5  Partial Fraction Expansion Method

The impedance $Z(s)$ is expanded by the *partial fraction method*. It may contain one polynomial and a proper fraction. The topic of partial fraction expansion was covered in Chapter 2, in sections 2.5 and 2.6. There may be a pole at the origin making the denominator a factor of $s$. Other denominator factors are of the form $(s + P_n)$. Thus a general form of $Z(s)$ is expanded as given by equation (11.2).

$$Z(s) = A + \frac{A_0}{s} + \frac{A_1}{s + P_1} + \frac{A_2}{s + P_2} + \ldots + \frac{A_n}{s + P_n} \qquad (11.2)$$

where $A$ is the result of a single division of the numerator by the denominator. This division is required to make the impedance a proper fraction when the number of poles are equal to the number of zeros. Each of the individual terms of equation (11.2) is an impedance. All of the impedances are connected in series. Recall that $R_1 + R_2$ implies a series connection between $R_1$ and $R_2$. There are three representative terms: $A$, $A_0/s$, and $A_n/(s + P_n)$.

1. $A$ is an impedance independent of $s$. There is only one such impedance which is the resistance $R$.

$$A = R \qquad (11.3)$$

2. The impedance $A_0/s = 1/(1/A_0)s$ and is of the form $1/Cs$.

$$C_0 = \frac{1}{A_0} \qquad (11.4)$$

3. Consider the network of Figure 11.6(a). Its impedance is $Z_n(s)$.

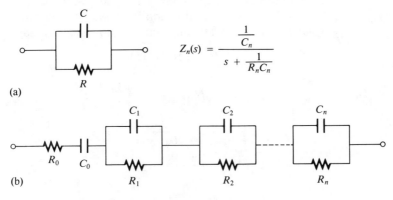

(a)

$$Z_n(s) = \frac{\dfrac{1}{C_n}}{s + \dfrac{1}{R_n C_n}}$$

(b)

FIGURE 11.6. (a) Network to obtain an impedance $A_n/(s + P_n)$. (b) Foster realization of $Z(s)$

$$Z_n(s) = \frac{R_n}{R_n C_n s + 1} = \frac{1/C_n}{s + 1/R_n C_n} \tag{11.5}$$

Comparing this equation of the impedance of Figure 11.6(a) with $A_n/(s + P_n)$:

$$A_n = \frac{1}{C_n} \quad \text{or} \quad C_n = \frac{1}{A_n} \tag{11.6}$$

and $P_n = 1/R_n C_n$ or $R_n = 1/C_n P_n$, hence

$$R_n = \frac{A_n}{P_n} \tag{11.7}$$

Thus, the representative term, $A_n/(s + P_n)$, is the impedance of a capacitor $C_n$ and resistor $R_n$ connected in parallel. The synthesized circuit is shown in Figure 11.6(b).

---

**Example 11.3**

For the following impedance functions, synthesize the Foster networks.

(a) $Z(s) = \dfrac{(s + 5)(s + 15)}{s(s + 10)}$     (b) $Z(s) = \dfrac{(s + 5)}{s(s + 10)}$

(c) $Z(s) = \dfrac{(s + 5)(s + 15)}{(s + 1)(s + 10)}$     (d) $Z(s) = \dfrac{(s + 5)}{(s + 1)(s + 10)}$

*Solution.*

(a) There are two poles, 0 and −10, and two zeros, −5 and −15. The impedance function starts with a pole and alternates with zeros. The impedance can be synthesized.

$$Z(s) = \frac{(s + 5)(s + 15)}{s(s + 10)}$$

is not a proper fraction.

$$s^2 + 10s \overline{\smash{\big)}\,\begin{matrix} 1 \\ s^2 + 20s + 75 \end{matrix}}$$
$$\underline{s^2 + 10s}$$
$$10s + 75$$

$$Z(s) = 1 + \frac{10s + 75}{s(s + 10)}$$

$$Z(s) = 1 + \frac{A_0}{s} + \frac{A_1}{s + 10} \tag{11.8A}$$

$A_0$ and $A_1$ are evaluated using the cover-up rule:

$$A_0 = \frac{75}{10} = 7.5 \qquad A_1 = \frac{-100 + 75}{-10} = 2.5$$

Substituting the values found using the cover-up rule into equation (11.8A), we have

$$Z(s) = 1 + \frac{7.5}{s} + \frac{2.5}{s + 10}$$

From this evaluation, we can now determine from equations (11.3), (11.4), (11.6), and (11.7) that $R = 1$, $C_0 = 1/7.5$, $C_1 = 1/2.5$, and $R_1 = 2.5/10$, respectively. The synthesized circuit is shown in Figure 11.7(a).

(b)  The following equation is a proper fraction:

$$Z(s) = \frac{s + 5}{s(s + 10)}$$

$$Z(s) = \frac{A_0}{s} + \frac{A_1}{s + 10} \tag{11.8B}$$

By the cover-up rule, we find that $A_0 = 0.5$ and $A_1 = 0.5$. Following the same evaluation as in part (a) of this solution, we can now determine from equation (11.4), (11.6), and (11.7) that $C_0 = 2$, $C_1 = 2$, and $R_1 = 0.5$. The synthesized circuit is shown in Figure 11.7(b).

(c)  The following equation is not a proper fraction:

$$Z(s) = \frac{(s + 5)(s + 15)}{(s + 1)(s + 10)}$$

$$= 1 + \frac{9s + 65}{(s + 1)(s + 10)}$$

$$Z(s) = 1 + \frac{A_1}{s + 1} + \frac{A_2}{s + 10} \tag{11.8C}$$

By the cover-up rule, we find that $A_1 = 56/9$ and $A_2 = 30/9$. Following the same evaluation as in part (a) of this solution, we can now determine from equations (11.3), (11.6), and (11.7) that $R = 1$, $C_1 = 9/56$ and $C_2 = 9/30$, and $R_1 = 56/9$ and $R_2 = 3/9$, respectively. The synthesized circuit is shown in Figure 11.7(c).

(d)  The following equation is a proper fraction:

$$Z(s) = \frac{s + 5}{(s + 1)(s + 10)}$$

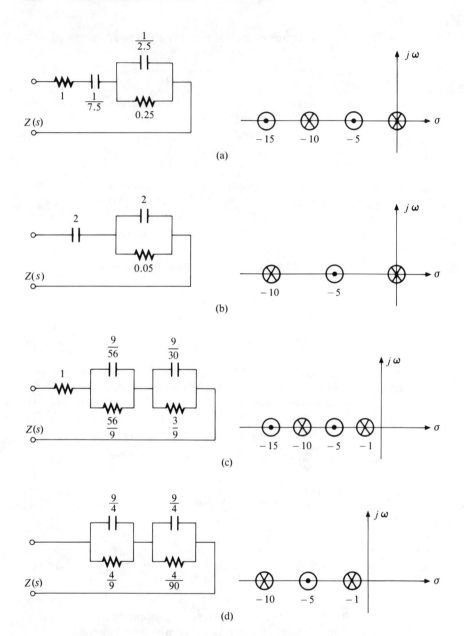

FIGURE 11.7. Designed circuits and pole-zero maps of the impedance functions of Example 11.3

$$Z(s) = \frac{A_1}{s+1} + \frac{A_2}{s+10} \tag{11.8D}$$

By the cover-up rule, we find that $A_1 = 4/9$, and $A_2 = 4/9$. Following the same evaluation as in part (a) of this solution, we can now determine from equation (11.6) that $C_1 = 9/4$ and $C_2 = 9/4$, and from (11.7) that $R_1 = 4/9$ and $R_2 = 4/90$. The synthesized circuit is shown in Figure 11.7(d).

## Problems

**11.4**  Synthesize the selected $Z_f$ and $Z_i = 1/Y_i$ of Problems 11.2 and 11.3.

## 11.6   Repeated Division Method

The *repeated division method* is another technique by which an impedance can be synthesized. This method is also known as the Cauer form of impedance synthesis. It leads to a ladder network realization. The numerator and denominator of $Z(s)$ are arranged in the increasing order of $s$. The numerator is then divided by the denominator for a dividend and a fraction. The dividend is left as an impedance and the fraction is reciprocated to make it an admittance. The process is repeated until the final dividend is infinity.

$$Z(s) = R_1 + \cfrac{1}{C_2 s + \cfrac{1}{R_3 + \cfrac{1}{C_4 s + \cfrac{1}{R_5 + \cfrac{1}{\ \ \ \ }}}}} \tag{11.9}$$

where $R$ and $Cs$ are the dividends of repeated division. The equation (11.9) may be realized by the network of Figure 11.8. Recall that the sum of admittances indicates a shunt connection.

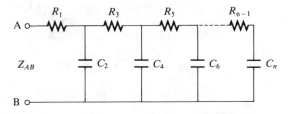

FIGURE 11.8. Network realization of impedance in Cauer form

**Example 11.4**

Synthesize the following impedance functions as Cauer networks.

(a) $Z(s) = \dfrac{s + 5}{s(s + 10)}$   (b) $Z(s) = \dfrac{(s + 5)(s + 15)}{s(s + 10)}$

(c) $Z(s) = \dfrac{s + 5}{(s + 1)(s + 10)}$   (d) $Z(s) = \dfrac{(s + 5)(s + 15)}{(s + 1)(s + 10)}$

*Solution.*

(a) Cauer network

$$Z(s) = \frac{0s^2 + s + 5}{s^2 + 10s}$$

The $0s^2$ term is added to the numerator to match the highest power of $s$ for the numerator and the denominator. The numerator is divided by the denominator.

$$
\begin{array}{r}
0 \quad \text{impedance} \\
s^2 + 10s \,\overline{)\,0s^2 + s + 5} \\
\underline{0s^2 + 0s} \\
s + 5
\end{array}
$$

$Z(s) \longrightarrow 0$ impedance $+ \dfrac{s + 5}{s^2 + 10s}$ impedance

$\longrightarrow 0$ impedance $+ \dfrac{s^2 + 10s}{s + 5}$ admittance

$\longrightarrow 0$ impedance $+ Y_1$ admittance

The numerator of $Y_1$ is divided by its denominator.

$$
\begin{array}{r}
1s \\
s + 5 \,\overline{)\,s^2 + 10s} \\
\underline{s^2 + \phantom{0}5s} \\
5s
\end{array}
$$

$Z(s) \longrightarrow 0$ impedance $+ \left(1s + \dfrac{5s}{s + 5}\right)$ admittance

$\longrightarrow 0$ impedance $+ 1s$ admittance

$\qquad\qquad + \dfrac{s + 5}{5s}$ impedance

$\longrightarrow 0$ impedance $+ 1s$ admittance $+ Z_2$ impedance

The numerator of $Z_2$ is divided by its denominator.

$$\begin{array}{r} 0.2 \\ 5s\overline{\smash{\big)}\,s + 5} \\ \underline{s\phantom{ + 5}} \\ 5 \end{array}$$

$Z(s) \longrightarrow$ 0 impedance + $1s$ admittance

$$+ \left(0.2 + \frac{5}{5s}\right) \text{ impedance}$$

$\longrightarrow$ 0 impedance + $1s$ admittance

$$+\ 0.2 \text{ impedance}$$

$$+\ \frac{5s}{5} \text{ admittance}$$

The division process is repeated.

$$\begin{array}{r} 1s \\ 5\overline{\smash{\big)}\,5s} \\ \underline{5s} \\ 0 \end{array}$$

$Z(s) \longrightarrow$ 0 impedance + $1s$ admittance

$$+\ 0.2 \text{ impedance}$$

$$+ \left(1s + \frac{0}{5}\right) \text{ admittance}$$

Repeating the process once more:

$Z(s) \longrightarrow$ 0 impedance + $1s$ admittance

$$+\ 0.2 \text{ impedance}$$

$$+\ 1s \text{ admittance} + \infty \text{ impedance}$$

The notation shown above is not an algebraic equation. The impedance + admittance does not mean that a resistance is added to an admittance, which of course is impossible. The plus sign indicates only the order and the type of connection between components. A plus sign indicates a series connection for impedances and a shunt connection for admittances. The admittance of capacitance $C$ is $sC$. An infinite admittance is a short circuit and an infinite impedance is an open circuit. Based on this information, the Cauer network is illustrated in Figure 11.9(a). The same network is redrawn in Figure 11.9(b).

The Cauer networks of (b), (c), and (d) are solved in a simplified manner.

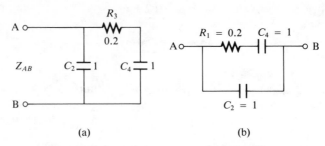

(a)                    (b)

FIGURE 11.9. Circuit of Example 11.4 (a). (b) Redrawn circuit of (a).

(b) Cauer network

$$Z(s) = \frac{s^2 + 20s + 75}{s^2 + 10s}$$

$$
\begin{array}{r}
1 \qquad \text{impedance} \\
s^2 + 10s \overline{)\, s^2 + 20s + 75} \\
-s^2 + 10s \qquad\qquad 0.1s \qquad \text{admittance} \\
\overline{\phantom{-s^2+}10s + 75 \,\overline{)\, s^2 + 10s}} \\
-s^2 + 7.5s \qquad\quad 4 \qquad \text{impedance} \\
\overline{\phantom{-s^2+}2.5s \,\overline{)\, 10s + 75}} \\
-10s \\
\overline{\phantom{-10s+}75}
\end{array}
$$

$$
\begin{array}{r}
0.03333s \;\text{admittance} \\
75 \overline{)\, 2.5s} \\
-2.5s \qquad \infty \;\text{impedance} \\
\overline{\phantom{-2.5}0 \,\overline{)\, 75}}
\end{array}
$$

The circuit is drawn in Figure 11.10(a)

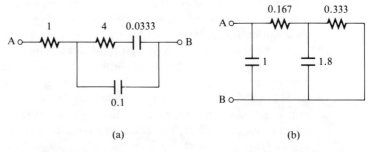

(a)                    (b)

FIGURE 11.10. (a) and (b) Synthesized circuit for Example 11.4 (b) and (c)

(c)  Cauer network

$$Z(s) = \frac{0s^2 + s + 5}{s^2 + 11s + 10}$$

$$
\begin{array}{r}
0 \quad\text{impedance} \\
s^2 + 11s + 10\overline{\big)\, 0s^2 + s + 5}
\end{array}
$$

$$
\begin{array}{r}
-0 \; + 0 + 0 \qquad\qquad 1s \qquad\text{admittance}\\
\overline{\qquad s + 5\,\big)\, s^2 + 11s + 10}
\end{array}
$$

$$
\begin{array}{r}
-s^2 + \; 5s \qquad\qquad (1/6) \quad\text{impedance}\\
\overline{\qquad 6s + 10\,\big)\, s + 5}
\end{array}
$$

$$
\begin{array}{r}
-s + 1.667\\
\hline
3.333
\end{array}
$$

$$
\begin{array}{r}
1.8s \quad\text{admittance}\\
3.333\overline{\big)\, 6s + 10}
\end{array}
$$

$$
\begin{array}{r}
-6s \qquad\qquad 0.333\;\text{impedance}\\
\overline{\qquad 10\,\big)\, 3.333}
\end{array}
$$

$$
\begin{array}{r}
-3.333 \qquad \infty\;\text{admittance}\\
\overline{\qquad 0\,\big)\, 10}
\end{array}
$$

The synthesized circuit is given in Figure 11.10(b)

(d)  Cauer network

$$Z(s) = \frac{s^2 + 20s + 75}{s^2 + 11s + 10}$$

$$
\begin{array}{r}
1 \qquad\text{impedance}\\
s^2 + 11s + 10\overline{\big)\, s^2 + 20s + 75}
\end{array}
$$

$$
\begin{array}{r}
-s^2 + 11s + 10 \qquad\qquad 0.111s \qquad\text{admittance}\\
\overline{\qquad 9s + 65\,\big)\, s^2 + 11s + 10}
\end{array}
$$

$$
\begin{array}{r}
-s^2 + 0.67s \qquad\qquad 0.87 \quad\text{impedance}\\
\overline{\qquad 10.33s + 10\,\big)\, 9s + 10}
\end{array}
$$

$$
\begin{array}{r}
-9s + \; 0.87\\
\hline
9.13
\end{array}
$$

$$
\begin{array}{r}
1.13s \quad\text{admittance}\\
9.13\overline{\big)\, 10.33s + 10}
\end{array}
$$

$$
\begin{array}{r}
-10.33s \qquad\qquad 0.913\;\text{impedance}\\
\overline{\qquad 10\,\big)\, 9.13}
\end{array}
$$

$$
\begin{array}{r}
-9.13 \qquad \infty\;\text{admittance}\\
\overline{\qquad 0\,\big)\, 10}
\end{array}
$$

The resulting network is given in Figure 11.11.

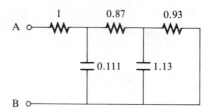

FIGURE 11.11. Network for Example 11.4 (d)

## Problems

**11.5**  Synthesize the selected $Z_f$ and $Z_i$ of Problems 11.2 and 11.3 in Cauer form.

**11.6**  Design the networks specified by Bode plots of Figure 11.2 and the P-Z maps of Problem 11.3 using Cauer impedances.

## 11.7  Synthesis of Transfer Function

In this section, an example of the synthesis of a transfer function is presented.

### Example 11.5

Design a network for the response curve shown by the magnitude Bode plot (approximate) of Figure 11.12(a). The output is to be inverted with respect to the input.

*Solution.*  From the straight-line approximation of the Bode plot given, the transfer function in the time-constant form is found as:

$$A(s) = \frac{0.1s(10^{-4}s + 1)(10^{-5}s + 1)}{(10^{-2}s + 1)^2(5 \times 10^{-6}s + 1)}$$

The transfer function is now changed to P-Z form.

$$A(s) = \frac{0.1 \times 10^{-4} \times 10^{-5}}{10^{-2} \times 10^{-2} \times 5 \times 10^{-6}} \frac{s(s + 10^4)(s + 10^5)}{(s + 100)^2(s + 2 \times 10^5)}$$

The pole-zero map is shown in Figure 11.12(b)

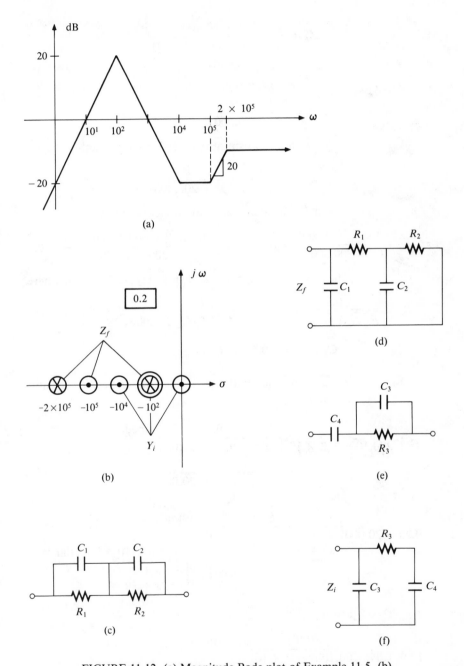

FIGURE 11.12. (a) Magnitude Bode plot of Example 11.5. (b)
Pole-zero map of (a). (c) $Z_f$ synthesized in Foster form. (d) $Z_f$
synthesized in Cauer form. (e) $Z_i$ synthesized in Foster form.
(f) $Z_i$ synthesized in Cauer form.

$$Z_f = \frac{0.2(s + 100,000)}{(s + 100)(s + 200,000)}$$

$$Y_i = \frac{s(s + 10,000)}{(s + 100)}$$

$$Z_i = \frac{(s + 100)}{s(s + 10,000)}$$

$Z_f$ is synthesized using the partial fraction method.

$$Z_f = \frac{A}{s + 100} + \frac{B}{s + 200,000}$$

$A$ and $B$ are calculated using the cover-up method.

$$A = \frac{0.2(-100 + 100,000)}{-100 + 200,000} = 0.1 \qquad B = \frac{0.2(-200,000 + 100,000)}{-200,000 + 100} = 0.1$$

The impedance layout is shown in Figure 11.12(c), where

$$R_1 = \frac{A}{R_1} = \frac{0.1}{100} = 10^{-3} \ \Omega \qquad R_2 = \frac{B}{P_2} = \frac{0.1}{200,000} = 5 \times 10^{-7}$$

$$C_1 = \frac{1}{A} = 10 \text{ F} \qquad C_2 = \frac{1}{B} = 10 \text{ F}$$

$Z_f$ can also be synthesized using the repeated division method.

$$
\begin{array}{r}
0 \qquad\qquad \text{impedance} \\
s^2 + 200,100s + 2 \times 10^7 \overline{\big)\ 0s^2 + 0.2s + 20,000} \\
\underline{-0 \ \ + 0} \\
0.2s + 20,000
\end{array}
$$

$$
\begin{array}{r}
5s \qquad\qquad \text{admittance} \\
0.2s + 20,000 \overline{\big)\ s^2 + 200,100s + 2 \times 10^7} \\
\underline{-s^2 + 100,000s} \qquad\qquad 1.998 \times 10^{-6} \ \text{impedance} \\
100,100s + 2 \times 10^7 \overline{\big)\ 0.2s + 20,000} \\
\underline{-0.2s + 39.96} \\
19,961.04
\end{array}
$$

$$
\begin{array}{r}
5.0148s \qquad \text{admittance} \\
19,961.04 \overline{\big)\ 100,100s + 2 \times 10^7} \\
\underline{-100,100s} \qquad\qquad 9.9805 \times 10^{-4} \ \text{impedance} \\
2 \times 10^7 \overline{\big)\ 19,961.04} \\
\underline{-19,961.04} \qquad \infty \quad \text{admittance} \\
0 \overline{\big)\ 2 \times 10^7}
\end{array}
$$

The impedance layout is given in Figure 11.12(d), where

$$R_1 = 2 \times 10^{-6} \ \Omega \qquad R_2 = 9.98 \times 10^{-4} \ \Omega$$
$$C_1 = 5 \ F \qquad C_2 = 5.01 \ F$$

$Z_i$ is synthesized using the partial fraction expansion method.

$$Z_i = \frac{A}{s} + \frac{B}{s + 10,000}$$

$$A = \frac{(0 + 100)}{(0 + 10,000)} = 0.01 \qquad B = \frac{-10,000 + 100}{-10,000} = 1$$

The impedance is shown in Figure 11.12(e), where

$$C_4 = 100 \ F \qquad C_3 = 1 \ F \qquad R_3 = 10^{-3} \ \Omega$$

$Z_i$ can be synthesized in Cauer form.

$$
\begin{array}{r}
0 \qquad\qquad \text{impedance} \\
s^2 + 10,000s \overline{\smash{\big)}\ 0s^2 + s + 100} \\
\underline{-0 \ +0 + \quad 0} \qquad\qquad\quad s \qquad\quad \text{admittance} \\
s + 100\ \overline{\smash{\big)}\ s^2 + 10,000s} \\
\underline{-s^2 + \qquad 100s} \quad 1.0101 \times 10^{-4} \quad \text{impedance} \\
9900s\ \overline{\smash{\big)}\ s + 100} \\
\underline{-s} \\
100
\end{array}
$$

$$
\begin{array}{r}
99s \quad \text{admittance} \\
100\ \overline{\smash{\big)}\ 9900s} \\
\underline{-9900s} \qquad \infty \ \text{impedance} \\
0\ \overline{\smash{\big)}\ 100}
\end{array}
$$

The impedance is configured in Figure 11.12(f), where

$$C_3 = 1 \ F \qquad C_4 = 99 \ F \qquad R_3 = 1.04 \times 10^{-4}$$

The required network can be implemented by any combination of $Z_f$ and $Z_i$ realizations. Figure 11.13 is one such combination, where $Z_f$ is synthesized in Foster form and $Z_i$ in Cauer form. The network is now scaled for practical values of impedance.

**Impedance scale**
**$10^9$**

| | |
|---|---|
| $R_1 = 10^{-3}$ | 1 M$\Omega$ |
| $R_2 = 5 \times 10^{-7}$ | 500 $\Omega$ |
| $R_3 = 1.04 \times 10^{-4}$ | 104 k$\Omega$ |

**Impedance scale**
$$10^9$$

$C_1 = 10$           10 nF
$C_2 = 10$           10 nF
$C_3 = 1$            1 nF
$C_4 = 99$          99 nF

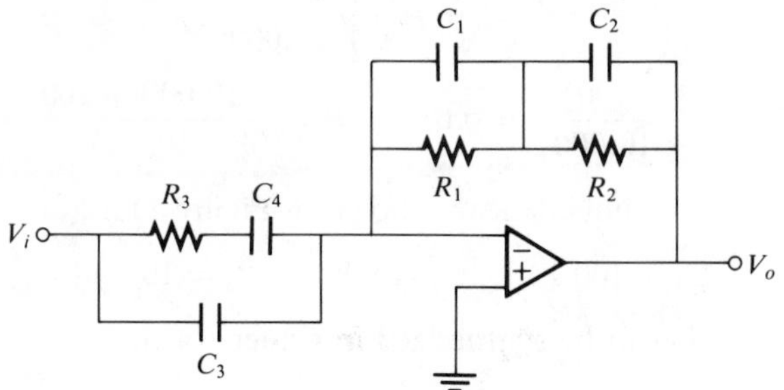

FIGURE 11.13. Designed circuit for Example 11.5

## 11.8  Summary

Two methods of impedance synthesis were investigated in this chapter. Two parallel methods can be used to synthesize admittance. One drawback of Foster and Cauer methods is that only networks with real poles and zeros can be implemented. Although operational amplifiers enable us to express the transfer function as a simple ratio of two impedances ($Z_f/Z_i$), thereby making the design procedure simple, the downside is that the frequencies will be low. Higher frequencies are possible with passive networks, but the transfer function, although a ratio, is not a simple ratio ($Z_2/(Z_1 + Z_2)$). This chapter attempts only to introduce the topic of network synthesis.

### Key Terms

Define the following terms:

Foster method                 canonic forms
Cauer method                driving point
partial fraction              synthesis
repeated division           analysis
ladder network

In Appendix A, you will find a further review of transfer function synthesis (see Lab 8).

# Labs

## Introduction

The following general objectives and other considerations apply to all the labs.

1. The objectives of all labs are either to analyze or to design the networks, given or specified.
2. A theoretical analysis will precede the design in order to obtain an expected or calculated performance of the system.
3. Measurements are to be made of the designed system so that they can be compared with the calculated response obtained by step 2.
4. The comparison of the two results, the calculated and the measured, will be the major objective of all the labs. If the lab calls for the design of a low-pass filter, the major objective is to show how well the response of the designed filter compares with the theoretical response of the same filter. The parameters are often stated to make a point, rather than to design a useful network. A second-order low-pass filter with a damping factor $z = 0.2$ is definitely not a good low-pass filter. But this filter will show dramatically the peaking of magnitude inside its pass band.
5. The frequency range of most of these labs is set well within the capabilities of 741-type op-amps. Unless otherwise specified, 741-type op-amps can be used.
6. Twenty-percent resistors and capacitors are enough to obtain reasonably accurate results. As a rule of thumb, restrict the resistance values for op-amp networks to 1 kΩ to 1 MΩ range and capacitance to 10 pF to 100,000 pF range.
7. Capacitors made of polystyrene and Teflon are the best choice. With a 741-type op-amp it is better to avoid electrolitic capacitors. If the op-amp is an FET input type, where its bias current is extremely small, large capacitors (electrolitic) can be used.
8. Do not use series and parallel combinations of resistors to make up the designed values of resistances. Use the nearest available manufactured resistance values. Likewise, do not use trim potentiometers (pots), unless otherwise stated.

9. The measured magnitude of gain is obtained by measuring the amplitudes of the input and output sine waves, and finding the ratio $V_o/V_i$. The magnitude of gain is supposed to be independent of the amplitude of the input. However, slew rate limiting may occur if the input signal is too large. This effect is more of a problem at higher frequencies. The moral of the story is to keep the input level low, especially at high frequencies.

10. The step response of the network is the output when the input is a unit step voltage (1 V dc). If we apply 1 V dc, the output displayed on the oscilloscope will contain only the steady-state component. In order to observe the transient component as well, a square wave (1 V) is used to simulate 1 V dc. A low-frequency square wave can be considered a dc signal, which is switched on and off at its half-period. As long as the half-period is larger than the settling time of the transients, we will be able to observe both the transient and steady-state components of the output on the oscilloscope.

11. The results of the lab must be graphically presented whenever possible, showing both the calculated and measured results. An alternative to the graphical presentation is to place the calculated and measured results in a tabular format.

12. Writing formal lab reports is a very good idea. In any case there must be a conclusion section, where the calculated and measured results are compared.

13. The following equipment and materials are required for each lab.
    (a) Balanced dual-power supply: 10-, 12-, or 15-volt supply can be used for 741-type op-amps. A single 20-volt supply can be configured as a 10-volt dual supply as indicated by Figure A.1. A more elegant network is presented in Figure A.2
    (b) oscilloscope
    (c) generator (sine wave and square wave)
    (d) spectrum analyzer (optional)
    (e) frequency counter (optional)
    (f) digital voltmeter (DVM) (optional)

14. The questions provided with each of the labs are included for one or more of the following reasons.
    (a) to refresh prerequisite topics
    (b) to extend the ideas of the lab topics
    (c) to create data for tabulation
    (d) to lead into the next lab.

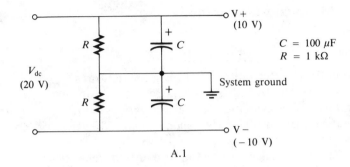

A.1

FIGURE A.1. Dual-power supply from a single supply

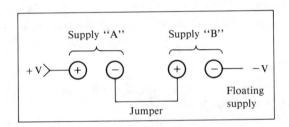

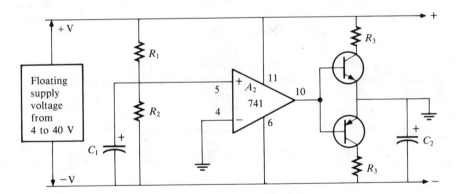

Parts List:
$A_1$   741 OP-AMP
$C_1;C_2$   50 V 22$\mu$F or larger
$R_1;R_2$   From 50 k to 100 k
$Q_{-1}$ : 2N3904
$Q_{-2}$ : 2N3906
$R_3 = 22\Omega$

$C_1$ reduces noise and prevents
    possible oscillations.

$C_2$ absorbs current transients.

Note pin numbers shown for $A_1$
    are for 14-PIN dip package.

Check for the proper pin numbers if you
    use 8-PIN mini-dip or 10-PIN flatpack
    or 8-PIN metal can.

A.2

FIGURE A.2. Dual-power supply from single supply

# Lab I   Magnitude Bode Plot

## Objectives

1. To find the transfer functions of the given networks.
2. To draw magnitude Bode plots (straight-line approximations).
3. To measure the magnitudes of gain at various frequencies in order to draw the measured frequency response curves (dB versus $\omega$) for the networks.
4. To compare the calculated and measured frequency response curves.
5. To calculate and draw the step response of the networks.
6. To observe the step response on the oscilloscope and to draw the actual step response of each.
7. To compare the calculated and measured step responses of the networks.

## Specifications and Directions

1. For each network of Figure A.3, find the transfer function in both the time-constant and P-Z forms.
2. Draw the magnitude Bode plot for each of the transfer functions.
3. Measure the magnitude of gain in dB of all of the networks at various frequencies (in rad/s). Draw the magnitude response curve (dB versus $\omega$) on the same semilog graph paper (step 2).
4. Compare the two graphs for each of the networks.
5. Calculate and draw the step response of each of the networks.
6. Draw the output waveform, as observed on the oscilloscope, when each network is excited by unit step. Refer to item 10 in the introduction to Appendix A for general observation techniques.
7. Compare the calculated and measured step responses of each network.

| Network | $A\,(s)$ Time constant form | $A\,(s)$ P-Z form | Bode plot | P-Z map | Comment |
|---|---|---|---|---|---|
| | $\dfrac{RCs}{RCs + 1}$ | $\dfrac{s}{s + \dfrac{1}{RC}}$ | | | High-pass filter |

## Questions

1. Find the transfer functions of all the networks of Problem 4.9 (Chapter 4, section 4.6).
2. Categorize the networks of Figure A.3 in a table as suggested on page 294.

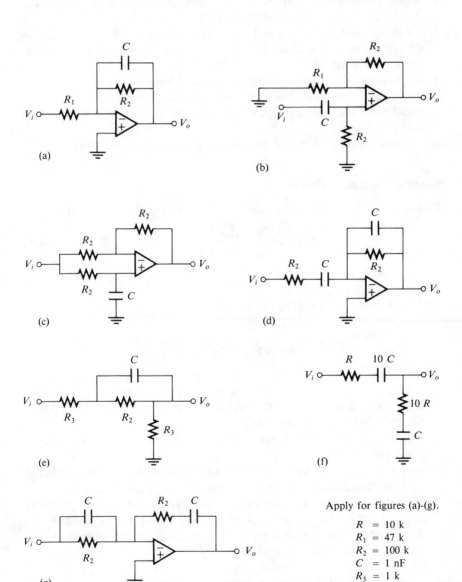

(a)

(b)

(c)

(d)

(e)

(f)

(g)

Apply for figures (a)-(g).

$R$ = 10 k
$R_1$ = 47 k
$R_2$ = 100 k
$C$ = 1 nF
$R_3$ = 1 k

FIGURE A.3. Networks for Lab 1

## Lab 2  Multiple Feedback Low-Pass Filter

### Objectives

1. To draw the frequency response curve for a second-order low-pass filter with a pass-band gain of $A_0 = -2$, a damping factor of $z = 0.707$, and a natural frequency of $\omega_n = 5000$ rad/s.
2. To design and build a second-order low-pass filter with $A_0 = -2$, $z = 0.707$, and $\omega_n = 5000$ rad/s, and to take measurements to draw the frequency response curve.
3. To compare the calculated and measured response curves.
4. To calculate and draw the step response of the filter.
5. To observe the step response on the oscilloscope and to draw its actual step response.
6. To compare the calculated and measured step response of the filter.

### Specifications and Directions

1. The transfer function of a second-order low-pass filter is given by:

$$A(s) = \frac{A_0 \omega_n^2}{s^2 + 2z\omega_n s + \omega_n^2} \tag{A.1}$$

   where $A_0$ is the pass-band gain, $z$ is the damping factor, and $\omega_n$ is the natural frequency.

   The magnitude $M(\omega)$ is given by:

$$M(\omega) = \frac{A_0 \omega_n^2}{\sqrt{(\omega^4 - 2(1 - 2z^2)\omega_n^2\omega^2 + \omega_n^4)}} \tag{A.2}$$

   where $A_0 = -2$, $z = 0.707$, and $\omega_n = 5000$ rad/s. Calculate the magnitude $M(\omega)$ for the following values of $\omega$ (rad/s): 50, 100, 200, 500, 1000, 2000, 3000, 4000, 4500, 5000, 5500, 6000, 7000, 10,000, 20,000, 50,000, 100,000, 200,000, and 500,000.

   Draw the magnitude response curve ($M(\omega)$ versus $\omega$) on semilog graph paper.
2. Design a multiple feedback low-pass filter with $A_0 = -2$, $z = 0.707$, and $\omega_n = 5000$ rad/s, and breadboard the circuit. Take measurements to draw the measured magnitude response curve on the same graph paper where the calculated response is drawn. Use 1-V sinusoidal waves as the inputs. Be sure to provide the proper conversion for the frequency indicated in Hz on the generators ($\omega = 2\pi f$).
3. Compare the two response curves.
4. Calculate and draw the step response of the filter.
5. Draw the output waveform, as observed on the oscilloscope, when the

network is excited by 1 V dc. Refer to item 10 in the introduction of Appendix A for general observation techniques.
6. Compare the calculated and measured step responses of the network.

### Questions

1. Derive equation (A.2).
2. Explain the significance of $z = 0.707$.
3. Using typical magnitude and time-domain response curves, describe the effect of changing $z$ to each of the following: 1, 2, 0, 0.4, $-0.4$.

## Lab 3    VCVS High-Pass Filter

### Objectives

1. To draw the frequency response curve for a second-order high-pass filter with a pass-band gain of $A_\infty = 2$, a damping factor of $z = 1$, and a natural frequency of $\omega_n = 5000$ rad/s.
2. To design and build a second-order high-pass filter with $A_\infty = 2$, $z = 1$, and $\omega_n = 5000$ rad/s, and to take measurements to draw the frequency response curve.
3. To compare the calculated and measured response curves.
4. To calculate and draw the step response of the filter.
5. To observe the step response on the oscilloscope and to draw its actual step response.
6. To compare the calculated and measured step response of the filter.

### Specifications and Directions

1. The transfer function of a second-order high-pass filter is given by:

$$A(s) = \frac{A_\infty s^2}{s^2 + 2z\omega_n s + \omega_n^2} \tag{A.3}$$

where $A_\infty$ is the pass-band gain, $z$ is the damping factor, and $\omega_n$ is the natural frequency.

The magnitude $M(\omega)$ is given by:

$$M(\omega) = \frac{A_\infty \omega^2}{\sqrt{(\omega^4 - 2(1 - 2z^2)\omega_n^2\omega^2 + \omega_n^4)}} \tag{A.4}$$

where $A_\infty = 2$, $z = 1$, and $\omega_n = 5000$ rad/s. Calculate the magnitude $M(\omega)$ for the following values of $\omega$ (rad/s): 50, 100, 200, 500, 1000, 2000, 3000, 4000, 4500, 5000, 5500, 6000, 7000, 10,000, 20,000, 50,000, 100,000, 200,000, and 500,000.

Draw the magnitude response curve ($M(\omega)$ versus $\omega$) on semilog graph paper.
2. Design a VCVS high-pass filter with $A_\infty = 2$, $z = 1$, and $\omega_n = 5000$ rad/s, and breadboard the circuit. Take measurements to draw the magnitude response curve on the same graph paper where the calculated response is drawn. Use 1-V sinusoidal waves as the inputs. Be sure to provide the proper conversion for the frequency indicated in Hz on the generators ($\omega = 2\pi f$).
3. Compare the two response curves.
4. Calculate and draw the step response of the filter.
5. Draw the output waveform, as observed on the oscilloscope, when the

network is excited by 1 V dc. Refer to item 10 in the introduction of Appendix A for general observation techniques.
6. Compare the calculated and measured step responses of the network.

## Questions

1. Derive equation (A.4).
2. Using typical magnitude and time-domain response curves, describe the effect of changing $z$ to each of the following: 0.707, 2, 0, 0.4, and $-0.4$.

## Lab 4   Multiple Feedback Band-Pass Filter

### Objectives

1. To draw the frequency response curve for a second-order band-pass filter with a pass-band gain of $A = -2$, a damping factor of $z = 0.1$, and a natural frequency of $\omega_n = 5000$ rad/s.
2. To design and build a second-order band-pass filter with $A = -2$, $z = 0.1$, and $\omega_n = 5000$ rad/s, and to take measurements to draw the frequency response curve.
3. To compare the calculated and measured response curves.

### Specifications and Directions

1. The transfer function of a second-order band-pass filter is given by:

$$A(s) = \frac{2zA\omega_n s}{s^2 + 2z\omega_n s + \omega_n^2} \tag{A.5}$$

where $A$ is the pass-band gain, $z$ is the damping factor, and $\omega_n$ is the natural frequency. The quality factor $Q$ is given by $Q = 1/2z$, and the bandwidth $B = \omega_n/Q = 2z\omega_n$.

The magnitude $M(\omega)$ is given by:

$$M(\omega) = \frac{2zA\omega_n \omega}{(\omega^4 - 2(1 - 2z^2)\omega_n^2\omega^2 + \omega_n^4)^{0.5}} \tag{A.6}$$

where $A = -2$, $z = 0.1$, and $\omega_n = 5000$ rad/s. Calculate the magnitude $M(\omega)$ for the following values of $\omega$ (rad/s): 50, 100, 200, 500, 1000, 2000, 3000, 4000, 45000, 5000, 5500, 6000, 7000, 10,000, 20,000, 50,000, 100,000, 200,000, and 500,000.

Draw the magnitude response curve ($M(\omega)$ versus $\omega$) on semilog graph paper.
2. Design a multiple feedback band-pass filter with $A = -2$, $z = 0.1$, and $\omega_n = 5000$ rad/s, and breadboard the circuit. Take measurements to draw the magnitude response curve on the same graph paper where the calculated response is drawn. Use 1-V sinusoidal waves as the inputs. Be sure to provide the proper conversion for the frequency indicated in Hz on the generators ($\omega = 2\pi f$).
3. Compare the two response curves.

### Questions

1. Derive equation (A.6).
2. Using typical magnitude response curves, describe the effect of changing $z$ to each of the following: 0.5, 0.1, and 0.05.

# Lab 5   Undamped Second-Order System — An Oscillator

## Objectives

1. To analyze the output of a second-order system with a zero damping factor.
2. To design and build an oscillatory system, and then measure the impulse response.
3. To compare the measured and calculated responses of the oscillatory system.

## Specifications and Directions

1. The transfer function of a second-order oscillatory system is given by:

$$A(s) = \frac{A_0 \omega_n^2}{s^2 + \omega_n^2} \tag{A.7}$$

The gain $A_0$ is left as a free parameter.
2. Calculate the output $V_o(t)$ when driven by:
   (a) a unit step input (1 V dc)
   (b) an impulse
   Draw the time-domain response curves ($V_o(t)$ versus $t$) for both cases.
3. For a VCVS low-pass filter:

$$A_0 = K = 1 + \frac{R_f}{R_i} \tag{A.8}$$

$$Y_1 = Y_2 = \frac{1}{R} \tag{A.9}$$

$$Y_3 = Y_4 = sC \tag{A.10}$$

The transfer function now becomes:

$$A(s) = \frac{K/(RC)^2}{s^2 + s(3 - K)/RC + 1/(RC)^2} \tag{A.11}$$

$$\omega_n = \frac{1}{RC} \tag{A.12}$$

$$2z\omega_n = (3 - K)/RC \tag{A.13}$$

Find the value of $K$ to make $z = 0$, so that the network will oscillate. Let $R_i = 10$ k$\Omega$. For $R_f$, use a 10-k$\Omega$ resistor in series with a 20-k$\Omega$ pot, connected as an adjustable resistor. Design the oscillator to oscillate at 5000 rad/s, such that

$$A(s) = \frac{25,000,000 A_0}{s^2 + 25,000,000}$$

Breadboard the network. Adjust the potentiometer to obtain the required $K$ for oscillation. Ground the input. The output should be an undistorted sine wave. The pot may have to be adjusted slightly. Observe the effect of varying the pot resistance in both directions. In addition, measure the output when the input is 1 V dc. The grounded input can be assumed to be an impulse input, not a unit impulse.

4. Compare the calculated and measured values of $V_o(t)$.

### Questions

1. For the transfer function of the oscillator given, calculate the two poles, the frequency of oscillation, and $A_0$.

$$A(s) = \frac{75,000,000}{s^2 + 25,000,000}$$

2. Calculate the time-domain response of the oscillator of question 1, when it is driven by:
   (a) sin 5000$t$
   (b) sin 4000$t$
3. Design a state variable network so that one resistor can be varied to change the damping factor $z$. Assume $\omega_n = 1$, such that

   (a) $A(s) = \dfrac{A_0}{s^2 + 2zs + 1}$

   (b) $A(s) = \dfrac{As^2}{s^2 + 2zs + 1}$

   (c) $A(s) = \dfrac{2Azs}{s^2 + 2zs + 1}$

   (d) $A(s) = \dfrac{A(s^2 + 1)}{s^2 + 2zs + 1}$

# Lab 6   Frequency-Domain Analysis of a Second-Order System

## Objectives

1. To analyze a second-order system in the frequency domain.
2. To design and build a second-order low-pass filter, and to measure its voltage gain.
3. To compare the calculated and measured results.

## Specifications and Directions

1. The transfer function of a second-order low-pass filter is given by:

$$A(s) = \frac{A_0 \omega_n^2}{s^2 + 2z\omega_n s + \omega_n^2} \tag{A.14}$$

where $A_0$ is the pass-band gain, $z$ is the damping factor, and $\omega_n$ is the natural frequency.

The magnitude $M(\omega)$ is given by:

$$M(\omega) = \frac{A_0 \omega_n^2}{\sqrt{(\omega^4 - 2(1 - 2z^2)\omega_n^2\omega^2 + \omega_n^4}} \tag{A.15}$$

where $A_0 = 4$, $z = 0.2$, and $\omega_n = 5000$ rad/s. Calculate the magnitude $M(\omega)$ for the following values of $\omega$ (rad/s): 50, 100, 200, 500, 1000, 2000, 3000, 4000, 4100, 4200, 4300, 4400, 4500, 5000, 5500, 6000, 7000, 10,000, 20,000, 50,000, 100,000, 200,000, and 500,000.

Draw the magnitude response curve ($M(\omega)$ versus $\omega$) on semilog graph paper (see Figure A.4).

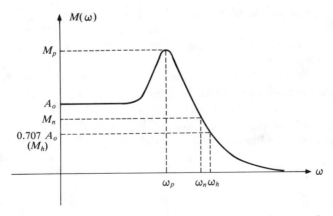

FIGURE A.4. Typical frequency response curve of a second-order low-pass filter when $z < 0.707$

From the graph of the magnitude response, find the following:

$\omega_p$    Peak frequency, where the gain is maximum.

$\omega_h$    Half-power frequency, where the gain is 0.707 of the pass-band gain.

$M_p$    The gain at the peak frequency.

$M_n$    The gain at natural frequency.

See section 8.4 of Chapter 8, and section 9.4 of Chapter 9.

Check the validity of the following equations (calculate and compare):

$$M_p = A_0/2z \sqrt{1 - z^2} \tag{A.16}$$

$$\omega_p = \omega_n \sqrt{(1 - 2z^2)} \tag{A.17}$$

$$M_h = 0.707 A_0 \tag{A.18}$$

$$\omega_h = \omega_n \sqrt{1 - 2z^2 + \sqrt{(2 - 4z^2 + 4z^4)}} \tag{A.19}$$

$$M_n = 0.5 A_0/z \tag{A.20}$$

2. Design a state variable low-pass filter with $A_0 = 4$, $z = 0.2$, and $\omega_n = 5000$ rad/s, and breadboard the circuit. Take measurements to draw the magnitude response curve on the same graph paper where the calculated response is drawn. Use 1-V sinusoidal waves as the inputs. Be sure to provide the proper conversion for the frequency indicated in Hz on the generators ($\omega = 2\pi f$). [Do not dismantle the circuit, it will be used again in Lab 8.]

3. Compare the two response curves. Compare the key frequencies such as $\omega_n$, $\omega_p$, and $\omega_h$, and the magnitudes such as $M_n$, $M_p$, and $M_h$. A typical frequency response curve is shown in Figure A.4.

## Questions

1. For an underdamped high-pass filter, derive equations for
   (a) $M_p$        (b) $\omega_p$        (c) $M_n$        (d) $\omega_h$

2. For an underdamped high-pass filter, find the value of $z$ to satisfy the condition $\omega_n = \omega_h$.

3. For a normalized 3-dB Chebyshave filter (fourth order), the following damping factors and natural frequencies are given.

    First stage:      $z = 0.464471$       $\omega_n = 0.442696$

    Second stage:   $z = 0.089624$       $\omega_n = 0.950309$

Assume $A_0 = 1$. Find the gain at 1 rad/s.

## Lab 7   Time-Domain Analysis of a Second-Order System

### Objectives

1. To calculate various characteristic quantities of the time-domain response of a second-order system excited by a unit step input.
2. To measure characteristic quantities of the time-domain response of a second-order system driven by a unit step input.
3. To compare the calculated and measured responses.

### Specifications and Directions

1. The transfer function of a second-order low-pass filter is given by:

$$A(s) = \frac{V_o(s)}{V_i(s)} = \frac{A_0 \omega_n^2}{s^2 + 2z\omega_n s + \omega_n^2} \qquad (A.21)$$

where $A_0$ is the pass-band gain, $z$ is the damping factor, and $\omega_n$ is the natural frequency.

For $A_0 = 4$, $\omega_n = 5000$ rad/s, and $z = 0.2$, calculate the following:

$$\omega_h = \omega_n [1 - 2z^2 + (2 - 4z^2 + 4z^4)^{0.5}]^{0.5} \qquad (A.22)$$

$$t_r = 2.2/\omega_n \qquad (A.23)$$

For further reference see sections 4.10, 8.4, and 9.4.

$$a = \sqrt{1 - z^2} \qquad (A.24)$$

$$\omega_d = a\omega_n \qquad (A.25)$$

$$T_d = \frac{2\pi}{\omega_d} \qquad (A.26)$$

$$T_s = \frac{3}{z\omega_n} \qquad (A.27)$$

$$MO = A_0 e^{-z\pi/a} \qquad (A.28)$$

$$TMO = 0.5 T_d \qquad (A.29)$$

where  $\omega_h$    is the half-power frequency where the gain is 0.707 of the pass-band gain

$t_r$    is the rise time; that is, the time required for the step response to go from 10% to 90% of the steady-state value

$\omega_d$    is the frequency of damped oscillations

$T_d$    is the period of damped oscillations

$T_s$    is the settling time; that is, the time required for the output to settle down to 5% band of the steady-state value.

MO     is the maximum overshoot; that is, the magnitude of the
       first peak above the steady-state value of the output
TMO    is the time to reach maximum overshoot.

Calculate $\omega_d$, $T_d$, $T_s$, MO, TMO, $\omega_h$, and $t_r$ for the second-order
system of equation (A.21). In addition, find an expression for $V_o(t)$ for
a unit step input.

$$V_o(t) = A_0 \left( 1 - \frac{e^{-z\omega_n t}}{a} \sin\left(\omega_d t + \phi\right)\right)$$

where    $\phi = \arctan(a/z)$
2. For the designed circuit of Lab 7, apply a low-frequency (about 50 Hz)
   square wave as the input. The period of the square wave applied must be
   at least two times larger than the settling time. *The square wave is considered a step input (dc) that is being switched on and off.* Due to the
   repeated operation, the transient can be observed on the oscilloscope.
3. Measure $\omega_d$, $T_d$, $T_s$, MO, TMO, and $t_r$. Compare the calculated and
   measured values. (See Figure A.5.)

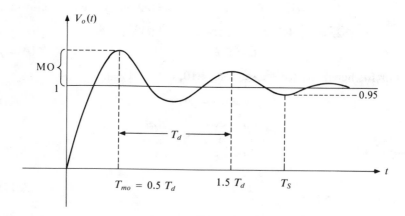

FIGURE A.5. Typical time-domain response curve

## Questions

1. For the following second-order system find the following:
   (a) maximum overshoot
   (b) settling time
   (c) phase shift
   (d) number of oscillations during settling time, and
   (e) the time it takes to reach maximum overshoot when excited by a unit
       step input.

$$A(s) = \frac{1,000,000}{s^2 + 100s + 1,000,000}$$

2. Prove that $z = \cos \phi$, where

$$\phi = \arctan \frac{\sqrt{1 - z^2}}{z}$$

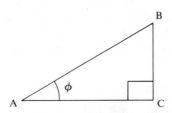

3. For the following second-order systems, find $\omega_n$, $z$, and the two poles.

(a) $A(s) = \dfrac{100}{s^2 + 5s + 100}$      (b) $A(s) = \dfrac{100}{s^2 + 10s + 100}$

(c) $A(s) = \dfrac{100}{s^2 + 14(14s) + 100}$      (d) $A(s) = \dfrac{100}{s^2 + 20s + 100}$

(e) $A(s) = \dfrac{100}{s^2 + 100}$      (f) $A(s) = \dfrac{100}{s^2 + 50s + 100}$

(g) $A(s) = \dfrac{100}{s^2 - 10s + 100}$      (h) $A(s) = \dfrac{100}{s^2 + 20s + 100}$

(i) $A(s) = \dfrac{100}{s^2 - 50s + 100}$      (j) $A(s) = \dfrac{100}{s^2 - 14(141s) + 100}$

4. Comment on the damping and stability of the systems represented by each of the transfer functions of question 3.

5. Draw the approximate step response of each of the systems represented by the transfer functions of question 3, without making any numerical calculations.

## Lab 8 Transfer Function Synthesis

### Objectives

1. To obtain the transfer function, in P-Z form, from the magnitude Bode plot (straight-line approximation) of the given desired response.
2. To design and build a network to produce the desired response.
3. To compare the measured and given responses.

### Specifications and Directions

Two networks are to be designed and evaluated in this lab.

1. (a) Draw the approximate magnitude Bode plot of Figure A.6(a) to scale on semilog graph paper.
   (b) Obtain the required transfer function from the desired magnitude Bode plot given in Figure A.6(a), in P-Z form.
   (c) Draw the pole-zero map and split the transfer function into $Z_f$ and $Z_i$, such that $Z_f/Z_i$ will provide the required transfer function.

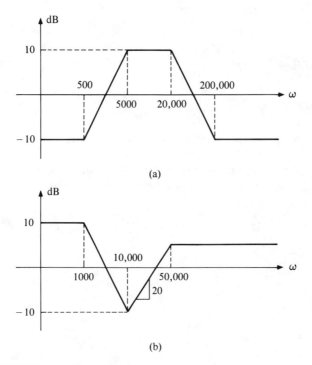

(a)

(b)

FIGURE A.6. (a) and (b) Desired magnitude response curve for the required networks

   (d) Synthesize both $Z_f$ and $Z_i$ in Cauer forms.

   (e) Scale for impedance and breadboard the inverting amplifier with the synthesized $Z_f$ and $Z_i$.

   (f) Take measurements to draw the frequency response curve (dB versus $\omega$) on the same graph of 1(a).

   (g) Compare the two graphs.

2. (a) Same as 1(a) except for Figure A.6(b)

   (b) Same as 1(b) except for Figure A.6(a)

   (c) Same as 1(c)

   (d) Same as 1(d) except synthesize in Foster forms.

   (e) Same as 1(e)

   (f) Same as 1(f)

   (g) Same as 1(g)

## Lab 9   Notch Filter

### Objectives

To design, build and investigate an inductor-less notch filter employing a gyrator to simulate the coil.

### Specifications and Directions

The network of Figure A.7(a) is a differential amplifier which rejects its common mode input signal. This is because the common mode signal experiences two cumulative gains of $-1$ (inverting) and $+1$ (noninverting). Suppose a capacitor and an inductor were added as shown in Figure A.7(b). At the resonance frequency, the inductive reactance negates the capacitive reactance and the output would be that of Figure A.7(a), namely, zero. At all other frequencies, the noninverting gain will not be the same as the inverting gain and, hence, there will be an output signal of varying magnitudes. The resistance and the inductance can be considered a coil. The coil can be simulated by the gyrator of Figure A.7(c). The network is shown in Figure A.7(d). The transfer function $A(s)$ of the network of Figure A.7(b) is given by:

$$A(s) = \frac{\left(s^2 + \dfrac{1}{LC_1}\right)}{s^2 + \dfrac{2R}{L}s + \dfrac{1}{LC_1}} \tag{A.30}$$

The transfer function of a second-order band-rejection filter is given by equation (8.5) of Chapter 8. Comparing equation (A.30) and equation (8.5):

$$A(s) = \frac{A(s^2 + \omega_n^2)}{s^2 + 2z\omega_n s + \omega_n^2} \tag{8.5}$$

$$\omega_n^2 = \frac{1}{LC_1} \tag{A.31}$$

$$2z\omega_n = \frac{2R}{L} = B \text{ (bandwidth)} \tag{A.32}$$

For the gyrator:

$$L = 0.25R^2C_2$$

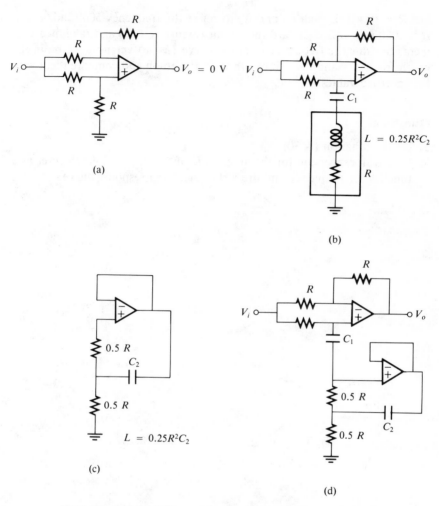

FIGURE A.7. (a) Differential amp. (b) Notch filter. (c) Gyrator. (d) Notch filter with a simulated coil.

Reject frequency:

$$\omega_n = \frac{2}{R(C_1 C_2)^{0.5}} \qquad (A.33)$$

Bandwidth:

$$B = \frac{8}{RC_2} \qquad (A.34)$$

Let $R = 10 \text{ k}\Omega$. Design $C_1$ and $C_2$ to reject the frequency 5000 rad/s, and $B = 1000$ rad/s. Breadboard the circuit (Figure A.7(d)) and take measurements to draw the frequency response curve ($M(\omega)$ versus $\omega$). Obtain the notch frequency and the bandwidth from the graph and compare them with the specified values.

## Questions

1. Derive equation (A.30).
2. Derive an expression for the magnitude of the designed notch filter as a function of frequency and draw the calculated response curve.

# Program Listings

In this appendix you will find several program listings of computer simulations for various forms of analysis discussed in this text. These listings provide the program simulations for inverse Laplace transformation, time-domain analysis, frequency-domain analysis, and multiple feedback and VCVS filter designs. You may find these programs helpful in the design process. These programs are written in Applesoft BASIC.

## Inverse Laplace Transformation

```
1   HOME
2   PRINT " INVERSE LAPLACE TRANSFORMATION": PRINT
5   PRINT : PRINT : PRINT :
6   PRINT "            CS + D        "
7   PRINT "   F(S) = ----------------"
8   PRINT "              2           "
9   PRINT "            S  + AS + B   "
15  PRINT : PRINT : PRINT
20  PRINT "INPUT A,B,C,D IN THE GIVEN ORDER"
30  PRINT : INPUT A,B,C,D: PRINT : PRINT : PRINT
31  IF A < 0 THEN 240
32  IF B < 0 THEN 240
40 WN = B ^ .5:Z = A / (2 * WN)
45  IF Z = 0 THEN 252
50  IF Z < 1 THEN 100
52  IF Z > 1 THEN 350
53  IF Z = 1 THEN 400
100  PRINT "UNDER DAMPED SYSTEM."

110 A = (1 - Z ^ 2) ^ .5:WD = A * WN
120 X = Z * WN:Y = D - C * X
130 AS = Y / WD:AC = C
135  PRINT
140  PRINT "THE INVERSE LAPLACE OF F(S) IS:"
150 A = (AS ^ 2 + AC ^ 2) ^ .5
155  IF AS = 0 THEN AS = .0000001
```

```
160 B = AC / AS
165  PRINT
166 X = X * 1000 + .5:X =  INT (X) / 1000
167 A = A * 1000 + .5:A =  INT (A) / 1000
168 WD = WD * 1000 + .5:WD =  INT (WD) / 1000
169 B = B * 1000 + .5:B =  INT (B) / 1000
170 U = ATN (B)

171 Z = Z * 1000 + .5:Z =  INT (Z) / 1000
175  PRINT
180  PRINT : PRINT A;"EXP(-";X;"T)";"SIN(";WD;"T+";U;")"
185  PRINT
186 WN = WN * 1000 + .5:WN =  INT (WN) / 1000
190  PRINT "WN=";WN;"RAD/SEC","Z=";Z
195  PRINT
197 TS = 3 / (Z * WN)
198 TS = TS * 1000 + .5:TS =  INT (TS) / 1000
200  PRINT "WD=";WD;"RAD/SEC","TS=";TS;"SEC"
205  PRINT
210 TD = 44 / (7 * WN)
220  PRINT "TD=";TD;"SEC": PRINT

230  PRINT
236  GOTO 500
240  PRINT
245  PRINT "THE SYSTEM IS UNSTABLE."
250  GOTO 500
252  PRINT "THE SYSTEM IS OSCILLATORY."
255  PRINT
260 A = (C ^ 2 + (D / WN) ^ 2) ^ .5:F = C * WN / D
265  PRINT
270  PRINT "THE INVERSE LAPLACE OF F(S) IS:"
275 A =  INT (1000 * A + .5) / 1000: PRINT
285 F =  INT (1000 * F + .5) / 1000
286 H =  ATN (F)
290  PRINT A;"SIN(";WN;"T+";H;")": PRINT
300  GOTO 500
350 K = - A / 2:L = ((A ^ 2) / 4 - B) ^ .5
360 R1 = K + L:R2 = K - L
361 Q = (C * R1 + D) / (R1 - R2)
362 R = (C * R2 + D) / (R2 - R1)
363  PRINT
364  PRINT "THE SYSTEM IS OVERDAMPED."
365 R =  INT (1000 * R + .5) / 1000: PRINT
```

```
366 Q =  INT (1000 * Q + .5) / 1000
367 R1 =  INT (1000 * R1 + .5) / 1000
368 R2 =  INT (1000 * R2 + .5) / 1000
370  PRINT "F(S) CAN BE REARRANGED AS:"
375  PRINT
380  PRINT R;"/(S+"; - R2;")"+";Q;"/(S+"; - R1;")"
381  PRINT : PRINT : PRINT
390  PRINT "THE INVERSE LAPLACE OF F(S) IS:"
391  PRINT
395  PRINT Q;"EXP(";R1;"T)";" +";R;"EXP(";R2;"T)"
398  GOTO 500
400  PRINT
410  PRINT "SYSTEM IS CRITICALLY DAMPED."
415  PRINT
425  PRINT "THE INVERSE LAPLACE OF F(S) IS:"
430  PRINT
435 K = Z * WN:K =  INT (1000 * K + .5) / 1000
440 L = D - C * Z * WN:L =  INT (1000 * L + .5) / 1000
450  PRINT "EXP(-";K;"T)";" (";C;"+";L;"T)"
500  PRINT
510  PRINT "DO YOU WANT TO TRY AGAIN?"
515  INPUT Y$
520  IF Y$ = "Y" THEN 5
521  IF Y$ = "YES" THEN 5
522  IF Y$ = "N" THEN 550
523  IF Y$ = "NO" THEN 550
525  PRINT
530  PRINT "PLEASE!!! PRESS Y FOR YES N FOR NO"
535  GOTO 510
550  END
```

## Time-Domain Analysis

```
10  HOME
20  PRINT "     TIME DOMAIN ANALYSIS": PRINT
30  PRINT "            OF          ": PRINT
40  PRINT "    A SECOND ORDER SYSTEM": PRINT
80  VTAB 22: PRINT "PRESS ANY KEY TO CONTINUE": GET V$
200  HOME
210  PRINT "            2          "
211  PRINT "        A0.WN          "
212  PRINT "  A(S) = ------------   "
213  PRINT "          2        2   "
```

```
214  PRINT "           S +2Z.WN.S+WN       "
220  PRINT : PRINT : PRINT "   WHERE": PRINT
230  PRINT "          WN IS THE NATURAL FREQ.": PRINT
240  PRINT "           Z IS THE DAMPING FACTOR.": PRINT
250  PRINT "          AO IS THE GAIN CONSTANT": PRINT
255  PRINT "THE SYSTEM IS DRIVEN BY A UNIT STEP": PRINT
260  INPUT "NATURAL FREQ.WN:";WN: PRINT
270  INPUT "DAMPING RATIO Z:";Z: PRINT

280  INPUT "GAIN CONSTANT AO:";AO: PRINT
290  IF Z < 0 THEN 600
300  IF Z = 0 THEN 800
310  IF Z = 1 THEN 1000
320  IF Z > 1 THEN 1200
330  PRINT "THE SYSTEM IS UNDER DAMPED": PRINT
331  PRINT
335  F = 2 - 4 * Z ^ 2 + 4 * Z ^ 4:F = F ^ .5:F = 1 - 2 * Z ^
     2 + F
340  F = F ^ .5:WH = WN * F
350  PRINT "THE HALF POWER FREQ.WH:";WH: PRINT
360  TR = 2.2 / WH
370  PRINT "THE RISE TIME TR:";TR;"SEC."
371  PRINT
380  A = (1 - Z ^ 2) ^ .5
390  WD = A * WN
400  PRINT : PRINT "THE FREQUENCY OF DAMPED OSCILLATIONS,WD:";WD
     ;" RAD/SEC": PRINT
401  PRINT
410  TD = 2 * 3.1416 / WD
420  PRINT : PRINT "THE PERIOD OF DAMPED OSC.";TD;"SEC": PRINT

421  PRINT
430  TS = 3 / (Z * WN)
435  PRINT "PRESS ANY KEY TO CONT.": GET V$: PRINT : PRINT
440  PRINT "SETTLING TIME, THE TIME IT TAKES FOR THE OUTPUT TO
     SETTLE DOWN TO 5% BAND OF THE STEADY STATE LEVEL,TS:";TS;
     " SEC.": PRINT
441  PRINT
450  K = - 3.1416 * Z / A
460  MO = AO *  EXP (K)
470  PRINT "THE MAXIMUM OVER SHOOT,MO:";MO: PRINT
471  PRINT
480  TMO = .5 * TD
```

```
490  PRINT "THE TIME TO REACH MAXIMUM OVER SHOOT,TMO:";TMO;
       " SEC.": PRINT
495  PRINT "PRESS ANY KEY TO CONT.": GET B$: PRINT
496  HOME
500  PRINT "THE OUTPUT IS GIVEN BY:": PRINT
575  X = Z * WN:K = 1 / A:P = A / Z
580  B =  ATN (P)
585  PRINT "VO=";AO;"-";AO * K;"EXP(-";X;"T) SIN(";WD;"T+";B;")"
       : PRINT
590  GOTO 2000
600  PRINT "THE SYSTEM IS UNSTABLE": PRINT
790  GOTO 2000
800  PRINT "THE SYSTEM IS OSCILLATORY": PRINT
810  A = AO:B =  - AO
820  PRINT : PRINT "VO(S)=A/S +B*S/(S^2+WN^2)": PRINT
830  PRINT "WHERE": PRINT
840  PRINT "        A=";AO
841  PRINT
850  PRINT "        B=";  - AO: PRINT


860  PRINT "VO(T)=";AO;"(1-COS";WN;"T)": PRINT
990  GOTO 2000
1000  PRINT "THE SYSTEM IS CRITICALLY DAMPED": PRINT
1010 A = WN
1015  PRINT "C(S)=K1/S +K2/(S+A) +K3/(S+A)^2": PRINT
1020  PRINT "WHERE": PRINT
1030  PRINT "        A=WN": PRINT
1040  PRINT "        K1=AO": PRINT


1050  PRINT "        K2=-AO": PRINT


1060  PRINT "        K3=-AO*WN": PRINT


1070 KI = AO:K2 =  - AO:K3 = K2 * WN
1080  PRINT "C(T)=";AO;"-";AO;"EXP(";A;"T)(1+T)": PRINT
1190  GOTO 2000
1200  PRINT "THE SYSTEM IS OVER DAMPED": PRINT
1210 P = Z ^ 2 - 1:P = P ^ .5:P =  - Z + P:A = WN * P:A =   - A

1220 P = Z ^ 2 - 1:P = P ^ .5:P =  - Z - P:B = WN * P:B =   - B

1230  PRINT "VO(S)= K1/S +K2/(S+A) +K3/(S+B)": PRINT
1240 P = B - A:P =  - P:P = A * P:K2 = AO * WN ^ 2 / P
```

```
1250 H = A0 * WN ^ 2:P = B ^ 2 - A * B:K3 = H / P
1255 K1 = A0 * WN * WN / (A * B)
1260  PRINT "WHERE": PRINT
1270  PRINT "        A=";A
1280  PRINT : PRINT "        B=";B

1290  PRINT : PRINT "        K1=";K1
1300  PRINT : PRINT "        K2=";K2
1310  PRINT : PRINT "        K3=";K3
1315  PRINT
1320  PRINT "VO(T)=";K1;"+";K2;"EXP(-";A;"T)";"+";K3"EXP(-";B;
        "T)": PRINT
2000  PRINT
2010  PRINT "WANT ANOTHER TRY?": GET P$: PRINT
2020  IF P$ = "Y" THEN 10
```

## Frequency-Domain Analysis

```
5   HOME
10  PRINT " FREQUENCY DOMAIN ANALYSIS": PRINT
20  PRINT "              OF            ": PRINT
30  PRINT "  A SECOND ORDER SYSTEM    ": PRINT
60  VTAB 22: PRINT "PRESS ANY KEY TO CONTINUE,E TO EXIT": GET A$
70  IF A$ = "E" THEN 1000
75  HOME
80  PRINT "THE TRANSFER FUNCTION OF A SECOND ORDER SYSTEM (LOW
      PASS FILTER) IS GIVEN BY:"

85  PRINT : PRINT
86  PRINT "              2          "
87  PRINT "         A0.WN          "
88  PRINT "  A(S) = --------------  "
89  PRINT "         2          2   "
90  PRINT "        S +2Z.WN.S + WN    ": PRINT : PRINT : PRINT

100  PRINT "A0 ---> PASS BAND GAIN": PRINT
110  PRINT "WN -----> NATURAL FREQ.": PRINT
120  PRINT "Z ---> DAMPING FACTOR:ALPHA =2Z": PRINT
130  PRINT "THE MAGNITUDE OF A(S) IS GIVEN BY:": PRINT
140  PRINT "M(W)=A0*WN^2/(W^4+2*WN^2*W^2(Z^2-1))^.5": PRINT
145  PRINT "PRESS ANY KEY TO CONTINUE": GET A$: HOME
150  INPUT "ENTER WN:";WC: PRINT

160  INPUT "ENTER DAMPING FACTOR:";Z: PRINT
```

```
170  INPUT "ENTER PASSBAND GAIN:";AO: PRINT
179  HOME
180  INPUT "ENTER ANY FREQUENCY W:";W
185  X = W / WC:X = X ^ 2:Y = 1 - X:Y = Y ^ 2
190  X = X * 4 * Z ^ 2:X = X + Y:X = X ^ .5
195  X = AO / X: PRINT
200  PRINT "FREQ.:";W,"M(W):";X: PRINT


210  VTAB 22: PRINT "PRESS ANY KEY FOR ANOTHER TRY, E TO
       CONTINUE": GET B$
220  IF B$ = "E" THEN 228
225  GOTO 179
228  HOME
229  IF Z > 0.707 THEN 1000
230  WP = WC * (1 - 2 * Z ^ 2) ^ .5
240  WH = WC * (1 - 2 * Z ^ 2 + (2 - 4 * Z ^ 2 + 4 * Z ^ 4) ^ .5)
       ^ .5
250  MC = .5 * AO / Z
260  MP = AO / (2 * Z * (1 - Z ^ 2) ^ .5)
270  MH = AO / 2 ^ .5
280  PRINT "THE PEAK FREQUENCY WP WHERE THE MAGNITUDE IS MAX:";
       WP: PRINT
290  PRINT "THE HALF POWER FREQUENCY WH WHERE THE GAIN HAS
       DROPPED 3DB BELOW THE PASSBAND GAIN IS:";WH: PRINT
300  PRINT "THE MAGNITUDE OF GAIN AT PEAK FREQUENCY,MP:";MP:
       PRINT


310  PRINT "THE MAGNITUDE OF GAIN AT THE NATURAL FREQUENCY,MN:";
       MC: PRINT
320  PRINT "THE MAGNITUDE OF GAIN AT HALF POWER FREQUENCY, MH:";
       MH: PRINT
1000 END
```

## Multiple Feedback and VCVS Filter Design

```
10   HOME
15   PRINT " 1. MULTIPLE FEEDBACK FILTERS.": PRINT
20   PRINT " 2. V.C.V.S FILTERS.": PRINT
25   PRINT : PRINT : PRINT : PRINT : PRINT "SELECT 1 OR 2 ": GET
       A$: PRINT : PRINT
30   IF A$ = "1" GOTO 50
35   IF A$ = "2" GOTO 80
40   GOTO 25
```

```
50   HOME : PRINT " 1. LOWPASS FILTER ": PRINT
55   PRINT " 2. HIGHPASS FILTER ": PRINT
60   PRINT " 3. BANDPASS FILTER ": PRINT
65   PRINT : PRINT : PRINT : PRINT "SELECT 1, 2 OR 3.": GET B$:
        PRINT : PRINT
70   IF B$ = "1" THEN 100
71   IF B$ = "2" THEN 300
72   IF B$ = "3" THEN 500
75   GOTO 65
80   HOME : PRINT "1. LOWPASS FILTER": PRINT
85   PRINT "2. HIGHPASS FILTER": PRINT

90   PRINT "3. BANDPASS FILTER": PRINT

92   PRINT : PRINT : PRINT : PRINT "SELECT 1, 2, OR 3.": GET C$:
        PRINT
94   IF C$ = "1" THEN 700
95   IF C$ = "2" THEN 900
96   IF C$ = "3" THEN 1100
97   GOTO 92


100  HOME : PRINT "   MULTIPLE FEEDBACK LOWPASS FILTER": PRINT :
        PRINT
110  INPUT "ENTER DAMPING FACTOR Z:";Z:A = 2 * Z: PRINT
115  PRINT :R1 = 1:R3 = 1:WN = 1
120  INPUT "ENTER PASSBAND GAIN AO:";AO: PRINT : PRINT
122  IF AO < 0 THEN AO =  - AO
125  R4 = AO * R1:Y1 = 1 / R1:Y3 = 1 / R3:Y4 = 1 / R4
130  YA = Y1 + Y3 + Y4:C2 = YA / A

135  C5 = 1 / (R3 * R4 * C2)
140  INPUT "ENTER NATURAL FREQ. IN RAD/SEC:";WN: PRINT : PRINT
145  PRINT "R1 = ";R1: PRINT
150  PRINT "R3 = ";R3: PRINT
155  PRINT "R4 = ";R4: PRINT
160  PRINT "C2 = ";C2 / WN: PRINT

165  PRINT "C5 = ";C5 / WN: PRINT

167  R1 = .001 * R1:R3 = .001 * R3:R4 = .001 * R4
168  C2 = 1000000 * C2 / WN:C5 = 1000000 * C5 / WN
170  INPUT "ENTER IMPEDANCE SCALE FACTOR:";KZ: PRINT : PRINT

175  PRINT "R1 = ";R1 * KZ;" K OHMS": PRINT
```

```
180   PRINT "R3 = ";R3 * KZ;" K OHMS": PRINT
185   PRINT "R4 = ";R4 * KZ;" K OHMS": PRINT
190   PRINT "C2 = ";C2 / KZ;" MICRO FARADS": PRINT
195   PRINT "C5 = ";C5 / KZ;" MICRO FARADS": PRINT
196 R1 = R1 * KZ:R3 = R3 * KZ:R4 = R4 * KZ:C2 = C2 / KZ:C5 = C5
      / KZ
200   INPUT "ARE THESE COMPONENTS SATISFACTORY ?";A$: PRINT
205   IF A$ = "N" THEN 170
210   END
300   HOME : PRINT "MULTIPLE FEEDBACK HIGHPASS FILTER": PRINT :
      PRINT
310 C4 = 1:C3 = 1:WN = 1
315   INPUT "ENTER PASSBAND GAIN :";B: PRINT : PRINT
316   IF B < 0 THEN B = - B
320   INPUT "ENTER DAMPING FACTOR Z:";Z: PRINT : PRINT
325 A = 2 * Z:C1 = B:R5 = (2 + B) / A:R2 = 1 / R5
330   INPUT "ENTER NATURAL FREQ. IN RAD/SEC:";WN: PRINT : PRINT

335   PRINT "R2 = ";R2: PRINT
340   PRINT "R5 = ";R5: PRINT
345   PRINT "C1 = ";C1 / WN: PRINT

350   PRINT "C3 = ";C3 / WN: PRINT

355   PRINT "C4 = ";C4 / WN: PRINT

357 C1 = C1 / WN:C3 = C3 / WN:C4 = C4 / WN
360   INPUT "ENTER IMPEDANCE SCALE FACTOR:";KZ: PRINT : PRINT
370   PRINT "R2 = ";.001 * R2 * KZ;" K OHMS": PRINT
375   PRINT "R5 = ";.001 * R5 * KZ;" K OHMS": PRINT
380   PRINT "C1 = ";1000000 * C1 / KZ;" MICRO FARADS": PRINT
385   PRINT "C3 = ";1000000 * C3 / KZ;" MICRO FARADS": PRINT
390   PRINT "C4 = ";1000000 * C4 / KZ;" MICRO FARADS": PRINT
395   PRINT "ARE THESE COMPONENTS SATISFACTORY ?": GET P$
396 R2 = R2 * KZ:R5 = R5 * KZ:C1 = C1 / KZ:C3 = C3 / KZ:C4 = C4
      / KZ
400   PRINT : IF P$ = "N" THEN 360

405   END
500   HOME : PRINT "MULTIPLE FEEDBACK BANDPASS FILTER": PRINT :
      PRINT
505   INPUT "ENTER BANDWIDTH IN RAD/SEC:";B: PRINT
510   INPUT "ENTER CENTER FREQ. IN RAD/SEC:";WN: PRINT
515 Q = WN / B:Z = 1 / (2 * Q)
520   INPUT "ENTER PASSBAND GAIN:";A: PRINT
```

```
525 X = 2 * Q ^ 2 - A
530  IF X > O THEN 545
535  PRINT "PASSBAND GAIN IS TOO LARGE": PRINT
540 A = O: GOTO 520
545 C3 = 1:C4 = 1:R1 = Q / A:R5 = 2 * Q
550 R2 = Q / (2 * Q ^ 2 - A)
560 C3 = C3 / WN:C4 = C4 / WN
565  PRINT "R1 = ";R1: PRINT
570  PRINT "R2 = ";R2: PRINT
575  PRINT "R5 = ";R5: PRINT
580  PRINT "C3 = ";C3: PRINT
585  PRINT "C4 = ";C4: PRINT
586 R1 = .001 * R1:R2 = .001 * R2:R5 = .001 * R5
588 C3 = 1000000 * C3:C4 = 1000000 * C4
590  INPUT "ENTER IMPEDANCE SCALE FACTOR:";KZ: PRINT
595 R1 = R1 * KZ:R2 = R2 * KZ:R5 = R5 * KZ
600 C3 = C3 / KZ:C4 = C4 / KZ
605  PRINT "R1 = ";R1;" K OHMS": PRINT

610  PRINT "R2 = ";R2;" K OHMS": PRINT

615  PRINT "R5 = ";R5;" K OHMS": PRINT

620  PRINT "C3 = ";C3;" MICRO FARADS": PRINT
625  PRINT "C4 = ";C4;" MICRO FARADS": PRINT
626  PRINT "ARE THESE COMPONENTS SATISFACTORY ?": GET H$
628  PRINT : IF H$ = "N" THEN 590


630  END
700  HOME : PRINT "      VCVS LOWPASS FILTER": PRINT : PRINT

705 C4 = 1:C3 = 1:WN = 1
710  INPUT "PASSBAND GAIN:";AO: PRINT

715  IF AO > 2 THEN 730
720  PRINT "PASSBAND GAIN IS TOO LOW. IT MUST BE GREATER THAN
       2": PRINT
725  GOTO 710
730  INPUT "ENTER DAMPING FACTOR Z:";Z: PRINT
735 A = 2 * Z:K = 4 * AO - 8:K = K / A ^ 2:K = K + 1
740 K = K ^ .5:K = K + 1:R2 = Z * K:R1 = 1 / R2
745  INPUT "ENTER NATURAL FREQ. IN RAD/SEC:";WN: PRINT
750 C3 = C3 / WN:C4 = C4 / WN
755  PRINT "R1 = ";R1: PRINT
```

```
757  PRINT "R2 = ";R2: PRINT
759  PRINT "C3 = ";C3: PRINT
760  PRINT "C4 = ";C4: PRINT
765 R1 = .001 * R1:R2 = .001 * R2:C3 = 1000000 * C3:C4 = 1000000
     * C4
770  INPUT "ENTER IMPEDANCE SCALE FACTOR:";KZ: PRINT
772 R1 = R1 * KZ:R2 = R2 * KZ:C3 = C3 / KZ:C4 = C4 / KZ
774  PRINT "R1 = ";R1;" K OHMS": PRINT

776  PRINT "R2 = ";R2;" K OHMS": PRINT

778  PRINT "C3 = ";C3;" MICRO FARADS": PRINT
780  PRINT "C4 = ";C4;" MICRO FARADS": PRINT
785  PRINT : PRINT "ARE THESE COMPONENTS SATISFACTORY ?": GET
      P$: PRINT
790  IF P$ = "N" THEN 770
795  PRINT : PRINT "RI = 10 K OHMS": PRINT
797  PRINT "RF = ";10 * (AO - 1);" K OHMS": PRINT
800  END
900  HOME : PRINT "     VCVS HIGHPASS FILTER": PRINT : PRINT

905 C1 = 1:C2 = 1:WN = 1
910  INPUT "ENTER DAMPING FACTOR:";Z: PRINT
915  INPUT "PASSBAND GAIN (>1):";A: PRINT
920  IF A < 1 THEN 915
925 R4 = .5 * Z + (.25 * Z * Z + .5 * A - .5) ^ .5
930 R3 = 1 / R4
935  INPUT "ENTER NATURAL FREQUENCY IN RAD/SEC:";WN: PRINT
940 C1 = C1 / WN:C2 = C2 / WN
945  PRINT "R3 = ";R3: PRINT
950  PRINT "R4 = ";R4: PRINT
952  PRINT "C1 = ";C1: PRINT
954  PRINT "C2 = ";C2: PRINT
955 R3 = .001 * R3:R4 = .001 * R4:C1 = 1000000 * C1:C2 = 1000000
     * C2
960  INPUT "ENTER IMPEDANCE SCALE FACTOR:";KZ: PRINT
965 R3 = R3 * KZ:R4 = R4 * KZ:C1 = C1 / KZ:C2 = C2 / KZ
970  PRINT "R3 = ";R3;" K OHMS": PRINT

975  PRINT "R4 = ";R4;" K OHMS": PRINT

980  PRINT "C1 = ";C1;" MICRO FARADS": PRINT
985  PRINT "C2 = ";C2;" MICRO FARADS": PRINT
990  PRINT "ARE THESE COMPONENTS SATISFACTORY ?": GET P$: PRINT
```

```
995   IF P$ = "N" THEN 960
1000  PRINT : PRINT "RI = 10 K OHMS": PRINT
1005  PRINT "RF = ";(A - 1) * 10; " K OHMS": PRINT
1010  END
1100  HOME : PRINT "          VCVS BANDPASS FILTER": PRINT :
        PRINT

1105  INPUT "ENTER BANDWIDTH IN RAD/SEC:";B: PRINT
1110  INPUT "ENTER CENTER FREQUENCY IN RAD/SEC:";WN: PRINT
1115  IF B < 2 * WN THEN 1130
1120  PRINT "BANDWIDTH IS TOO LARGE. IT MUST NOT BE MORE THAN
        TWICE THE CENTER FREQUENCY.": PRINT : GOTO 1105
1125  PRINT "THE PASSBAND GAIN IS LEFT AS A FREE PARAMETER IN
        THAT YOU TAKE WHAT YOU GET.": PRINT
1130 C1 = 1 / WN:C2 = 1 / WN:R1 = 1:R2 = 1
1135 Q = WN / B:Z = .5 / Q
1140 K = (3 * Q - 1) / (2 * Q - 1)
1150  PRINT "R1 = R2 = ";R1: PRINT

1155  PRINT "C1 = C2 = ";C1: PRINT

1160 R1 = R1 * .001:R2 = R2 * .001:C1 = C1 * 1000000:C2 = C2 *
        1000000
1165  INPUT "ENTER IMPEDANCE SCALE FACTOR:";KZ: PRINT
1170  PRINT "R1 = R2 = ";R1 * KZ; " K OHMS": PRINT
1175  PRINT "C1 = C2 = ";C1 / KZ; " MICRO FARADS"
1176 R1 = R1 * KZ:C1 = C1 / KZ
1180  PRINT : PRINT "ARE THESE COMPONENTS SATISFACTORY ?": PRINT
        : GET P$
1185  IF P$ = "N" THEN 1165
1190  PRINT "THE AMPLIFIER GAIN K = ";K: PRINT
1195 A = 3 * Q - 1
1200  PRINT "THE PASSBAND GAIN A = ";A: PRINT
1205  PRINT "RI = 10 K OHMS": PRINT

1210  PRINT "RF = ";10 * (K - 1); " K OHMS": PRINT

2500  END
```

# Table of Laplace Transform Pairs

| No. | $F(s)$ | $f(t)$   $f(t) = 0$ for $t < 0$ |
|-----|--------|----------------------------------|
| 1. | $1$ | $\delta(t)$ |
| 2. | $\dfrac{1}{s}$ | $1$ |
| 3. | $\dfrac{1}{s^2}$ | $t$ |
| 4. | $\dfrac{1}{s^3}$ | $0.5t^2$ |
| 5. | $\dfrac{1}{s^n}$ | $\dfrac{t^{(n-1)}}{(n-1)!}$ |
| 6. | $\dfrac{1}{s+P}$ | $e^{-Pt}$ |
| 7. | $\dfrac{s+b}{s+P}$ | $\delta(t) + (b-P)e^{-Pt}$ |
| 8. | $\dfrac{1}{(s+P)^n}$ | $\dfrac{e^{-Pt}t^{(n-1)}}{(n-1)!}$ |
| 9. | $\dfrac{1}{s^2+\omega^2}$ | $\dfrac{1}{\omega}\sin \omega t$ |
| 10. | $\dfrac{s}{s^2+\omega^2}$ | $\cos \omega t$ |
| 11. | $\dfrac{s+a}{s^2+\omega^2}$ | $A \sin(\omega t + B)$ where $A = \sqrt{(\omega^2 + a^2)}/\omega$ |

$\dfrac{t}{s+8l} = e^{-8t}$

| | | |
|---|---|---|
| **11. cont.** | | and $$B = \arctan \frac{\omega}{a}$$ |
| **12.** | $$\frac{1}{s(s^2 + \omega^2)}$$ | $$\frac{1}{\omega^2}(1 - \cos \omega t)$$ |
| **13.** | $$\frac{s + a}{s(s^2 + \omega^2)}$$ | $$\frac{a}{\omega^2} - \frac{A}{\omega^2} \cos(\omega t + B)$$ where $$A = \sqrt{a^2 + \omega^2}$$ and $$B = \arctan \frac{\omega}{a}$$ |
| **14.** | $$\frac{1}{(s + a)^2 + \omega_d^2}$$ | $$\frac{1}{\omega_d} e^{-at} \sin \omega_d t$$ |
| **15.** | $$\frac{s + b}{(s + a)^2 + \omega_d^2}$$ | $$A e^{-at} \sin(\omega_d t + B)$$ where $$A = \frac{\sqrt{(b - a)^2 + 1}}{\omega_d}$$ and $$B = \arctan \frac{\omega_d}{b - a}$$ |
| **16.** | $$\frac{1}{s^2 + 2z\omega_n s + \omega_n^2}$$ | Same as **14**, where $$a = z\omega_n$$ and $$\omega_d = \omega_n \sqrt{1 - z^2}$$ |
| **17.** | $$\frac{s + b}{s^2 + 2z\omega_n s + \omega_n^2}$$ | Same as **15**, where $$a = z\omega_n$$ and $$\omega_d = \omega_n \sqrt{1 - z^2}$$ |
| **18.** | $$\frac{as + b}{(s + P_1)(s + P_2)}$$ | $$\frac{b - aP_1}{P_2 - P_1} e^{-P_1 t} + \frac{b - aP_2}{P_1 - P_2} e^{-P_2 t}$$ |
| **19.** | $$\frac{b}{(s + P_1)(s + P_2)}$$ | Same as **18**, where $$a = 0$$ |

| 20. | $\dfrac{as + b}{s(s + P_2)}$ | Same as **18**, where $$P_1 = 0$$ |
|---|---|---|
| 21. | $\dfrac{as^2 + bs + c}{(s + P_1)(s + P_2)(s + P_3)}$ | $K_1 e^{-P_1 t} + K_2 e^{-P_2 t} + K_3 e^{-P_3 t}$ where $$K_1 = \frac{aP_1^2 - bP_1 + c}{(P_2 - P_1)(P_3 - P_1)}$$ $$K_2 = \frac{aP_2^2 - bP_2 + c}{(P_1 - P_2)(P_3 - P_2)}$$ and $$K_3 = \frac{aP_3^2 - bP_3 + c}{(P_1 - P_3)(P_2 - P_3)}$$ |
| 22. | $\dfrac{bs + c}{s(s + P_2)(s + P_3)}$ | Same as **21**, where $$a = 0 \text{ and } P_1 = 0$$ |
| 23. | $\dfrac{bs + c}{(s + P)(s^2 + 2z\omega_n s + \omega_n^2)}$ | $Ke^{-Pt} + \dfrac{A}{b\omega_d} e^{-at} \sin(\omega_d t + B)$ where $$a = z\omega_n$$ $$\omega_d = \omega_n \sqrt{1 - z^2}$$ $$K = \frac{c - bP}{(a - P)^2 + \omega_d^2}$$ $$A = \frac{\sqrt{(c - ba)^2 + \omega_d^2}}{\sqrt{(P - a)^2 + \omega_d^2}}$$ $$B = \arctan \frac{b\omega_d}{c - ab} - \arctan \frac{\omega_d}{P - a}$$ |
| 24. | $\dfrac{bs + c}{s(s^2 + 2z\omega_n s + \omega_n^2)}$ | Same as **23**, where $$P = 0$$ |
| 25. | $\dfrac{1}{s(s^2 + 2z\omega_n s + \omega_n^2)}$ | Same as **23**, where $$P = 0, \ b = 0, \text{ and } c = 1$$ |
| 26. | $\dfrac{bs + c}{s^2(s + P)}$ | $\dfrac{c - Pb}{P^2} e^{-Pt} + \dfrac{c}{P} t + \dfrac{Pb - c}{P^2}$ |
| 27. | $\dfrac{1}{s^2(s + P)}$ | Same as **26**, where $$b = 0 \text{ and } c = 1$$ |

| 28. | $\dfrac{s^2 + bs + c}{s^2(s + P)}$ | $\dfrac{P^2 - bP + c}{P^2}\,e^{-Pt} + \dfrac{c}{P}\,t + \dfrac{bP - c}{P^2}$ |
|---|---|---|
| 29. | $\dfrac{bs + c}{(s + P)^2}$ | $(c - Pb)te^{-Pt} + be^{-Pt}$ |
| 30. | $\dfrac{bs + c}{s^2(s^2 + \omega^2)}$ | $\dfrac{c}{\omega^2}\,t + \dfrac{1}{\omega^2} - \dfrac{1}{\omega^3}\sqrt{c + b\omega^2}\,\sin\,(\omega t + B)$ <br> $B = \arctan\dfrac{b\omega}{c}$ |
| 31. | $\dfrac{1}{s^2(s^2 + 2z\omega_n s + \omega_n^2)}$ | $\dfrac{1}{\omega_n^2}\,t - \dfrac{2a}{\omega_n^2} + \dfrac{1}{\omega_d}\,e^{-at}\,\sin\,(\omega_d t - B)$ <br> $\omega_d = \omega_n\sqrt{1 - z^2}$ <br> $a = z\omega_n$ <br> $B = -2\arctan\dfrac{\omega_d}{a}$ |
| 32. | $\dfrac{s}{(s^2 + \omega_1^2)(s^2 + \omega_2^2)}$ | $\dfrac{1}{\omega_1^2 - \omega_2^2}\,(\cos\,\omega_2 t - \cos\,\omega_1 t)$ <br> if $\omega_1 \neq \omega_2$ <br> $\dfrac{t}{2\omega}\,\sin\,\omega t$ <br> if $\omega_1 = \omega_2 = \omega$ |
| 33. | $\dfrac{1}{(s^2 + \omega^2)^2}$ | $\dfrac{1}{2\omega^3}\,(\sin\,\omega t - \omega t\,\cos\,\omega t)$ |

# Answers to Selected Problems

## Chapter 1

**1.1.** (C)

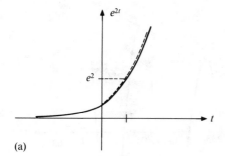

(a)

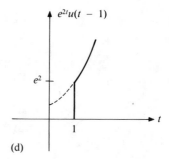

(d)

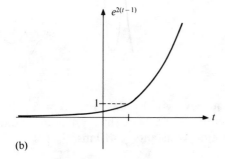

(b)

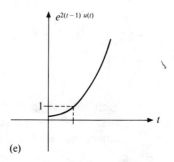

(e)

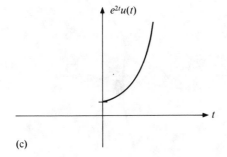

(c)

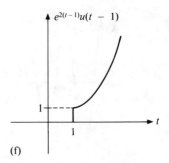

(f)

**1.3.**

| | *Initial value* | *Time constant* |
|---|---|---|
| **(a)** | 1 | 0.333 s |
| **(b)** | −4 | 8.000 s |
| **(c)** | 20 | 0.020 s |
| **(d)** | −1 | 0.050 s |

**1.5.** **(c)** Amplitude $= 8t$, Frequency $= 500$ rad/s, Period $= 2\pi/500 = 12.6$ ms, Phase shift $= 0$, Time shift $= 0$ s

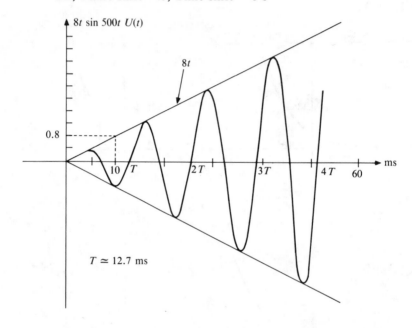

$T \simeq 12.7$ ms

**(o)** Amplitude $= e^{-12t}$, Frequency $= 100$ rad/s, Period $= 2\pi/100$ rad/s $= 62.8$ ms, Phase shift $= 270°$, Time shift $= 47.1$ ms, Time constant $= 82.5$ ms, Five time constants $= 410$ ms

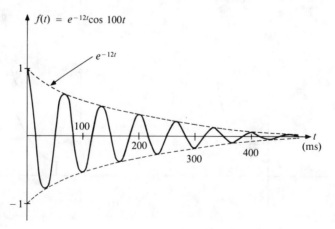

**1.6. (a)** $RC = \dfrac{\text{Volt}}{\text{Ampere}} \cdot \dfrac{\text{Coulomb}}{\text{Volt}} = \dfrac{\text{Coulomb}}{\text{Coulomb/Second}} = \text{Second}$

**(b)** $\dfrac{L}{R} = \dfrac{\text{Volt} \cdot \text{Second}}{\text{Ampere}} \cdot \dfrac{\text{Ampere}}{\text{Volt}} = \text{Second}$

**(c)** $LC = \dfrac{L}{R} \cdot CR = \text{Second}^2$ or $(LC)^{-0.5} = \dfrac{1}{\text{Second}} = \text{Frequency}$

**(d)** $R^2 C = \dfrac{R}{L} \cdot RC \cdot L = \dfrac{1}{\text{Second}} \cdot \text{Second } L = L \text{ (inductance)}$

**1.7.**

|  | (a) | (b) | (c) | (d) | (e) |
|---|---|---|---|---|---|
| Driving function | N | (NM) | P | °C | M |
| Driven function | M | rad | kg | cal | M³ |
| Rate function | M/s | rad/s | kg/s | cal/s | M³/s |
| Rate of rate function | M/s² | rad/s² | kg/s² | cal/s² | M³/s² |
| Resistance | Ns/M | (NM)s/rad | Ps/kg | °Cs/cal | s/M² |
| Capacitance | M/N | rad/(NM) | kg/P | cal/°C | M² |
| Inductance | Ns²/M | (NM)s²/rad | Ps²/kg | °Cs²/cal | s²/M² |

**1.8. (a)** $y(t) = 10 - e^{-0.5t}(10 \cos 0.867t + 5.77 \sin 0.867t)$

**(c)** $x(t) = 1 - e^{-t}(1 + t)$

**(e)** $y(t) = 0.0625 - 0.0625 \cos 4t$

**(g)** $y(t) = -0.16 + 1.6t + 0.16e^{-10t}$

**(i)** $x(t) = 0.05(1 - e^{-20t})$

**1.9. (b)** $p(t) = 1 - 1.15e^{0.5t} \sin 0.87t$

**(d)** $z(t) = 1 + 0.29(e^{-0.27t} - e^{-3.73t})$

**(f)** $y(t) = 10t^2 - t + 1$

**(h)** $x(t) = 18t^2 - t + 1$

**(j)** $x(t) = 2t + 1$

# Chapter 2

**2.1. (a)** 20 **(b)** $30/s^2$ **(c)** $45/s^7$ **(d)** $\dfrac{400}{s^2 + 160{,}000}$ **(e)** $\dfrac{s}{s^2 + 16}$

**(f)** $23 + 18/s^4 + 4/s^3 - 1/s^2 - 7/s$ **(g)** $12/(s + 5)$

**(h)** $12/(s - 27)$    **(i)** $\dfrac{-0.867s + 4.5}{s^2 + 81}$    **(j)** $\dfrac{0.707(s - 4)}{s^2 + 16}$

**(k)** $\dfrac{4}{s^2 + 16} - \dfrac{4s}{s^2 + 4} + \dfrac{1}{s + 2}$    **(l)** $\dfrac{11s - 40}{s(s - 4)}$

**(m)** $\dfrac{96}{s^5} + \dfrac{18}{s^4} - \dfrac{4}{s^3} - \dfrac{4}{s^2} + \dfrac{12}{s} + 1$    **(n)** $\dfrac{1}{s - 3}$

**2.2.** **(a)** $20\delta(t)$    **(b)** $4u(t)$    **(c)** $5\delta(t)$    **(d)** $(4 - 6e^{-4t})u(t)$

**(e)** $(4 \cos 9t + 0.89 \sin 9t)u(t)$    **(f)** $2e^{8t}u(t)$

**(g)** $(8 \sin 5t - 4 \cos 9t)u(t)$    **(h)** $-4\delta(t) + 37e^{-8t}u(t)$

**(i)** $\delta(t) - 4u(t)$    **(j)** $6\delta(t) + (20 \cos 2t - 8 \sin 2t)u(t)$

**(k)** $(7 \cos 6t - 1.5 \sin 6t)u(t)$    **(l)** $\delta(t) + 16e^{8t}u(t)$

**2.4.** **(a)** $1 + \dfrac{A}{s + 10} + \dfrac{B}{s + 2}$    **(b)** $20 + \dfrac{A}{s} + \dfrac{B}{s + 1}$    **(c)** $\dfrac{A}{s + 1} + \dfrac{B}{s + 3}$

**(d)** $\dfrac{A}{s} + \dfrac{Bs + C}{s^2 + 9}$    **(e)** $\dfrac{A}{s + 1} + \dfrac{B}{(s + 1)^2} + \dfrac{C}{s - 3}$

**(f)** $\dfrac{A}{s + 1} + \dfrac{B}{s + 3} + \dfrac{C}{(s + 3)^2}$

**(g)** $\dfrac{A}{s + 1} + \dfrac{B}{s - 3} + \dfrac{C}{(s - 3)^2} + \dfrac{Ds + E}{s^2 - 4s + 4}$

**(h)** $\dfrac{A}{s + 3} + \dfrac{B}{(s + 3)^2} + \dfrac{C}{(s + 3)^3} + \dfrac{D}{s - 3} + \dfrac{E}{(s - 3)^2} + \dfrac{F}{(s - 3)^3}$

**(i)** $\dfrac{A}{s + 1} + \dfrac{B}{s + 2} + \dfrac{C}{s + 6}$    **(j)** $1 - \dfrac{100}{s + 100}$    **(k)** $\dfrac{4}{s^2 + 4s + 4}$

**2.5.** **(a)** $(0.023 - 0.03e^{-2t} - 0.038e^{8t} - 0.39e^{-10t} + 0.085e^{10t})u(t)$

**(b)** $(8.95 - 8.95e^{-20t})u(t)$

**(c)** $(0.069 - 5.425e^{-4t} + 1.120e^{6t} + 8.240e^{-6t})u(t)$

**(d)** $\delta(t) - 240e^{-240t}u(t)$

**(e)** $(0.0025 + 0.0089e^{200t} - 0.011e^{-20t})u(t)$

**(f)** $(0.0008 + 0.013e^{49t} - 0.0140e^{-25t})u(t)$

**(g)** $(-0.019e^{-t} - 0.074e^{2t} - 0.154e^{5t} - 0.099e^{-4t})u(t)$

**(h)** $\delta(t) - 102e^{-100t}u(t)$    **(i)** $(-0.028 + 0.347e^{-6t} + 0.681e^{6t})u(t)$

**(j)** $(-8.53e^{-4t} - 0.050e^t + 0.021e^{-t} + 9.370e^{-5t})u(t)$

**(k)** $(0.5e^{4t} - 0.5e^{-4t})u(t)$    **(l)** $(0.5e^{4t} + 0.5e^{-4t})u(t)$

**2.7.**  **(a)** $1 - \dfrac{11.25}{s + 10} + \dfrac{2.25}{s + 2}$    **(b)** $20 + \dfrac{9}{s} - \dfrac{37}{s + 1}$

**(c)** $\dfrac{1.5}{s + 3} - \dfrac{0.5}{s + 1}$    **(d)** $\dfrac{0.222}{s} + \dfrac{-0.222s + 9}{s^2 + 9}$

**(e)** $\dfrac{-0.625}{s + 1} - \dfrac{1.5}{(s + 1)^2} + \dfrac{1.625}{s - 3}$    **(f)** $\dfrac{2.5}{s + 1} - \dfrac{2.5}{s + 3} - \dfrac{5}{(s + 3)^2}$

**(i)** $\dfrac{-24}{s + 1} - \dfrac{45}{s + 2} + \dfrac{41}{s + 6}$    **(j)** $1 - \dfrac{100}{s + 100}$    **(k)** $\dfrac{4}{s^2 + 4s + 4}$

**(l)** $\dfrac{1}{s} - \dfrac{1}{s + 2} - \dfrac{2}{(s + 2)^2}$    **(m)** $\dfrac{1}{s + 2} - \dfrac{2}{(s + 2)^2}$    **(n)** $\dfrac{1}{s} - \dfrac{4}{(s + 2)^2}$

# Chapter 3

**3.1.**  **(a)** $\dfrac{2!}{(s + 3)^3}$    **(b)** $\dfrac{s + 4}{(s + 4)^2 + 16}$    **(c)** $\dfrac{20}{(s + 1)^2 + 400}$

**(d)** $\dfrac{4!}{(s - 4)^5}$    **(e)** $\dfrac{1}{s}$    **(f)** $\dfrac{1}{s + 1}$    **(g)** $1$    **(h)** $\dfrac{1613.72}{s^2 + 16}$    **(i)** $\dfrac{e}{s}$

**3.2.**  **(a)** $e^{-3t}(1 - 3t)u(t)$    **(b)** $e^{-1.5t}(\cos 2.4t - 0.626 \sin 2.4t)u(t)$

**(c)** $1.15e^{-0.5t} \sin 0.876t \, u(t)$    **(d)** $0.407e^{-3.73t} - 0.407e^{-0.27t}u(t)$

**(e)** $\dfrac{1}{5!} e^{-4t}t^5 u(t)$    **(f)** $e^{-0.5t}(\cos 0.87t - 2.9 \sin 0.87t)u(t)$

**(g)** $e^{-t}t \, u(t)$    **(h)** $e^{-t}(9 - 13t)u(t)$    **(i)** $(e^{-t} + 5e^{-3t})u(t)$

**(j)** $10\delta(t) - e^{-5t}(10 \cos 8.7t + 5.8 \sin 8.7t)u(t)$

**(k)** $e^{-5t}(20 \cos 8.7t - 11.5 \sin 8.7t)u(t)$

**(l)** $9\delta(t) - e^{-5t}(10 \cos 8.7t - 97.7 \sin 8.7t)u(t)$

**3.4.**  **(a)** $F(s) = \dfrac{32}{s^2 + 4}$

**(b)** $F(s) = \dfrac{12}{s^2 + 16}(s^2 + 2s + 8) - 12$    **(c)** $F(s) = P(s)(s^6 - 1)$

**(d)** $F(s) = \dfrac{4s}{(s+3)^2 + 16}$  **(e)** $F(s) = \dfrac{s(s-3)}{(s-3)^2 + 4} - 1$

**(f)** $F(s) = \dfrac{2s}{(s+4)^3}$  **(g)** $F(s) = \dfrac{2}{(s+4)^2}$

**3.5.** **(a)** i. $3.33e^{-5t} \sin 3t\, u(t)$  ii. $e^{-5t}(61.67 \sin 3t - \cos 3t)u(t)$

  **(b)** i. $25(e^{-t} - e^{-5t})u(t)$  ii. $(31.5e^{-t} - 32.5e^{-5t})u(t)$

**3.10.** **(a)** $y(t) = 0.2(e^{3t} - e^{-2t})u(t)$  **(b)** $y(t) = 0.167e^{-t}t^3 u(t)$

  **(c)** $x(t) = 0.5(e^{-t} - e^{-2t}(\cos t + \sin t))u(t)$

  **(d)** $z(t) = (t - \sin 10t)u(t)$

**3.12.** **(a)** $\dfrac{2}{s^2}$  **(b)** $2e^{-s}\left(\dfrac{1}{s^2} + \dfrac{1}{s}\right)$  **(c)** $\dfrac{1}{s^2} - \dfrac{1}{s}$  **(d)** $\dfrac{e^{-s}}{s^2}$  **(e)** $\dfrac{1}{(s+2)^2}$

  **(f)** $\left(\dfrac{1}{(s+2)^2} + \dfrac{1}{s+2}\right)e^{-(s+2)}$  **(g)** $\dfrac{1}{(s+2)^2} - \dfrac{1}{s+2}$

  **(h)** $\dfrac{1}{(s+2)^2}e^{-(s+2)}$  **(i)** $e^2\,\dfrac{1}{(s+2)^2}$  **(j)** $e^{-s}\,\dfrac{1}{(s+2)^2}$

**3.13.** **(a)** $\delta(t-1) - 10e^{-10(t-1)}u(t-1)$

  **(b)** $0.5(-e^{-4(t-1)} + e^{-2(t-1)})u(t-1) + 0.5(-e^{-4(t-2)} + e^{-2(t-2)})u(t-2)$

  **(c)** $0.5e^t \sin 2(t-1)u(t-1)$

  **(d)** $0.45e^{-(t-1)} \sin 2.25(t-1)u(t-1)$

  **(e)** $1.33e^{-(t-1)} \sin 3(t-1)u(t-1)$

  **(f)** $\dfrac{5}{\sqrt{6e}}^{-2(\pm -2)} \sin \sqrt{6}(\pm -1)u(\pm -1)$

**3.14.** **(a)** $F(s) = \dfrac{\omega(1 + 2e^{-0.5Ts} + e^{-Ts})}{s^2 + \omega^2}$

  **(b)** $F(s) = \dfrac{3}{Ts^2}(1 - e^{-0.33Ts} - e^{-0.67Ts} + e^{-Ts})$

  **(c)** $F(s) = \dfrac{1}{s}(1 - e^{-0.1Ts})$  **(d)** $\dfrac{1}{Ts^2}(1 - e^{-Ts}(1 + Ts))$

  **(e)** $F(s) = \dfrac{4}{s^2 + \omega^2}(1 - e^{-0.5Ts}) - \dfrac{1}{s}(e^{-0.5Ts} - e^{-Ts})$

  **(f)** $F(s) = \dfrac{1}{(s+100)}(1 - e^{-(s+100)})T$

**3.15.**  **(a)** $F(s) = \dfrac{\omega(1 + e^{-Ts})}{(s^2 + \omega^2)(1 - e^{-Ts})}$

**(b)** $F(s) = \dfrac{3(1 - e^{-0.33Ts} - e^{-0.67Ts} + e^{-Ts})}{Ts^2(1 - e^{-Ts})}$

**(c)** $F(s) = \dfrac{(1 - e^{-0.1Ts})}{s(1 - e^{-Ts})}$    **(d)** $F(s) = \dfrac{(1 - e^{-Ts} - Tse^{-Ts})}{Ts^2(1 - e^{-Ts})}$

**3.16.**  **(e)** $\dfrac{8(s + 4)e^{-(s+2)}}{(s^2 + 8s + 32)^2}$

**3.17.**  **(a)** $\dfrac{1}{t}(e^{-4t} - e^{-3t})u(t)$   **(b)** $\dfrac{1}{t}(1 + e^{2t} + e^{-3t} - e^{-4t})u(t)$

**3.18.**  **(a)** Initial value = 4, Final value = $\dfrac{-1}{14}$

**(b)** Initial value = 1, Final value = 0

# Chapter 4

**4.1.**  $A(s) = \dfrac{1/(LC)}{s^2 + (R/L)s + 1/(LC)}$

**4.2.**  $A(s) = \dfrac{(R/L)s}{s^2 + (R/L)s + 1/(LC)}$

**4.3.**  **(a)** $V_o(t) = 10(1 - e^{0.5t}(\cos 0.87t + 0.574 \sin 0.87t)u(t)$

**(b)** $V_o(t) = 11.5e^{-0.5t} \sin 0.87t\, u(t)$

**(c)** $V_o(t) = 10e^{-0.5t}(\cos 0.87t - 0.58 \sin 0.87t)u(t)$

**4.6.**  **(a)** $0.042\dfrac{(s + 10)(s + 100)}{(s + 1.25)(s + 1.67)}$   **(b)** $\dfrac{0.15(s + 3.33)}{s(s + 2.5)(s + 0.5)}$

**(c)** $\dfrac{20(s + 100)(s^2 + 2s - 20)}{s^2(s + 30)^2(s + 0.1)}$   **(d)** $\dfrac{5000(s^2 + 12s + 40)}{s^2(s^2 + 2000s + 100,000)}$

**4.7.**  **(a)** $\dfrac{0.0075s(0.1s + 1)(0.167s + 1)}{(0.05s + 1)^2}$   **(b)** $\dfrac{0.015(0.33s^2 + 0.667s + 1)}{s(0.05s + 1)(0.05s - 1)}$

**(c)** $\dfrac{0.933(0.1s + 1)}{(0.067s + 1)}$   **(d)** $\dfrac{0.071}{s(0.5s + 1)(0.143s - 1)}$

**(e)** $\dfrac{1}{0.000001s^2 + 0.001s + 1}$   **(f)** $\dfrac{10(0.001s + 1)}{0.001s^2 + 0.02s + 1}$

(g) $\dfrac{2 \times 10^{-4}s}{10^{-6}s^2 + 10^{-4}s + 1}$  (h) $\dfrac{0.0005s^2}{(0.01s + 1)(0.005s + 1)}$

(i) $\dfrac{\dfrac{R_3}{R_1 + R_2 + R_3}(R_2Cs + 1)}{\dfrac{(R_1 + R_3)}{R_1 + R_2 + R_3}R_2Cs + 1}$

**4.8.** A summary of the poles and zeros illustrated below appears on page 337.

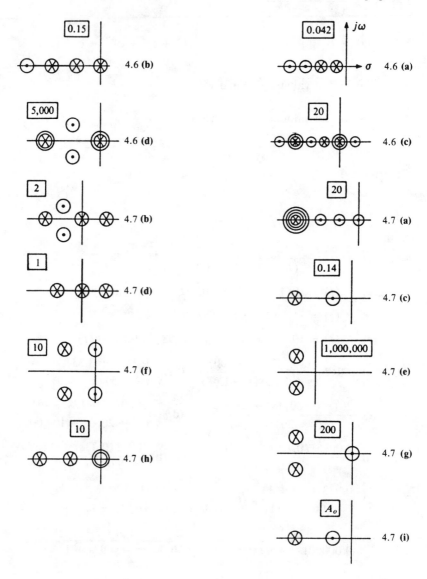

**4.8.** **(4.6)** **(a)** Zeros at $-10$, $-100$
Poles at $-1.25$, $-1.67$

**(b)** Zero at $-3.33$
Poles at $0$, $-2.5$, $-0.5$

**(c)** Zeros at $-100$, $-5.7$, $3.7$
Poles at $0, 0$, $-0.1$, $-30$, $-30$

**(d)** Zeros at $-6 + 2j$, $-6 + 2j$
Poles at $0$, $0$, $-1000$, $-1000$

**(4.7)** **(a)** Zeros at $0$, $-10$, $-6$
Poles at $-20$, $-20$, $-20$, $-20$

**(b)** Zeros at $-1 + 1.414j$, $-1 - 1.414j$
Poles at $0$, $-20$, $20$

**(c)** Zero at $-10$
Pole at $-15$

**(d)** Zero $-$ none
Poles at $-2$, $7$, $0$

**(e)** Poles at $-500 + 870j$, $-500 - 870j$

**(f)** Zeros at $31.6j$, $-31.6j$
Poles at $-10 + 30j$, $-10 + 30j$

**(g)** Zero at $0$
Poles at $-50 + 998j$, $-50 - 998j$

**(h)** Zeros at $0$, $0$
Poles at $-100$, $-200$

**(i)** Zero at $-1/(R_2 C)$
Pole at $-(R_1 + R_2 + R_3)/((R_1 + R_3)R_2 C)$

**4.12.** **(a)** $A(s) = \dfrac{-10s}{(s + 10)^2}$, $V_o(t) = -10e^{-10t}t\, u(t)$

**(c)** $A(s) = -1$, $V_o(t) = -u(t)$

**4.14.** **(a)** $A(s) = -RCs$     Zero at the origin

**(b)** $A(s) = \dfrac{-2RCs}{RCs + 1} = \dfrac{-2s}{s + 1/(RC)}$     Zero at the origin
Pole at $-1/RC$

**(c)** $A(s) = \dfrac{-2}{2RCs + 1} = \dfrac{-1/(RC)}{s + 1/(2RC)}$     Pole at $-1/2RC$

**(d)** $A(s) = \dfrac{3RCs}{RCs + 1} = \dfrac{3s}{s + 1/(RC)}$     Zero at the origin
Pole at $-1/RC$

(e) $A(s) = \dfrac{-RCs + 1}{RCs + 1} = \dfrac{-s + 1}{-RCs + 1}$    Zero at $1/RC$
Pole at $-1/RC$

(f) $A(s) = 5$    No pole and no zero.

**4.17.**

|  | $z$ | $\omega_d$ in rad/s | $T_s$ in seconds | Number of oscillations during $T_s$ |
|---|---|---|---|---|
| (a) | 0.25 | 96.80 | 0.12 | 1.85 |
| (b) | 0.125 | 99.21 | 0.24 | 3.79 |
| (c) | 0.05 | 99.87 | 0.60 | 9.54 |
| (d) | 0.025 | 99.96 | 1.20 | 19.09 |
| (e) | 0.05 | 99.87 | 0.60 | 9.54 |
| (f) | 0.025 | 99.96 | 1.20 | 19.09 |

# Chapter 5

**5.7.** (a) $\dfrac{C(s)}{R(s)} = \dfrac{G_1 G_2 G_3}{1 + G_2 H_1}$

(b) $\dfrac{C(s)}{R(s)} = \dfrac{G_3 G_4 (G_1 + G_2)}{1 + G_4 H_1 - G_3 G_4 (G_1 + G_2)}$

**5.8.** $X(s) = \dfrac{G_1 G_2}{1 + G_1 G_2 G_3} F_1 + \dfrac{G_2}{1 - G_1 G_2 G_3} F_2$

**5.9.** (a) $\dfrac{C(s)}{R(s)} = \dfrac{200}{21}$    (b) $\dfrac{0.5(s + 1)}{s(s + 2)}$

**5.10.** (a) No solution.    (b) $G(s) = 45$

# Chapter 6

**6.1.** (a)  $K = 10$, $Z$ at $-1000$, and $P$ at $-100$

(b)  $K = 2$, $Z$ at $1000$, and $P$ at $-1000$

(c)  $K = 5 \times 10^7$, and $P$ at $-1250 + j4841$ and $-1250 - j4841$

(d)  $K = 10{,}000$, $Z$ at $0$, and $P$ at $-1250 + j4841$ and $-1250 - j4841$

(e)  $K = 2$, $Z$ at $0$, and $0$ and $P$ at $-1250 + j4841$ and $-1250 - j4841$

(f)  $K = 5 \times 10^7$ and $P$ at $-2500 + j4330$ and $-2500 - j4330$

**6.4.** For all parts: $\omega = 1000$ rad/s, $z = 0.5$, and pass-band gain $= 1$

    **(a)** low-pass filter  **(b)** band-pass filter  **(c)** high-pass filter

    **(d)** band-elimination filter

## Chapter 7

**7.1.** **(a)** $A(s) = \dfrac{1/RC}{s + 1/RC}$,    $\omega_c = 1/RC$

    **(b)** $A(s) = \dfrac{R/L}{s + R/L}$,    $\omega_c = R/L$

    **(c)** $A(s) = \dfrac{(1 + R_2/R_1)(1/RC)}{s + 1/RC}$,    $\begin{array}{l}\omega_c = 1/RC \\ A_o = 1 + R_2/R_1\end{array}$

    **(d)** $A(s) = \dfrac{-(R_2/R_1)(R_1/L)}{s + R_1/L}$,    $\begin{array}{l}\omega_c = R_1/L \\ A_o = -R_2/R_1\end{array}$

    **(e)** $A(s) = \dfrac{(1 + R_2/R_1)(R/L)}{s + R/L}$,    $\begin{array}{l}\omega_c = R/L \\ A_o = 1 + R_2/R_1\end{array}$

**7.2.** **(a)** Assume $C$, Calculate $R$ from $\omega_c = 1/RC$

    **(c)** Assume $C$, Calculate $R$ from $\omega_c = 1/RC$
        Assume $R_2$, Calculate $R_1$ from $A_o = 1 + R_2/R_1$

    **(e)** Assume $L$, Calculate $R$ from $\omega_c = R/L$
        Assume $R_2$, Calculate $R_1$ from $A_o = 1 + R_2/R_1$

**7.3.** **(a)** $A(s) = -\dfrac{L}{R}\left(s + \dfrac{R_2}{L}\right)$    It is not a high-pass filter.

    **(b)** $A(s) = -(R_2/R_1)s/(s + 1/R_1/R_1C)$,    $\begin{array}{l}\omega_c = 1/RC \\ A_o = -R_2/R_1\end{array}$

    **(c)** $A(s) = \dfrac{s}{(s + L/R)}$,    $\omega_c = L/R$

    **(d)** $A(s) = \dfrac{(1 + R_2/R_1)s}{s + L/R}$,    $\begin{array}{l}\omega_c = L/R \\ K = 1 + R_2/R_1\end{array}$

**7.4.** **(a)** $A(s) = \dfrac{RCs - 1}{RCs + 1}$    **(c)** $A(s) = \dfrac{0.5(RCs - 1)}{RCs + 1}$

**7.5.** **(a)** $A(s) = \dfrac{1}{RCs}$    **(b)** $A(s) = \dfrac{1}{0.5RCs}$

(c) Positive feedback. The output will be $V_{sat}$. If the input polarities of the first op-amp were interchanged, then $A(s) = \dfrac{1}{KRCs}$, where $K$ is $R_1/R_2$.

(d) $A(s) = \dfrac{-1}{RCs}$

**7.12.** (a) $A(s) = \dfrac{R_2 Cs}{(R_1 + R_2)Cs + 1}$ (b) $A(s) = \dfrac{R_2 Cs + 1}{(R_1 + R_2)Cs + 1}$

(c) $A(s) = \dfrac{-R_2 Cs}{R_1 Cs + 1}$ (d) $A(s) = \dfrac{R_2/L}{s + (R_1 + R_2)/L}$

(e) $A(s) = \dfrac{(R_2/(R_1 + R_2))(RCs + 1)}{(R_1 R_2 Cs/(R_1 + R_2)) + 1}$

**7.13.** (a) $A(s) = R_2/(R_1 + R_2)$ (b) $A(s) = -1$

(c) $A(s) = -R_2/R_1$

# Chapter 8

**8.1.** (a) $\omega_n = 100$ rad/s, $A_o = 2$, $z = 1$

(b) $\omega_n = 100$ rad/s, $A_o = 1$, $z = 0.5$

(c) $\omega_n = 100$ rad/s, $A_o = 2$, $z = 2.5$

**8.2.** $z = 0.477$, $\omega_n = 771$ rad/s, $\omega_p = 738$ rad/s, $M_n = 10.5$

$$A(s) = \dfrac{5,944,410}{s^2 + 735s + 594,441}$$

**8.3.** $\omega_n = 3150$ rad/s, $A_o = 10$, $z = 0.16$, $\omega_p = 3068$ rad/s, $M_n = 31.25$, $\omega_h = 4805$ rad/s

**8.4.** (a) $\omega_h = 60.3$ rad/s, $M_n = 1$, $\omega_p$ and $M_p$ do not exist ($z > 0.707$)

(b) $\omega_h = 127.2$ rad/s, $M_n = 1$, $\omega_p = 70.7$ rad/s, $M_p = 1.15$

(c) $\omega_h = 20.8$ rad/s, $M_n = 0.4$, $\omega_p$ and $M_p$ do not exist ($z > 0.707$)

**8.6.** 1. Assume $C_3 = C_4 = C$

2. Calculate $R_1$ from (8.51)

3. Calculate $R_5$ from (8.52)

4. Calculate $R_2$ from (8.53)

**8.8.** $z = 0.05$, $Q = 20$

## Chapter 9

**9.3.** (a) High-pass  (b) Low-pass  (c) Lag-lead  (d) All-pass

**9.6.** $A(s) = \dfrac{1}{0.5RCs}$

## Chapter 10

**10.1.** $C = 10^{-7}$ F, $R_1 = 200$ k$\Omega$, and $R_2 = 500$ $\Omega$

## Chapter 11

**11.1.** (a) $A(s) = \dfrac{0.1s}{(0.01s + 1)^2} = \dfrac{1000s}{(s + 100)^2}$ $\quad$ $K = 1000$

$\qquad\qquad\qquad\qquad\qquad\qquad\qquad\qquad\qquad$ $Z$ at $0$

$\qquad\qquad\qquad\qquad\qquad\qquad\qquad\qquad\qquad$ $P$ at $-100$ and $-100$

(b) $A(s) = \dfrac{(0.01s + 1)^2}{0.1s(0.001s + 1)} = \dfrac{1(s + 100)^2}{s(s + 1000)}$

$\qquad$ $K = 1$, $Z$ at $-100$ and $-100$, $P$ at $0$ and $-1000$

(c) $A(s) = \dfrac{3.16(0.01s + 1)(0.005s + 1)}{(0.0005s + 1)(0.1s + 1)}$

$\qquad\quad = \dfrac{3.16(s + 100)(s + 200)}{(s + 2000)(s + 10)}$

$\qquad$ $K = 3.16$, $Z$ at $-100$ and $-200$, $P$ at $-10$ and $-2000$

(d) $A(s) = \dfrac{0.1(0.01s + 1)^2}{(0.001s + 1)^2} = \dfrac{10(s + 100)^2}{(s + 1000)^2}$

$\qquad$ $K = 10$, $Z$ at $-100$ and $-100$, $P$ at $-1000$ and $-1000$

(e) $A(s) = \dfrac{0.316(0.02s + 1)(0.0002s + 1)}{(0.002s + 1)^2}$

$\qquad\quad = \dfrac{0.316(s + 50)(s + 5000)}{(s + 500)^2}$

$\qquad$ $K = 0.316$, $Z$ at $-50$ and $-5000$, and $P$ at $-500$ and $-500$

(f) $A(s) = \dfrac{3.16(0.002s + 1)}{(0.02s + 1)} = \dfrac{0.316(s + 500)}{(s + 50)}$ $\quad$ $K = 0.316$

$\qquad\qquad\qquad\qquad\qquad\qquad\qquad\qquad\qquad$ $Z$ at $-500$

$\qquad\qquad\qquad\qquad\qquad\qquad\qquad\qquad\qquad$ $P$ at $-50$

**(g)** $A(s) = \dfrac{10(0.002s + 1)}{(0.1s + 1)} = \dfrac{0.2(s + 500)}{(s + 10)}$    $K = 0.2$

$Z$ at $-500$

$P$ at $-10$

**(h)** $A(s) = \dfrac{0.1s(0.01s + 1)(0.005s + 1)}{(0.1s + 1)^2}$

$\qquad = \dfrac{0.005s(s + 100)(s + 200)}{(s + 10)^2}$

$K = 0.005$, $Z$ at $0$, $-100$ and $-200$, and $P$ at $-10$ and $-10$

# Bibliography

Bateson, Robert. *Introduction to Control System Technology*. Columbus, OH: Charles Merrill Publishing Co., 1973.

Bogart, Theodre F. *Laplace Transforms and Control Systems*. New York: John Wiley & Sons, 1982.

Budack, Aram. *Circuit Theory*. Englewood Cliffs, NJ: Prentice-Hall, 1978.

Burton, Leonard T. *R-C Active Circuits*. Englewood Cliffs, NJ: Prentice-Hall, 1980.

Cadsow, James A. *Signals, Systems, and Transforms*. Englewood Cliffs, NJ: Prentice-Hall, 1985.

Clark, Robert. *Introduction to Automatic Control Systems*. New York: John Wiley & Sons, 1964.

Daryanani, Gobind. *Active and Passive Network Synthesis*. New York: John Wiley & Sons, 1976.

Deltoro, Vincent. *Engineering Circuits*. Englewood Cliffs, NJ: Prentice-Hall, 1987.

Dorf, Richard C. *Modern Control Systems*. Boston: Addison-Wesley, 1980.

Eveleigh, V. W. *Introduction to Control Systems*. New York: McGraw-Hill, 1972.

Gayakward, R. A. *Op-Amps and Linear Integrated Technology*. Englewood Cliffs, NJ: Prentice-Hall, 1983.

Hostetter, G. H., C. J. Savant, and R. T. Stefan. *Design of Feedback Systems*. New York: Holt, Rinehart, and Winston, 1982.

Johnson, David E. *Introduction to Filter Theory*. Englewood Cliffs, NJ: Prentice-Hall, 1976.

Johnson, David E., J. R. Johnson, and H. P. Moore. *A Handbook of Active Filters*. Englewood Cliffs, NJ: Prentice-Hall, 1980.

Karni, Shlomo and William Byatt. *Mathematical Methods in Continues and Discrete Systems*. New York: Holt, Rinehart, and Winston, 1982.

Lathi, B. P. *Signals, Systems, and Communication*. New York: John Wiley & Sons, 1967.

Lynn, Paul A. *The Analysis and Processing of Signals*. Indianapolis, IN: Howard W. Sams & Co., 1983.

Maddock, R. J. *Poles and Zeros*. Englewood Cliffs, NJ: Prentice-Hall, 1982.

McGillem, Clare and George Cooper. *Continues and Discrete Signal and System Analysis*. New York: Holt, Rinehart, and Winston, 1984.

Needler, Marvin and Don Baker. *Digital and Analog Controls*. Reston, VA: Reston Publishing Co., 1985.

Oppenheim, Willsky, and Young. *Signals and Systems*. Englewood Cliffs, NJ: Prentice-Hall, 1983.

Papoulis, Athanasios. *Circuits and Systems*. New York: Holt, Rinehart, and Winston, 1980.

Roberge, James K. *Operational Amplifiers*. New York: John Wiley & Sons, 1975.

Rowlant, J. R. *Linear Control Systems*. New York: John Wiley & Sons, 1986.

Sedra, Adel S. and Peter O. Brackett. *Filter Theory and Design*. Forest Grove, OR: Matrix Publishers, 1978.

Sedra, Adel S. and K. C. Smith. *Microelectronic Circuits*. New York: Holt, Rinehart, and Winston, 1982.

Stanley, William D. *Transform Circuit Analysis*. Englewood Cliffs, NJ: Prentice-Hall, 1968.

Stanley, William D. *Operational Amplifiers with Linear Integrated Circuits*. Columbus, OH: Charles Merrill Publishing Co., 1984.

Stanley, William D. *Network Analysis with Applications*. Reston, VA: Reston Publishing Co., 1985.

Stout, D. F. and Milton Kaufman. *Handbook of Operational Amplifier Circuit Design*. New York: McGraw-Hill, 1976.

Temes, G. C. and S. K. Mitra. *Modern Filter Theory and Design*. New York: John Wiley & Sons, 1973.

Tobey, G. E., J. G. Green, and L. P. Huelsman. *Operational Amplifiers—Design and Applications*. New York: McGraw-Hill, 1971.

Van Valkenburg. *Analog Filter Design*. New York: Holt, Rinehart, and Winson, 1982.

Williams, Arthur B. *Electronic Filter Design Handbook*. New York: McGraw-Hill, 1981.

Zverev, A. I. *Handbook of Filter Synthesis*. New York: John Wiley & Sons, 1967.

# Index